Storybook ART

Great Words from Great People

Wow! **Storybook Art** *is amazing—chock full of all sorts of how-to illustrator inspired art projects. This book is great for ALL ages. I want a copy of my own!*
~ Denise Fleming , illustrator & author
Mama Cat Has Three Kittens (Holt),
CHARLOTTE ZOLOTOW AWARD
In the Small, Small Pond (Holt),
1994 CALDECOTT MEDAL
Barnyard Banter, and more

I wish this book had been available when we were raising our children. I sincerely recommend it!
~ John Schoenherr, illustrator
Owl Moon (Philomel),
1988 CALDECOTT MEDAL

I have great respect for the art of imitation— to learn to saw or hammer by watching a good carpenter—a highly perceptive process. **Storybook Art** *honors this ability of creativity and perception within the child.*
~ Marvin Bileck, illustrator
Rain Makes Applesauce (Holiday),
1965 CALDECOTT HONOR BOOK
ALA NOTABLE BOOK
NEW YORK TIMES 10 BEST ILLUSTRATED
BOOKS

Storybook Art *takes kids inside the mind and soul of picture book illustrators, offering them a bridge of hands-on art connecting them to their favorite books. Every teacher of early readers—and every parent—should have a copy.*
~ Karen Katz, author & illustrator
Counting Kisses (Margaret McElderry Books), Oppenheim Toy Portfolio Gold Award 2002, NAPPA Gold 2001

I can't wait to try projects from **Storybook Art** *with my children and their friends. It's a thrill to be included with the other 99 illustrators. How fun to learn that Patrick Benson* **(Elmer)** *and I were born only one day apart!*
~ Beth Krommes, illustrator
Grandmother Winter (Houghton Mifflin)

Arithmetic lesson from illustrator, Susan L. Roth:
100 great picture book illustrators
X 100 great **Storybook Art** *activities*
=100,000 inspirations.
~ Susan L. Roth, illustrator
My Love For You All Year Round (Dial)

What a fantastic way to bridge the gap between literature and real-life hands-on fun!
~ Robert Bender, author & illustrator
The A to Z Beastly Jamboree (Puffin)

What an amazing book and great resource! I am sure **Storybook Art** *will bring inspiration and fun to many young artists and older ones too! (Hmm, I think I will make a Crictor snake with all my orphan socks.)*
~ Barbara Garrison, illustrator
Only One (Dutton)

MaryAnn Kohl continues to make children's lives richer through her newest book **Storybook Art** *(with Jean Potter). We are adding it to our library shelves and to those of our grandchildren. We highly recommend it.*
~ Robert and Marlene McCracken,
"Literacy Through Teaching" consultants

I want to encourage my students to read and enjoy what they read. **Storybook Art** *is the golden ticket.*
~ Gail Jensen
reading specialist
Seabreeze Elementary School

I like to do art and read everyday. **Storybook Art** *is really fun. It has good ideas to help me learn about my favorite illustrators. If you like to read, you will like this book.*
~ Vivianne Davis, age 8
Jefferson Elementary School

As an author, I know illustrations often speak louder than words. Connecting children to illustrators through their first means of written communication – their artwork – is an exciting way to make story books more meaningful. What a great idea!!!
~ Pam Schiller, author
A Chance for Esperanza; Sing a Song of Opposites (SRA/McGraw-Hill)

Storybook Art *creates, for adults and children alike, a heightened awareness of the role illustrations play in literacy development. Kohl and Potter inspire children to explore their favorite books in new and creative ways.*
~ Cecile Culp Mielenz, Ph.D.
Early Childhood Literacy Specialist
Bureau of Education and Research

Storybook ART

Hands-On Art for Children
in the Styles of
100 Great
Picture Book
Illustrators

MaryAnn F. Kohl
Jean Potter

Illustrations
Rebecca Van Slyke

BRIGHT IDEAS
FOR LEARNING

Bright Ring
Publishing, Inc.

Credits

Illustrations.. Rebecca Van Slyke
Graphic Production.................................... Dorothy Tjoelker-Worthen, Textype
Cover Design.. MaryAnn Kohl
Cover Preparation..................................... Joe Shahan, Textype
Art by Children (Cover & More).......... See pages 5 & 140 for credit listing
Art Idea Contributions by Educators.... See individual art activity for credit listing

ISBN 0-935607-03-X

Library of Congress Catalog Card Number: 2001119111

© copyright 2003 MaryAnn F. Kohl and Jean Potter

Manufactured in the United States of America   First Printing May 2003
20   19   18   17   16   15   14   13   12   11   10   9   8   7   6   5   4   3   2   1

Bright Ring Publishing, Inc
PO Box 31338, Bellingham, WA 98228-3338
800-480-4278 • fax 360-383-0001
artbooks@brightring.com • www.brightring.com

Attention: Schools and Businesses

Bright Ring Publishing, Inc.'s books are available for quantity discounts with bulk purchase for educational, business, or sales promotion use. Please contact the publisher.

Disclaimer

The Publisher/Bright Ring Publishing, Inc., & The Authors/MaryAnn Kohl & Jean Potter, resolutely affirm that proper adult supervision of any & all children doing the art projects in *Storybook Art* **must** be utilized at all times, & that appropriate & safe use of art materials **must** be be employed at all times. The aforementioned assume no responsibility whatsoever for mishap due to lack of child supervision or because of misuse or inappropriate use of art materials by or with children. *Thank you for using caution at all times & knowing the abilities of the children* involved in art projects selected from *Storybook Art*. Children must never be left unattended; art materials must be under the supervision of an adult, & children using them must be supervised at all times.

Publisher's Cataloging-in-Publication
(Provided by Quality Books, Inc.)

Kohl, MaryAnn F.
    Storybook art: hands-on art for children in the styles of 100 great picture book illustrators / MaryAnn F. Kohl, Jean Potter; illustrations, Rebecca Van Slyke.
    p. cm. -- (Bright ideas for learning ; 7)
    includes index.
    LCCN 2001119111
    ISBN: 0-935607-03-X

    1. Art--Study and teaching (Elementary--Activity programs--United States. 2. Creative activities and seatwork. 3. Children's literature--Miscellanea. 4. Illustrators--United States--Miscellanea. I. Potter, Jean, 1947- II. Van Slyke, Rebecca. III. Title. IV. Series: Kohl, MaryAnn F. Bright ideas for learning ; 7.

N362.K64 2003   372.5'044
                                             QBI33-1304

With Thanks

Dedicated to...

... my childhood teachers from Converse Street School, Longmeadow, Massachusetts, who encouraged me in art, writing, and responsibility ~ gentle Mrs. Flood, courageous Mrs. Priest, gracious Miss Paier, inspiring Mrs. Stetson, steadfast-loving Mrs. Nesbitt, and creative Mrs. Coffey.
– MaryAnn

...Thomas E. Potter, my husband and Prince Charming, who has made my life a fairy tale.
– Jean

Illustrators of Tomorrow ~

Thank you, great children/artists/illustrators (and your teachers and parents) for contributing your amazing art, used as part of the cover design and within the pages. You are each an inspiration! On the cover - from left top corner moving clockwise - the artists & their works are:

Shiny Castle............................ Carley Roddy, age 8	The Snowy Day Girl.............. Jazmin Mendoza, age 8
Little Man Blue................... £ Marty Finkbonner, age 7 (1973)	Rainbow Fish........................≈ Taylor Thompson, age 8
Little House........................ Δ Rachel, age 8, kidsart.org.uk	House by the Sea................≈ James Tennant, age unknown
A Cat in a Hat.................. ≈ Taylor Thompson, age 8	Diving Turtle........................ ≈ Shannon Baker, age 6
Corduroy.............................≈ student of Michal Austin	Olivia's Horse........................◊ Olivia Herbert, age 8
Butterfly...........................§ student of Martha D. Rogala (reprinted with permission from SchoolArts, issue 12/97)	Squiggle Ducks.................... Kayla Johnston, age 8
Happy Sun......................... £ Vivianne Fisher, age 3	Caroline's Collage..................◊ Caroline Gibson, age 8
Clone Collage.....................£ Megan Kohl, age 7 (1985)	Drummer Hoff Tree............. Adriana Mitchell, age 8
Snow Owl............................Δ Margaryta Lypova, age 7	Outlined Watercolor.............£ Hannah Kohl, age 6 (1981)
Happy Cat...........................≈ Chelsea M., Kindergarten	Bold Airplane........................ Jalani Phelps, age 8
Rainbow Bright Fish.............. Henry Dotson III age 8 (with Eleanor Davis, age 12)	Resting Cat............................ ≈ Courtney Jackson, age 7
Ducks in a Row.................. Hannah Robinson, age 8	Self Portrait.......................... Δ Megan Jones, age 7
Fruit Bowl Collage.............. Kayla Comstock, age 8	Blue Reflection.....................§ Michael Dudek, grade 6 reprinted with permission from Arts&Activities, issue 4/03 (www.artsandactivities.com)
Flamingo Reflection.............. unidentified artist	Pressed Clay......................... Kayla Comstock, age 8
Elephant Parade................... Carley Roddy, Valeria Quiroz-Nava, Molly Koker (age 8)	Floral Painting....................... ◊ Paige Albert, age 8
Collage Miss Spider..............≈ Kelsey Switzer, age 7	Tar Beach Bridge................ contributing artist unknown, age 8
Polar Bear.............................§ Joshua Christopher, age 9 reprinted with permission from Arts&Activities, issue 4/03 (www.artsandactivities.com)	Seastars................................. Δ Ruxandra Raileanu, age 13

Credit details for children's book cover art –
- students of **Rebecca Van Slyke** – grade 2 teacher – Lynden, Washington
- £ students & friends of **MaryAnn Kohl** – Bellingham, Washington
- § *SchoolArts* or *Arts&Activities* magazines – children's art from various issues
- § student work of **Barbara Valenta**, *SchoolArts* issue 12/97, p. 15.
- § Maurice Woodley, age 13 reprinted with permission from *Arts&Activities*, issue 2/98 (www.artsandactivities.com)
- Δ **kidsart.org.uk** – Kids Art galley, contests – directed by **John Conway**
- ~ students of **Michal Austin** – art teacher, The Art Kids – Cassoday, Kansas
- ◊ students of **Linda Woods** – art teacher, St. John's School – Houston, Texas
  ◊ John Naruk, age 8, see p. 24.
  ◊ Rita Herzog, age 8, see p. 32.

Acknowledging special people –
- **Picture Book Illustrators** – Thank you to each one of you who were able to take the time to share your thoughts & kind approvals in letters, emails, and phone calls. All of Bright Ring, and the children involved, hope you enjoy the representation.
- **Dee Jones** – Curator, deGrummond Children's Literature Collection, for priceless assistance locating illustrators' photographs and biographies.
- **Helen Scholtz** – Bellingham Public Children's Library assistant, for sharing her art ideas for books integrating the styles of children's picture book illustrators.
- **Teachers & Educators** contributed art ideas throughout this book – individual credits are listed on each applicable activity page.
- **Michael, Hannah, & Megan Kohl** - thanks for creative input and support

 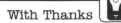

The artworks on pages 5 and 6 are provided for the enjoyment of all, with compliments from children who love art, love books, and treasure the art *within* those books.

Artists, ages 5–12

Kayla Comstock, age 8
clay

Storybook Art offers over 100 companion art activities matched to children's favorite picture books (ages 4-12) and the wonderful illustrators of those books.

Literacy
Reading – and enjoying – books has always been the key to success in school. Literacy is the basis for learning well, with enjoyment. Comfort with art is natural for most children. Couple art with books, and literacy becomes inspired.

Lynette Robertson, age 8
collage, 2 colors

Storybook Art allows children to become more aware of book illustration by experiencing hands-on art techniques as part of easy art projects. Children are thereby encouraged to read – and re-read – their favorite books with new awareness and enjoyment. Children will be inspired to create individual, self-authored stories expressed through their choice of artistic style, such as, drawing, painting, crafts, collage, assemblage, sewing, and construction. Reading and books take on new meaning for a child when integrated with creative art in everyday life.

John Naruk, age 9
outlined watercolor

Harry Jeffries, age 5
melted crayon

Storybook Art invites children to explore hands-on art activities with materials readily available in most homes and schools. The wide variety of activities require no expertise, and are equally appropriate for ages 4-12. Each activity builds new awareness about books, illustrators, and their art techniques. Each illustrator is paired with a book, and presented to the child artist for an art activity of value.

Rita Herzog, age 7
pastels

Companions: Art & Books

Storybook Art introduces children to picture book illustrators — some familiar and others new; to books that are classics and others destined to become classics. Most of the books and illustrators chosen are award-winning and of the highest quality and inspiration.

Morgan Van Slyke, age 7
outlined markers

Joshua Christopher, age 9, chalk
reprinted with permission from *Arts&Activities*, issue 4/03, page 59 (www.artsandactivities.com)

Tanya Taylor, age 11
marking pen, watercolor

Enjoy a peek at a short list of the wonderful illustrators and beautiful books brought to children in **Storybook Art:**

Maurice Sendak..*Where the Wild Things Are*
Ian Falconer...*Olivia*
Ezra Jack Keats.................*The Snowy Day*
Molly Bang..............*When Sofie Gets Angry*
Eric Carle..............*Brown Bear, Brown Bear*
Wanda Gág.........................*Millions of Cats*
Donald Crews.....................*Ten Black Dots* and *Carousel*
Don Freeman................................*Corduroy*
Pat Hutchins.................*The Doorbell Rang*
Anita Lobel............................*Alison's Zinnia*
Patricia Polacco..............*The Keeping Quilt*
Lynd Ward........................*The Biggest Bear*
Leo Lionni.....................................*Inchworm* and *Fish is Fish*
Chris Van Allsburg.........*The Polar Express*
Ed Emberley.........................*Drummer Hoff*
Jan Brett ....*Goldilocks & the 3 Bears*
David McKee ....*Elmer*
Joan Steiner ....*Look-Alikes, Jr.*
Shel Silverstein...*Where the Sidewalk Ends*
Clement Hurd..............*Good Night, Moon*
Faith Ringgold............................*Tar Beach*
David Wiesner...............................*Tuesday*
Tomie dePaola.......................*Strega Nona*
Robert McCloskey........*Blueberries for Sal*
Tomi Ungerer.....................................*Crictor*
and 75 more!

A special feature of **Storybook Art** is the amazing portrait work of book illustrators sketched by kids. A book synopses adds familiarity to the art project. Get to know the illustrators through their personal quotes.

David Williams, age 8
collage, watercolor

Storybook Art encourages children to love books, to learn by doing hands-on art, and to become familiar with new ideas. Children will see a relationship of book illustrations to their own art explorations. A new awareness and appreciation for books is sure to blossom and flourish.

Adults – Your assignment is:
- keep children surrounded with good books
- keep the art corner stocked
- read to children every day

Jim Tennant, age 8
crayon, collage, chalk

Enjoy reading and art,
right alongside your children.
Sharing together
gives learning importance.

Caroline Gibson, age 9
collage

Recipe for Learning:
Stir together generous scoops of kids, art, & books. Cook-up life-long readers, with creative-filled centers. – MaryAnn Kohl

On each activity page, ICONS *are positioned in the upper corner to help the parent, teacher, or young artist evaluate art projects or activity attributes. Other icons are found throughout the pages.*

CHILD EXPERIENCE ICON

Because age and skill do not necessarily go hand in hand, the *starred experience icons* indicate projects which are *easiest, moderate,* or *most involved* for children. All children are welcome to experience all projects, regardless of their skill levels. Beginning artists will need more help or supervision with involved projects. More advanced artists will work independently on easier projects. *Use these icons as guides, not as rules.*

 one star for beginning artists with little experience (easiest art activity)

 two stars for artists with some experience and moderate skill (intermediate art activity)

 three stars for artists who are more experienced with a variety of art methods (most challenging art activity)

ADULT PLANNING & PREPARATION ICON

Indicates the degree of involvement & planning time expected for the adult in charge, ranging from *quick or little* involvement/planning, to *moderate* involvement/planning, and to *significant* involvement/planning.

 little adult planning and preparation

moderate adult planning and preparation

involved adult planning and preparation

HELPING HANDS ICON

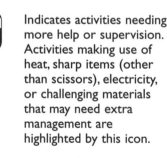 Indicates activities needing more help or supervision. Activities making use of heat, sharp items (other than scissors), electricity, or challenging materials that may need extra management are highlighted by this icon.

AWARD ICON

Indicates art activities based on award-winning books, like Caldecott Medal or Horn Book Award.

TECHNIQUE – STYLE ICON

Art icons help the reader quickly assess the key art technique, style, or material that is the focus of the art activity. When activities have more than one technique or style, the main one will be listed first, followed by others.

DRAW

TAPE ASSEMBLE

GLUE

PAINT

JOIN BUILD

STAPLE

PRINT

SEW WEAVE

GLUE GUN [ADULT HELP]

CUT COLLAGE

MIXTURE DOUGH

PHOTOCOPY

CRAFT CONSTRUCT

PHOTOGRAPHY CAMERA

OUTDOOR ICON

Indicates activities well-suited to outdoor set-up, or may be completed indoors as well.

GROUP ACTIVITY ICON

Indicates activities suited for groups of two or more children.

OTHER HELPFUL ICONS

TABLE OF CONTENTS EASY INDEX

INDEX OF BOOK TITLES

 INDEX OF ILLUSTRATORS

INDEX OF WEBSITE & BOOKS RESOURCES

INDEX OF ACTIVITIES PAGE ORDER

INDEX OF AUTHORS

INDEX OF PUBLISHERS

 INDEX OF ART ACTIVITIES

ILLUSTRATOR BIRTHDAY LISTING

INDEX OF YOUNG ILLUSTRATORS

 INDEX OF ILLUSTRATOR WEBSITES

 AUTHOR PAGE CREDITS SOURCES INTRODUCTION OTHER

Storybook Art © 2003 Bright Ring Publishing, Inc.

Chart of Contents

The Chart of Contents is designed to offer a quick appraisal of important elements and companion information about each art activity, illustrator, and book title.

The Chart of Contents is useful as a reference and for selecting activities suitable to the needs of individual children and groups.

PAGE	ILLUSTRATOR	AUTHOR	BOOK TITLE	ART PROJECT	ART STYLE	CHILD LEVEL	ADULT INVOLVEMENT
13	**CHAPTER 1: PAINT**						
14	Molly Bang	Molly Bang	*When Sophie Gets Angry*	Color Outline	Paint	**	•
15	Robert Bender	Robert Bender	*The A to Z Beastly Jamboree*	Acetate Layers	Paint	***	••
16	Eric Carle	Bill Martin, Jr.	*Brown Bear, Brown Bear*	Multi Paint Picture	Paint / Cut-Collage	**	•
17	Donald Crews	Donald Crews	*Carousel*	Motion Effect	Paint	**	•
18	Ian Falconer	Ian Falconer	*Olivia*	Jackson Piglet Wall Painting	Paint	*	••
19	Don Freeman	Don Freeman	*Corduroy*	Corduroy Print Bear	Paint / Cut-Collage / Draw	*	••
20	Wanda Gág	Wanda Gág	*Millions of Cats*	Cat & Mouse Prints	Paint / Print	**	••
21	Stephen Gammell	Stephen Gammell	*Is that You, Winter?*	Winter Mist	Paint / Draw	*	••
22	Barbara Garrison	Marc Harshman	*Only One*	Collagraph	Paint / Glue-Collage	***	••
23	Pat Hutchins	Pat Hutchins	*The Doorbell Rang*	Decorating Cookies	Paint / Cut-Collage / Group	*	•
24	Thea Kliros	Shannon Brenda Yee	*Sand Castle*	Pencil Watercolor	Paint / Draw	**	•
25	Anita Lobel	Anita Lobel	*Alison's Zinnia*	Alpha Baggie Book	Paint / Craft	**	•••
26	Bernard Lodge	Bernard Lodge	*There Was an Old Woman Who Lived in a Glove*	Glue Block Print	Paint / Print	**	••
27	Robert McCloskey	Robert McCloskey	*Blueberries for Sal*	Blue Fingerdots	Paint / Print	*	•
28	David McKee	David McKee	*Elmer*	Patchwork Parade	Paint / Print / Collage / Group	*	••
29	Pierr Morgan	Carole Lexa Schaefer	*The Squiggle*	Brown Bag Painting	Paint / Glue	*	•
30	Diana Pomeroy	Diana Pomeroy	*One Potato*	Shaded Potato Print	Paint / Print	**	•
31	Rémi Saillard	Fanny Joly	*Mr. Fine, Porcupine*	Wipe Away Fingerpaints	Paint / Draw	**	••
32	John Schoenherr	Jane Yolen	*Owl Moon*	Stencil Trees	Paint / Draw	**	••
33	Charles G. Shaw	Charles G. Shaw	*It looked Like Spilt Milk*	Shaving Cream Puffs	Paint / Mixture	*	•
34	Chris Van Allsburg	Chris Van Allsburg	*The Polar Express*	Lights & Snow	Paint / Cut-Collage	*	•
35	Neil Waldman	Sarah Waldman, retold by	*Light*	Window Letters	Paint / Draw / Cut-Collage	**	••
36	Ellen Stoll Walsh	Ellen Stoll Walsh	*Mouse Paint*	Mixing Mouse Tracks	Paint / Print	*	•
37	Lynd Ward	Lynd Ward	*The Biggest Bear*	Mono Color Painting	Paint	*	••
38	Taro Yashima	Taro Yashima	*Seashore Story*	Etch and Paint Plaster	Paint / Draw / Craft	***	•••
39	**CHAPTER 2: DRAW**						
40	Jim Arnosky	Dale Fife	*The Empty Lot*	Border Extension	Draw	*	•
41	Muriel Batherman	Jan Garten	*The Alphabet Tale*	See Through Scribbles	Draw / Cut-Collage	**	•
42	Patrick Benson	Martin Waddell	*Owl Babies*	Cross-Hatch & Stipple	Draw	**	•
43	Marvin Bileck	Julian Scheer	*Rain Makes Applesauce*	Fancy Words	Draw	**	•
44	Jan Brett	Jan Brett	*Goldilocks and the Three Bears*	Behind the Scene	Draw	**	•
45	Virginia Lee Burton	Virginia Lee Burton	*The Little House*	Four Square Seasons	Draw	**	•
46	Donald Crews	Donald Crews	*Ten Black Dots*	Spot Dots	Draw / Cut-Collage	*	•
47	Bruce Degen	Joanna Cole	*The Magic School Bus Lost in the Solar System*	Talking Bubbles	Draw / Cut-Collage	**	••
48	Ed Emberley	Barbara Emberley	*Drummer Hoff*	Bold Marking	Draw	**	•
49	Marie Hall Ets	Marie Hall Ets	*Gilberto and the Wind*	Accented Pencil	Draw	**	•
50	Paul Goble	Paul Goble	*The Girl Who Loved Wild Horses*	Mirror Reflection	Draw / Cut-Collage	***	•

Storybook Art © 2003 Bright Ring Publishing, Inc.

Chart of Contents continued

Chris Knight style

Dare Wright style

Stephen Johnson style

Did you know photography is an art form young artists can explore with any kind of camera – from instamatic to digital? Three photographers who illustrate picture books – Knight, Wright, and Johnson – show three ways to be creative with cameras.

Celebrate a favorite illustrator's birthday. Enjoy a special art project on that special day! **Illustrator Birthdays**

Birthdays by Month & Day

January
2	1935	McKee, David
2	1949	Brett, Jan
5	1956	Benson, Patrick
6	1956	Krommes, Beth
10	1943	Knight, Christopher
12	1908-1988	Hurd, Clement
28	1932	Jonas, Ann
31	1950	Fleming, Denise

February
5	1956	Wiesner, David
6	1923	Wexler, Jerome
8	–	Whitman, Candace
10	1943	Gammell, Stephen
11	1949	Saint James, Synthia
19	1903-1975	Slobodkin, Louis
24	1956	Jocelyn, Marthe
27	1935	Shulevitz, Uri
29	1944	Roth, Susan
29	1943	Bang, Molly

March
1	1955	Reisberg, Mira
2	1904-1991	Seuss, Dr. (Geisel, Ted)
2	1920	Marvin Bileck
3	1940	MacDonald, Suse
4	1957	Carter, David A.
8	1965	Sabuda, Robert
11	1893-1946	Gág, Wanda
11	1916-1983	Keats, Ezra Jack
17	1944	Minor, Wendell
21	1953-2002	Wisniewski, David
31	1926-2001	Montresor, Beni
31	1952	Jenkins, Steve

April
10	1903-1970	Newberry, Clare Turlay
20	1947	Beaton, Clare
22	1887-1974	Wiese, Kurt
25	1955	Kirk, David

May
1	1892-1974	Shaw, Charles G.
1	1962	Bender, Robert
2	1952	Morgan, Pierr
3	1934	Lobel, Anita
4	1945	Wood, Don
19	1950	Dorros, Arthur

June
5	1910-1999	Lionni, Leo
10	1928	Sendak, Maurice
12	1949	McGraw, Sheila
14	1945	Degen, Bruce
18	1942	Hutchins, Pat
18	1949	Van Allsburg, Chris
19	1928	Bunting, Eve
20	1964	Johnson, Stephen T.
25	1929	Carle, Eric
26	1905-1985	Ward, Lynd

5	1935	Schoenherr, John
11	1925	Mills, Yaroslava
11	1944	Polacco, Patricia
20	1959	Buehner, Mark
30	1960	Pfister, Marcus

August
6	1917-2000	Cooney, Barbara
11	1908-1978	Freeman, Don
15	1934	dePaola, Tomie
16	–	Kliros, Thea
25	1959	Falconer, Ian
28	1904-1980	Duvoisin, Roger
28	1937	Say, Allen
30	1909-1968	Burton, Virginia Lee
30	1938	Crews, Donald

September
1	1956	Arnosky, Jim
2	1942	Walsh, Ellen Stoll
14	1956	Meade, Holly
15	1914-1972	McCloskey, Robert
15	1952	Donohue, Dorothy
16	–	Katz, Karen
19	1952	Mullins, Patricia
20	1941	Geisert, Arthur
21	1908	Yashima, Taro
25	1930-1999	Silverstein, Shel
27	1933	Goble, Paul

October
2	1958	Diaz, David
8	1930	Ringgold, Faith
10	–	Steiner, Joan
11	–	Gerberg, Mort
19	1931	Emberley, Ed
19	1933	Lodge, Bernard
20	1906-1975	Johnson, Crockett
22	1947	Waldman, Neil
22	1931	Garrison, Barbara
30	1930	Parker, Nancy Winslow
31	1960	Saillard, Rémi

November
9	1934	Ehlert, Lois
14	1907	Steig, William
15	1941	Pinkwater, Daniel Manus
16	1957	Reid, Barbara
23	1915	Simont, Marc
23	1945	Pomeroy, Diane
28	1931	Ungerer, Tomi
28	–	Young, Ed

December
3	1914-2001	Wright, Dare
16	1895-1984	Ets, Marie Hall

Full Birthday Information Unavailable
–	–	Martin, Josephine
–	1926	Batherman, Muriel

Birthdays – Earliest to Present

1880-1899
1887-1974	April 22	Wiese, Kurt
1892-1974	May 1	Shaw, Charles
1893-1946	March 11	Gág, Wanda
1895-1984	December 16	Ets, Marie Hall

1900-1909
1903-1970	April 10	Newberry, Clare T.
1903-1975	February 19	Slobodkin, Louis
1904-1991	March 2	Seuss, Dr. (Geisel)
1904-1980	August 28	Duvoisin, Roger
1905-1985	June 26	Ward, Lynd
1906-1975	October 20	Johnson, Crockett
1907	November 14	Steig, William
1908-1988	January 12	Hurd, Clement
1908-1978	August 11	Freeman, Don
1908	September 2	Yashima, Taro
1909-1968	August 30	Burton, Virginia Lee

1910-1919
1910-1999	June 5	Lionni, Leo
1914-1972	September 15	McCloskey, Robert
1914-2001	December 3	Wright, Dare
1915	November 23	Simont, Marc
1916-1983	March 11	Keats, Ezra Jack
1917-2000	August 6	Cooney, Barbara

1920-1929
1920	March 2	Bileck, Marvin
1923	February 6	Wexler, Jerome
1925	July 11	Mills, Yaroslava
1926	–	Batherman, Muriel
1926-2001	March 31	Montresor, Beni
1928	June 10	Sendak, Maurice
1928	June 19	Bunting, Eve
1929	June 25	Carle, Eric

1930-1939
1930-1999	September 25	Silverstein, Shel
1930	October 8	Ringgold, Faith
1930	October 30	Parker, Nancy W.
1931	October 19	Emberley, Ed
1931	October 22	Garrison, Barbara
1931	November 28	Ungerer, Tomi
1932	January 28	Jonas, Ann
1933	September 27	Goble, Paul
1933	October 19	Lodge, Bernard
1934	May 3	Lobel, Anita
1934	August 15	dePaola, Tomie
1934	November 9	Ehlert, Lois
1935	January 2	McKee, David
1935	February 27	Shulevitz, Uri
1935	July 5	Schoenherr, John
1937	August 28	Say, Allen
1938	August 30	Crews, Donald

1940-1949
1940	March 3	MacDonald, Suse
1941	September 20	Geisert, Arthur
1941	November 15	Pinkwater, Daniel
1942	June 18	Hutchins, Pat
1942	September 2	Walsh, Ellen Stoll
1943	January 10	Knight, Chris
1943	February 10	Gammell, Stephen
1943	February 29	Bang, Molly
1944	February 29	Roth, Susan L.
1944	March 17	Minor, Wendell
1944	July 11	Polacco, Patricia
1945	May 4	Wood, Don
1945	June 14	Degen, Bruce
1945	November 23	Pomeroy, Diana
1947	April 20	Beaton, Clare
1947	October 22	Waldman, Neil
1949	January 2	Brett, Jan
1949	February 11	Saint James, Synthia
1949	June 12	McGraw, Sheila
1949	June 18	Van Allsburg, Chris

1950-1959
1950	January 31	Fleming, Denise
1950	May 19	Dorros, Arthur
1952	March 31	Jenkins, Steve
1952	May 2	Morgan, Pierr
1952	September 15	Donohue, Dorothy
1952	September 19	Mullins, Patricia
1953-2002	March 21	Wisniewski, David
1955	March 1	Reisberg, Mira
1955	April 25	Kirk, David
1956	January 5	Benson, Patrick
1956	January 6	Krommes, Beth
1956	February 5	Wiesner, David
1956	February 24	Jocelyn, Marthe
1956	September 1	Arnosky, Jim
1956	September 14	Meade, Holly
1957	March 4	Carter, David A.
1957	November 16	Reid, Barbara
1958	October 2	Diaz, David
1959	July 20	Buehner, Mark
1959	August 25	Falconer, Ian

1960-1969
1960	July 30	Pfister, Marcus
1960	October 31	Saillard, Rémi
1962	May 1	Bender, Robert
1964	June 20	Johnson, Stephen T.
1965	March 8	Sabuda, Robert

Year of Birth a Secret
–	February 8	Whitman, Candace
–	August 16	Kliros, Thea
–	September 16	Katz, Karen
–	October 10	Steiner, Joan
–	October 11	Gerberg, Mort
–	November 28	Young, Ed

Happy Birthday, Dr. Seuss ~ March 2 ~ We Love You!

Storybook Art © 2003 Bright Ring Publishing, Inc.

Painting

chapter 1

Angry Seas Painting by Hannah Kohl, age 5 (1980)
based on
When Sofie Gets Angry - Really, Really Angry by Molly Bang

Elephant Parade by Carley Roddy, age 8,
Valeria Quiroz-Nava, age 8, and Molly Koker, age 9
based on
Elmer by David McKee

Cat with Roses by Olivia, age 5
based on
Millions of Cats by Wanda Gàg

Dancing Cow in Motion by Jordon Drost, age 11 (1998)
based on
Carousel by Donald Crews

Molly Bang February 29, 1943

Molly Bang uses broadly stroked, intensely painted pictures. On each page, her illustrations are rendered on a different colored background. Each object on the page is highlighted with an outline in a contrasting paint color. Imitate Bang's outlining style using thick tempera paint on colored construction paper.

"I made the pictures of gouache, a thick mud-like paint which feels nice and gucky when painted thickly. It is very satisfying to paint exuberant feelings with gouache. I began the book with bright pinks and purples and chartreuse, turning to reds and oranges when Sophie gets angry, then turning to browns, then blues and greens as she calms down, and then using the full palette when she returns home, "whole" again. It was interesting to notice how angry I felt while I was making the angry pictures, and how much calmer I felt when I was painting with the blues and greens."

by Molly Brandt, age 7

- MOLLY BANG
Molly Bang's website,
www.mollybang.com,
request through email

When Sophie Gets Angry - Really, Really Angry • *Molly Bang, author*

Sophie gets very angry when her sister takes her toy. Her feelings intensify as the story progresses, expressed through Molly Bang's use of color. Eventually Sofie learns how to control her anger.

CALDECOTT HONOR 2000 • CHARLOTTE ZOLOTOW AWARD - JANE ADDAMS BOOK AWARD 2000

Color Outline

Materials
colored construction paper
thick tempera paints
paintbrushes

Process
1. Paint a picture using the thick tempera paints. Let the paint dry overnight.
2. The next day, study the painting and choose a color to highlight and outline the painting.
3. Paint a contrasting outline around each object in the painting.

Variation
• Draw a picture, fill in the drawing with watercolor paint, and when dry, outline the painting with black marker.

Robert Bender May 1, 1962

The A to Z Beastly Jamboree • *Robert Bender, author*

Wacky creatures fill the pages of this delightful children's alphabet book. Kids explore their ABC's as they watch ants anchor an *A*, lions launch an *L*, and zebras zipper a *Z* in this fun-filled beastly jamboree. The bright colors and snappy scenes bring children into a world where animals do the strangest things. Don't miss the lively border – it holds more beastly surprises!

Acetate Layers

Imitate Bender's technique of painting bright, glowing illustrations on both sides of a sheet of clear acetate. Place the acetate painting on a black background to give the colors contrast. Though this activity requires special supplies, it is worth the extra effort to experience this amazing technique.

Materials
thin sheets of acetate (clear overhead transparency sheet)
choice of paint (from art supply store, rubber stamp supply, or hobby/craft store)
choices of tools for painting –
    paintbrushes, variety
    stencil brushes (hobby or art store)
    cotton swabs
    toothpicks
    draw directly from a tube of paint
vinyl animator's paint (best choice, from art supply store or drafting/architectural store)
acrylic paint
Gallery Glass Textured Paints™
choice of tape -
    masking tape, duct tape, library tape
3D Fabric Dimensional Paint™
transparency markers (Vis-à-Vis™, other brands for writing on transparencies)

Process
1. Think about a picture, design, or scene to paint. Decide what will be the main focus of the painting, and what will be the background.
2. First, with the paint on hand, brush in background colors, designs, or scene on the back of the acetate. Use any chosen tools for painting, such as those listed to the left.
3. Keep lifting the background painting, peeking to see how the painting looks from the front side. Remember that any words or letters will look reversed, so paint them in reverse, and they will look just right when the acetate is turned over. Then let this painting dry completely - overnight is recommended.
4. When dry, turn the acetate over and place it on a piece of clean paper, ready for the next step.
5. Now paint the main objects and focus of the painting on the front of the acetate, using any choice of painting tools or paints. The background will fit into the general layout scene of the painting, as it shows through from the back of the clear acetate. Let this painting dry completely.
6. When both sides are dry, place the acetate on a sheet of black paper like Robert Bender does, or try other colors of paper and see what is most appealing. Tape all four edges down with tape, making a frame that holds the acetate to the background paper.

by Eleanor Davis, age 12

"I drew a lot as a kid. I was fortunate that my mother always encouraged me. She was against coloring books—I had some, but she felt they inhibited my imagination, so she always kept me supplied with paper, magic markers, and crayons."

— ROBERT BENDER
letter to Jean Potter 2002

1. Paint or draw the lettering (in reverse) and a scene or design on the back of the clear acetate.

2. Turn the acetate over. Paint a picture on the front. Display on a black or dark background.

Eric Carle June 25, 1929

Imitate Eric Carle's illustration technique. Fill glossy sheets of paper with painted designs. Then cut the colorful paper into shapes to create a collage picture which is glued to a sturdy background base.

Brown Bear, Brown Bear, What Do You See? • *Bill Martin, Jr., author*

One animal sees another in a progressive sequence of chanting and bright collage pictures that have entertained and delighted children for years.

by David Williams, age 8

"My pictures are collages. I didn't invent the collage. Artists like Picasso and Matisse and Leo Lionni and Ezra Jack Keats made collages. Many children have done collages at home or in their classrooms. In fact, some children have said to me, "Oh, I can do that." I consider that the highest compliment."

— ERIC CARLE

Eighth Book of Junior Authors & Illustrators, *autobiographical sketch, 2000©HW Wilson Co.*

Multi Paint Picture

Materials
glossy paper (fingerpainting paper) or construction paper
tempera paints in flat dishes or trays
choice of things to use as painting
    tools —
        feather duster
        sponge
        potato cut in half
        ball of crumbled foil
        burlap scrap
        collect more items of choice
paintbrush
glue
scissors
heavy paper or matboard

Process
1. Paint on paper with any choice of painting tool. For example, the feather duster, sponge and crumbled paper can be dipped in paint and lightly dabbed on the paper. The burlap can be painted with a brush and pressed onto the paper. A paintbrush in varying widths and sizes is always a versatile choice. Experiment with different techniques and materials. There will be many textures and designs in the paintings.
2. Then let the paint dry well.
3. To create a collage picture like Eric Carle, cut the painted papers into shapes or animals to assemble in a picture.
4. Glue them into a collage picture on a fresh piece of heavy paper or matboard.

Variations
- Plan a sequence of animals or objects that "see" each other, just like in *Brown Bear*. Staple the pictures together to make a book.
- Fingerpaint on slick paper. When the paint is dry, cut the paper into shapes and glue them on a fresh sheet of paper to make a picture or collage.
- Paint with a mixture of several colors of watercolor paints on damp paper so that the colors blur. Then cut the paper into shapes and glue a picture or collage on fresh paper.
- Cut and glue wrapping paper into a collage on a sheet of paper or matboard.

Donald Crews August 30, 1938

Carousel • *Donald Crews, author*

The carousel stands waiting for children. The music begins, the children arrive and climb on, and then the spinning begins, moving the carousel faster, faster and faster. The blurred illustrations confirm how fast the carousel is moving.

Motion Effect

Materials
tempera paints, several colors
paintbrushes
paper
damp sponge

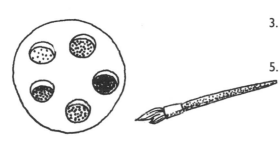

Process
1. Paint one object or subject on the paper with tempera paints. Something that is often in motion will be a good subject, such as, a horse, car, sailboat, or Ferris wheel.
2. While the paint is wet, take the damp sponge and with a light touch, wipe the object in one direction (from left to right) to gently smear the paint.
3. Paint another object on the paper, such as a house. While the paint is wet, use the sponge to wipe in the same direction again, smearing the paint.
5. Continue drawing objects and smearing the paint from left to right in one direction until the picture is completed. This will give the same effect of movement as the train illustrated in the book. Perhaps this is what the children see as they spin past objects on the carousel.

Variations
• Draw a picture or design with pastel chalks, and then brush the colors in one direction with a cotton ball or tissue. This will create the look of motion.
• Another book by Donald Crews with this art style is *Freight Train*.

The illustration of movement found in Donald Crews' art can be imitated by smearing the wet paint of the picture in one direction. This will communicate the impression that objects are moving very, very faaaaaast.

by Molly Brandt, age 7

"I wouldn't be in picture books if it weren't for the fact that they are books that are primarily stories that can be told without the words. Ideally, if the pictures are done well enough you shouldn't need the words; the pictures should tell the story. The story should be full and fulfilling and interesting even without any words."

- DONALD CREWS
interview by George Bodmer,
Professor of English, Indiana University Northwest
©1998 African American Review

Ian Falconer August 25, 1959

Olivia • Ian Falconer, author

Olivia is a headstrong little girl piglet who is good at singing loud songs and generally wearing her family out, but they love her anyway. She is particularly skilled at imitating Jackson Pollock's art on the walls of her home. CALDECOTT HONOR 2001 • ABA BOOKSENSE BOOK OF THE YEAR • PARENTS' CHOICE GOLD AWARD 2000

See Olivia's daring Jackson Pollock (a painter famous for his splattered and drippy paintings) red and black spattered artwork in Ian Falconer's story. Then imitate Ian Falconer's charcoal drawings with highlights done in the brightest of red and black gouache.

"I think black and white can be just as arresting as color. It can also be much less information going on — into your eye, your brain — so that you pay attention to subtler detail in, say, facial expressions."

- IAN FALCONER
Something About the
Author®Vol.125 p.67, ©2003
The Gale Group, Inc.

by Abby Brandt,
age 5

Jackson Piglet Wall Painting

Materials
white drawing paper, large and heavy (cardboard also works well)
newspaper or other covering for work area
tape
paintbrushes
gouache paint, red and black (gouache is a heavy, opaque watercolor paint producing a more strongly colored picture than watercolor. Tempera paints may be substituted.)

Process
1. Protect the floor with a large covering of newspaper. Tape the corners to help hold it in place.
2. Place the sheet of large white drawing paper in the center of the newspaper. Tape the corners of the drawing paper to the newspaper to keep it from slipping.
3. Start with red paint, imitating Olivia's favorite great master painter, Jackson Pollock. Dip a brush in paint and then gently spatter, drip, shake, or dribble paint on the paper. Work lightly and carefully to place paint with thought and care.
4. When satisfied with the red design, add black in the same manner. Let dry overnight.
5. When the painting is completely dry, tape it on the wall to give the impression that Olivia has painted directly on the wall!

Variations
• Experiment with other ways to apply paint in a "Jackson Pollock/Olivia style", as in —
  - rolling a ball dipped in paint across the paper
  - slapping a fly-swatter dipped in paint on the paper
  - spraying paint from a hand-misting bottle
  - squirting paint from a squirt gun
• Ian Falconer's other books include: *Olivia Saves the Circus, Olivia Counts, Olivia's Opposites.*

Don Freeman
August 11, 1908 –1978

Corduroy • *Don Freeman, author*

Corduroy is a stuffed bear for sale in a department store waiting for someone to buy him and take him to a real home. Even though Corduroy is missing a button on his overalls and feels less than desirable, he finds a special new home at the end of his adventure.

Replicate the delightful details of Don Freeman's characterization of *Corduroy*, the lonely little bear. Capture a bear design print made from corduroy fabric. Remember his precious button!

Corduroy Bear Print

Materials
thin layer of thick brown paint in a flat baking pan
piece of corduroy fabric
cut in a bear shape (corrugated cardboard is a good substitute)
tagboard or other heavy paper
one button
green paper scraps plus other paper scraps
glue
crayons, markers, or paints
scissors, optional

Process
1. Press the bear-shaped corduroy fabric into the paint and then press paint side down on a sheet of tagboard. Pat gently to make a nice print with corduroy texture. (Another idea: Paint the corduroy with a paintbrush, and then press it onto the paper.)
2. Remove the fabric and place it on a sheet of newspaper or a tray until ready to make another print. Make additional corduroy bear prints if desired. Let each print dry.
3. Decorate the dry bear print with green paper cut into overalls or other creative clothing.
4. Glue on one button (or two!), just like Corduroy's precious button in Don Freeman's book. Dry briefly.
5. Add a face or other features with crayons, markers, or paints.
6. Cut out the shape of the bear around the decorated corduroy print, or leave uncut.

Variation
- Read the sequel, *A Pocket for Corduroy,* and create another bear print, but this time, add a pocket cut from fabric for Corduroy.
- Some other books by Don Freeman are: *Beady Bear , Fly High, Fly Low* - a Caldecott Honor Book, *Norman the Doorman, Come Again Pelican, The Guard Mouse, Tilly Witch, Inspector Peckit, Bearymore* and many more.

~ art idea generously contributed by
Gail Hariton, Port Washington, New York

"I love the flow of turning the pages, the suspense of what's next. Ideas just come at me and after me. It's all so natural. I work all the time, long into the night, and it's such a pleasure. I don't know when the time ends. I've never been happier in my life!"
- DON FREEMAN
www.edupaperback.org

by Molly Brandt, age 7

originally excerpted from print volumes ©HW Wilson Company

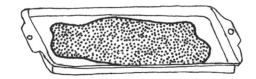

Wanda Gág March 11, 1893 –1946

Imitate Wanda Gág's wood-cut style. Construct printing blocks with shapes cut from worn computer mouse pads glued to cardboard or wood.

"My Own Motto - Draw to Live and Live to Draw." (Diary 10, 28 October 1910)
- WANDA GÁG
Denise Ortakales©1999–2002
www.ortakales.com/illustrators/Gag.html
& letters to Denise Ortakales

by Jennifer Reinstra, age 9

Millions of Cats • *Wanda Gág, author*

Once upon a time there was a very old man and a very old woman who lived in a nice clean house with flowers all around it. But they were not happy because they were lonely. Finding a pet kitten should surely cure the loneliness they share.   NEWBERY HONOR 1929 • LEWIS CARROLL SHELF AWARD 1958

Cat & Mouse Prints

Materials
squares of thick cardboard or
   blocks of wood
old computer mouse pad
scissors
glue
tempera paint
paintbrush
heavy paper

Process
1. Cut a cat shape or other design from the mouse pad. Glue the shape on the cardboard square or block of wood. Glue the colorful side of the pad, and leave the plain textured side of the pad facing up (see illustrations for cutting effects).
2. After the glue has dried, brush paint onto the cat shape. Then press it on paper to make a print. Will there be hundreds of cats, thousands of cats, millions or billions or trillions of cats?
3. Make several different stamps of cats or other designs cut out from a mouse pad. Glue on cardboard or on a block of wood.
4. When the prints are dry, highlight the cat's features with a marker, if desired.

Variations
- Cut intricate cat designs with more definition and features such as whiskers, eyes, and stripes or spots.
- To make a raised design, cut out the outline of the cat instead of the whole cat shape.
- A few of the many books Wanda Gág has written are: *The Funny Thing, Snippy and Snappy,* and *Nothing at All.*

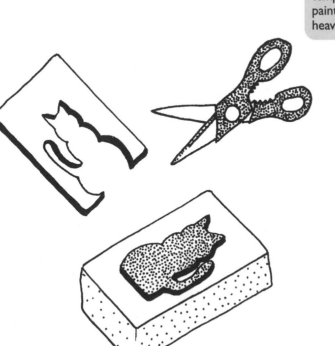

White Glue

Stephen Gammell February 10, 1943

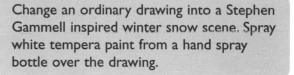

Is That You, Winter? • *Stephen Gammell, author*

Old Man Winter grumbles about who else will make the snow, but he is the only one who can do it (which he does while complaining and grumbling the entire time).

SOCIETY OF SCHOOL LIBRARIANS INTERNATIONAL BOOK AWARD 1998

Change an ordinary drawing into a Stephen Gammell inspired winter snow scene. Spray white tempera paint from a hand spray bottle over the drawing.

Winter Mist

"I love my work. I love drawing and making books. In a deep sense, I am my work — what is seen on the page is really me."
- STEPHEN GAMMELL
Something About the Author®
Vol.128 p.78 ©2003
The Gale Group, Inc.

by John Asplund, age 13

Materials
colored markers or crayons
drawing paper
outdoor area or indoor art area
newspapers to cover work area
white liquid tempera paint in a hand spray or misting bottle

Process
1. Draw a picture of any outdoor scene with markers or crayons on drawing paper.
2. Take the drawing outdoors and place it on a grassy spot, or place on newspapers held down with rocks. (Indoor work: prepare an area covered with newspaper.)
3. Fill a misting bottle with white tempera paint. White liquid shoe polish will also work.
4. Spray the paint in the space above and over the painting so the paint droplets fall onto the painting in small dots and splashes that look like snow. Hint for success: Practice the spraying step on newspaper with plain water to get the idea before spraying the actual art work. Then spray the white paint to make snow.
5. The painting will only need to dry briefly.

Variation
• Dip a toothbrush into white paint with one hand, and then brush the bristles with the thumb of the other hand over the painting. Make the paint spatter *towards* the paper and not toward the artist! Practice with water first to get the idea. Placing the artwork inside a cardboard box and then splattering the paint is a good way to contain spatters.

Barbara Garrison August 22, 1931

Explore Barbara Garrison's "collagraph" technique, a combination of collage and graphics. Collage materials are glued on cardboard. A print is made from the collage and then colored. Create a collagraph and print it on cloth.

by Sarah Wiley-Jones, age 14

"My interest in collage may have begun as a very young child happily occupied carefully tearing paper into shapes. My homework was always decorated with drawings. In fact, the drawings on the wall behind Miss Shackelton in One Room School were copied from letters my mother saved, commemorating my third grade trip to the Museum of Natural History. Only One was the first book I illustrated with collagraphs."
— BARBARA GARRISON
letter to MaryAnn Kohl 2003

Only One • Marc Harshman, author

The county fair is a great place to see many wonderful things to count. See five hundred seeds in one pumpkin and eleven cows in one herd! But there is also only one of the special something at the end of the book!

Collagraph

Materials
collage items (fairly flat objects) —

contact paper	stickers & stars
glitter	feathers
paper stars	matboard
paper shapes	sandpaper
sequins	string
corrugated	foil
cardboard	paper doilies
lace	seeds
ribbons	thread

glue
cardboard for backing
tempera paints
plain white cotton fabric
colored markers
watercolor paints, paintbrushes

Process
1. Arrange selected collage items on the cardboard in any pattern or design. Make a simple design, abstract pattern, or form a scene. Move the objects around until satisfied with the design. (Materials can also be cut into shapes.)
2. Glue the collage materials onto the cardboard and then let dry for at least an hour so the glue is not wet.
3. After the design is dry, decide on a color to paint over all the scraps — one color or many. Then paint over all the scraps.
4. While the paint is still wet, place a piece of cotton cloth over the top of the entire design. Lay it out smoothly using a steady hand to pat it in place.
5. Gently lift the cloth to see the print transferred to the cloth. Let the cloth print dry overnight or several hours.
6. When dry, add more color to the printed fabric with colored markers or watercolor paints.

Variations
- Glue collage items on a piece of wood. Spray paint the collage all the same color. Feel the textures and see the shapes. Add more design and sparkle to the collage with glue and glitter, confetti, faux jewels, and/or sequins.
- Stretch the dried fabric print on an embroidery hoop for display.

Pat Hutchins June 18, 1942

The Doorbell Rang • Pat Hutchins, author

Ma bakes wonderful cookies. Each time the doorbell rings, more and more people arrive who have come to share her irresistible treats.

Pat Hutchins story and illustrations inspire creative cookie decorating. Create unique paper cookies with paints, scraps and squeezy "artsy-icing".

Decorating Cookies

Materials
3"-4" [8cm-10cm] heavy paper circles (small paper plates with the edges cut away work well, or cake circle bases from a restaurant supply store)
saved materials for decorating the pretend cookies –
    paper-punch holes from red, yellow, brown, blue, and green paper
    sequins
    stickers
  squeeze bottle (from mustard)
  construction paper
  scraps of paper
  other odds and ends (real candy sprinkles?) to decorate cookies
crayons
tempera paints and paintbrushes
white glue, gluestick, tape
foil rectangles, optional
  (about 12"x18") [about 30cmx38cm] or baking sheet size

Process
1. Glue hole-punched dots on a paper circle, just like decorating a real cookie with M&M's, candy sprinkles, or chocolate chips.
2. Think of more ways to decorate the paper cookies. Some ideas are:
   - write or draw with "squeezy icing" made from tempera paint mixed with white glue. Squeeze the mixture from a mustard bottle. Let dry for about one hour.
   - fancy paper scraps can be cut into squiggles, squirts, dots, and dollops and glued onto the paper cookies
   - add glitter, glitter glue, confetti, sequins
   - glue on real baking sprinkles
   - spread thickened paint like icing
3. Optional idea: Glue the pretend cookies to a square of aluminum foil to look like they are on a baking sheet.

Variation
- Make sugar cookies from any favorite recipe and decorate them in fun designs and colors. Share with all the people who drop by for a visit – and ring the doorbell.

by Morgan Van Slyke, age 7

"I like to build my stories up, so the reader can understand what is happening and, in some cases, anticipate what is likely to get quite complicated ideas across to small children as long as they are presented in a simple, satisfying way."

- PAT HUTCHINS
Hutchins Film Company letter to MaryAnn Kohl 2002,
& www.hutchinsfilm.co.uk

~ art idea generously contributed by Bobbi Capwell, League City, Texas

Thea Kliros August 16

Imitate the breezy style of Thea Kliros by first creating a drawing with a pencil. Add highlight and focus by filling in the drawing with watercolor paints.

Sand Castle • *Shannon Brenda Yee, author*

Jen starts to build a castle at the beach and others come one by one to help with the sunny-day project, sharing their ideas and their tools. They enjoy putting the finishing touch on the castle together.

by Shon Gorsuch, age 7

"One of my earliest childhood memories: my father reading Alice in Wonderland *and loving the story and at the same time being fascinated and frightened by the original Tenniel etchings, particularly the one where Alice grows tall – and her neck is very long. Also, I always loved drawing and painting by myself on the floor. I have never stopped, but I did get up off the floor!"*

- THEA KLIROS
letter to MaryAnn Kohl 2002
from Hilary Kliros, Thea's daughter

Pencil Watercolor

Materials
white drawing paper
masking tape
pencil
watercolor paints and brush
jar or water for rinsing
tissues for blotting wet paint

Undersea Outline Watercolor
by John Naruk, age 8

Process
1. Gently press tape around the border of the drawing paper, covering all four edges of the paper. This will make a frame. The tape will remain on the painting until it dries, helping keep it flat.
2. Draw a bold and spacious picture lightly with pencil on the white paper. It can be a seashore picture, another scene, or an abstract design. The drawing should primarily be in outline form without much detail. It will be easier to paint if it isn't too complicated or detailed.
3. Paint-in the pencil outline drawing with watercolor paints. (Tip: Mixing colors with water in the lid of the paintbox is a good technique to achieve thin colors. Paint-in areas that do not touch one another to begin; let those dry, and then paint-in the remaining areas. (If wet areas touch, the colors will run together. Dab and blot very wet areas with tissues for a muted look or to pick up excessive paint.)
5. When the painting is completely dry, gently peel off the masking tape, and a nice white border will remain.

Variations
• Draw with permanent markers, and paint-in with watercolor paints.
• Outline or fill-in some parts of a dry seashore painting with white glue, like the beach area or a sandcastle. Sprinkle with real sand, and then shake off excess. The sand will stick to the glued areas giving it a fun, sandy beach look.

Anita Lobel May 3, 1934

Alison's Zinnia • *Anita Lobel, author*

Each child is named alphabetically in the Anita Lobel's book, giving a flower to the next child listed. This progressive alphabet book cleverly ranges from amaryllis to zinnia and matches with children's names from A to Z.

Create a collection of painted flowers those richly depicted by Lobel — or paint a collection of unique ideas. Arrange the collection in a protective ziplock baggie book that will last for years.

Alpha-Baggie Book

Materials
14 ziplock style baggies, all the same size (sandwich, quart, or gallon size)
stapler
choice of sewing machine, or needle and thread
26 paintings (30 papers cut to fit baggies, any kind of paint, paintbrush)
scissors
permanent marker

Process
To prepare –
1. Stack the 14 the ziplock baggies together with edges and corners matching. An adult can staple these to hold them in place. Sew through the stack on the closed ends (not the zipper ends) by hand with needle and thread, or have an adult sew them together with a zigzag stitch on the sewing machine. Sometimes it helps to punch holes along the edge to make sewing easiest. (See illustrations.) If all this seems too complicated, staple all the bags together instead!
2. Leave the first baggie blank to be used for the cover of the book. Use a permanent marker to label each baggie-page of the book beginning with A and ending with Z. Then set aside.

The paintings – It make take some time to create and collect paintings for all 26 letters of the alphabet, but it's a satisfying experience to create the collection over time.
1. Begin thinking of what to paint for each alphabet letter. Anything that starts with that letter of the alphabet is suitable, or work with a category like "animals" or "flowers" or "insects" for another approach. Begin by painting one alphabet painting on each paper. For example, paint an apple on the first paper for A, banana for B, and so on. Start with any letter of the alphabet that comes to mind first. Little by little, all 26 letters will have a painting.
2. When each painting is dry, slip it into the labeled baggie for the correct alphabet page.
3. Remember to make a cover painting and a "The End" painting. (Don't forget to label the cover with the name of the book's author and illustrator.)

Variations
• Create a Number Baggie Book, painting 1 object on the first page, 2 objects on the second page, 3 objects on the third page, and so on.
• Create a very easy book by simply stapling a grouping of paintings together, whether it is alphabetical or not. Papers should be the same size or trimmed to be the same size.

"It is the 'drama' in a picture book that interests me most. I stage the story the way a director might work on a theater piece."

- ANITA LOBEL
Anita Lobel's website,
www.anitalobel.com
& email request February 2003

by Jennifer Reinstra, age 9

Bernard Lodge October 19, 1933

Imitate the style of Bernard Lodge's wood cut illustrations. Squeeze glue designs on blocks of wood. When the glue is hard and dry, make prints with the glue blocks.

There Was an Old Woman Who Lived in a Glove • *Bernard Lodge, author*

There is an old woman who lives in a glove, not a shoe. Readers follow her daily excursions as she finds out how other people live.

by Laura Sanchez, age 9

"There Was an Old Woman Who Lived in a Glove *was my first children's book as author and illustrator. Previous to that I'd had a 30 year career as a graphic designer in the TV industry."*

— BERNARD LODGE
letter to MaryAnn Kohl 2002

Glue Block Print

Materials
white glue in squeeze bottle (some brands are Elmer's™ Glue, Elmer's™ School Glue, LePages™, & RoseArt™)
block of wood
tempera paint and brush
paper
pad of newspaper

Process
1. Squeeze a thick design of glue on one side of the block of wood. Make several wood block designs to have a variety of designs. Then set aside to dry for several days until the glue is hard, dry, and clear.
2. Place a sheet of paper on a thick pad of newspapers.
3. Paint the glue design with tempera paint, and press the design onto paper. Make several prints from the painted design. Then, repaint and make more prints.

Variations
- To make prints with a bar of soap, scratch, dig, and carve a design into a bar of soap, dip in paint, and press on paper. Use a cuticle stick to dig out designs.
- Glove prints: Pull on a rubber glove. Make a glove print by painting the hand of the glove with tempera, and then pressing the rubber glove onto paper. Make many prints with different hand positions.
- Funny Glove Prints: Stick corn pads or bunion pads on the fingers of a latex glove, press in paint, and then on paper, making the prints while wearing the glove. For added design, cut the pads into different shapes.

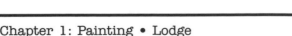

~ art idea generously contributed by
Fall River Elementary School,
Fall River Mills, California

Storybook Art © 2003 Bright Ring Publishing, Inc.

Robert McCloskey September 15, 1914 –1972

Blueberries for Sal • Robert McCloskey, author

In this true story (the real Sal lives in Maine), Sal and her mother go out for a day of blueberry picking carrying their little tin buckets. Sal meets up with another youngster who is out picking berries – a bear cub. The little cub also has a mother - a very big *bear* mother!

CALDECOTT HONOR 1949

Enjoy and appreciate Robert McCloskey's blueberry story illustrations with their familiar blue-and-gold colors. Press fingers in blue paint to make quick and easy dots that look like blueberries, or paint with fresh blueberries instead!

Blue Fingerdots

Materials
white paper
blue paint in shallow dish
fingers
green and brown marking pens or crayons, optional
fresh blueberries, optional

Process
1. Dip a fingertip in blue paint and make "fingerdot" prints on the paper resembling blueberries. Add green leaves and brown twigs with markers or crayons to complete the blueberry designs. Feel free to create any design on the paper. Try making borders, patterns, or simple random prints.
2. As an optional idea, make prints with real blueberries on white paper!

Variation
• Wrap the blue-dot paper around a cardboard paint bucket and tape to hold. Trim the blue-dot paper to fit. Poke two holes in the edge of the bucket and add a wire handle or string. Use the blue-dot bucket for picking blueberries or as a great place to store crayons or toys.

by Taylor Niemi, age 11

"I get a lot of letters. Not only from children but from adults, too. Almost every week, every month, clippings come in from some part of the world where ducks are crossing the street."(McCloskey also wrote Make Way for Ducklings, among many other award-winning titles.)

— ROBERT MCCLOSKEY
reprinted with permission from The Horn Book, Inc.,
www.hbook.com, interview by Anita Silvey, Horn Book Radio Review, Virtual History Exhibit

~ art idea generously contributed by
  Laurel Rancitelli, Springfield, Massachusetts

David McKee January 2, 1935

Experience what David McKee might have thought as he imagined and then illustrated the story of *Elmer*, the patchwork elephant. Create a unique patchwork parade of elephants designed with bright "junk-prints".

"I deplore the fact that picture books are automatically labeled as young children's books, and I like to work for adults and children at the same time; I am proud of being called the Master of the Modern Fable."

- DAVID MCKEE
Andersen Publishing and David McKee letter to MaryAnn Kohl 2003
London - original publisher
HarperCollins - USA editions
www.andersenpress.co.uk

by Andrew DeMann
age 10
*Andrew is very proud to sketch his favorite picture book illustrator

Elmer • *David McKee, author*

All the elephants paint themselves to look like Elmer, an unusual patchwork elephant.

Patchwork Parade

Materials
heavy paper for template
colored paper for elephants
scissors, glue, pencil
tempera paints, puddles poured in
   Styrofoam grocery trays
collect "junk" for printing –
   potato masher
   sponges
   blocks
   eraser of pencil
   bristle block
   comb
   fork
   strawberry basket
   hair curler
   string
   thumb
   pinecone
wide black marker
long piece of cardboard or roll of
   butcher paper

Process
1. An adult can help draw a large elephant shape on heavy paper and cut it out with scissors. This will be the elephant stencil or template for tracing more elephant shapes.
2. Trace the elephant template on different sheets of colored paper, but do not cut them out yet. Make as many as desired, but make at least five. More can be made later, if needed.
3. Spread all the colored elephants on a worktable. Draw large open criss-cross sections on the elephants with a pencil to make the big patchwork shapes (see illustration).
4. Next, make prints inside the patchwork shapes by dipping a junk item into paint and then pressing it into a patchwork space on the elephant. Decorate all the elephants and their patchwork spaces in different ways with different colors. Then let them dry.
5. Trace the patchwork lines on each elephant with a heavy black marker to make the patches stand out.
6. Cut out each elephant with scissors. Glue the patchwork elephants in a long, joyful procession on the piece of cardboard or on a long roll of butcher paper. Add as many elephants as desired - enough to parade all the way around the room would be a significant accomplishment!

Variations
Decorate or paint the cardboard before gluing the elephants on, with ideas such as –
- first paint the background black to show off the elephant colors
- cover the background with aluminum foil, metallic or regular wrapping paper, butcher paper, fabric, or burlap

The Squiggle • *Carole Lexa Schaefer, author*

A young girl finds a simple red string and thinks, imagines, and discovers all it could be.

Imitate the cheerful style of Pierr Morgan. Paint with tempera paints on a brown paper grocery bag.

Brown Bag Painting

Materials
brown paper grocery bag
scissors
iron and ironing area (adult help)
tempera paints and paintbrush
jar of water for rinsing
red string and glue, optional

Process
1. Cut away the bottom section of a brown paper grocery bag (discard or save for other projects). Cut apart the remaining bag on its center seam.
2. Open the bag and smooth it out flat. (An adult can iron out the wrinkles with a very warm iron, with or without steam. Cool briefly before continuing.)
3. Paint designs or a picture on the brown paper to imitate the look of the illustrations in the book.
4. Consider gluing a red string onto the brown paper in the shape of something like a snake, house, ball, bear, or any other idea. Then paint around the outside edges of the string, or paint inside the borders of the string to fill in the rest of the picture.

Variations
- Glue a red string on the brown grocery bag paper, and then draw with crayons, incorporating the string design into the picture.
- Play "What could it be?" with homemade game cards. With a red marker, make a squiggle or shape on a white index card. Make a whole set of cards, perhaps ten to twenty in the set. To play, hold up one card for a friend to guess "What could it be?" Then take turns guessing with different cards.
- Another book by the author-illustrator team is *Snow Pumpkin*.

by Kailey Olson, age 9

"As a child I began drawing pictures. Now I like to work with kids, and drawing on paper bags. The Squiggle *took 22 years to find its words: Carole Lexa came out of the shower one morning with the words in her mind, and called me to say she had them - finally! I had originally pictured* The Squiggle *as a wordless book."*

— PIERR MORGAN
interview by MaryAnn Kohl 2002

Squiggle Yarn Clouds & Painted Ducks
by Kayla Johnston, age 7

Diana Pomeroy November 23, 1945

Working artfully with everyday potatoes imitates the style of Diana Pomeroy's fruit and vegetable illustrations. Making shaded potato prints is a novel way to take potato printing one step further. Explore printing with other objects, fruits, and vegetables in addition to the versatile potato.

by Derek DeMann, age 12

"My designs all start with an X-acto blade and a cut potato. I then carefully carve a detailed image to create a bas-relief surface similar to a rubber stamp. The next step is to carefully paint the images with a small brush and acrylics. All the shading and detail is done directly onto the potato through either the carving or the painting process – nothing is added once the image is stamped."
- DIANA POMEROY
interview by MaryAnn Kohl 2003
excerpt from www.potatoprint.com

One Potato • Diana Pomeroy, author

Bright potato prints show groups of fruits and vegetables for counting 1 through 20, counting by 10's up to 50, and finishing with 100.

Shaded Potato Prints

Materials
knife (adult)
potato
pencil
grapefruit spoon or other digging
   utensils
tempera paints and brush
paper

Process
1. With the help of an adult, cut a potato in half. With a pencil, draw a simple geometric shape, letter, or any created design on the sliced portion of the potato.
2. With the spoon, scrape away the part of the potato that is not part of the shape. The shape will be raised; the background will be cut and scraped away.
3. Paint any color on the remaining raised shape. Then, firmly press the potato on the paper to make a print. Make several prints before repainting. Each print will be lighter than the first.
4. Shading Step: With the spoon or other digging utensil, scoop away a little more of the remaining shape. Paint a different color on the potato shape and press the potato on the prints already made. Try to print exactly on the area of the first print. This will produce the look of dual colored shading. Continue this method to make more shaded prints or additional prints.

Variations
• Explore making prints with other objects from around the house, such as these suggestions:

bar of soap	eraser on a pencil
hands, fingers, toes	rubber glove
carrot	toy, or part of toy
block	crumpled foil
nuts and bolts	

• Use this technique to make wrapping paper and note cards.

Rémi Saillard · October 31, 1960

Mr. Fine, Porcupine · *Fanny Joly, author*

Mr. Porcupine's prickly quills prevent him from making friends, leading him to unsuccessfully flatten and smooth them. It takes someone special to appreciate him and show him that he can be loved just for being himself.

Rémi Saillard's illustrations resemble a lino-style wood cut with distinctive patterns. He uses a scratching technique along with colored ink. Imitate this playful look of Rémi Saillard's work by scraping details in a fingerpainted picture.

Wipe Away Fingerpaints

by Geneva Faulkner
age 14

"I'm glad to know that Mr. Fine's life is going on over the ocean. In France, there is a second part to Mr. Fine called Mr. Fine's Wedding. I work on "scratching card" and use ink for the colour. I also use the computer a great deal."

- RÉMI SAILLARD
letter to MaryAnn Kohl 2003

Materials

pencil
sheet of finger paint paper
fingerpaint (squeeze 1 squirt of liquid tempera into a puddle of liquid starch directly on the paper to make an easy fingerpaint)
craft stick, cuticle stick, pencil without point
permanent marker

Process

1. Draw a large simple shape or animal on the fingerpaint paper. Draw the object with outlines like those found find in a coloring book, without details. Some suggestions are –

chicken	sheep
cat	barn
house	church

2. Carefully spread fingerpaint with fingers on the paper keeping within the lines of the drawings. Different colors can be used. When done, wash hands.
3. Add features and details to the painting with a stick.. For example, a chicken might need detailed feathers, a sheep might need curly swirled wool, a house might need a textured roof or brick wall. With a craft stick or other tool, scratch away the detailing lines. Wipe the stick on a rag between each scratched design. When satisfied with the detailing, let the painting dry.
4. Use a permanent marker to add final details to the painting, such as eyes for animals.

Variations

- Place an outline-style drawing under waxed paper. Smear fingerpaint on the waxed paper, staying within the lines. Then add details to the paint with fingers or a stick.
- Use several colors for each outlined drawing under the waxed paper. For example, a chicken might have red feathers, yellow beak and orange feet.
- Use the same technique freehand without outlines.

Spread fingerpaint in a simple design or shape, and add scratched details with a stick.

John Schoenherr July 5, 1935

John Schoenherr's illustrations are a delicate watercolor interpretation of a cold winter night. Imitate his wintry watercolor technique with blue washes over white paper, masking out some areas to remain white. Black crayon lines will give this crayon resist strong contrast.

by Brittany Peterson, age 9

"I have always tried to draw what I could see. That lets me draw what I can imagine. When I was very young, every kid of my age in the neighborhood spoke a different language. I remember hearing French, Italian, German, Chinese and even Mohawk. I was trying to explain something, grabbed a piece of sidewalk chalk, and drew what I meant. It worked, and still does."

— JOHN SCHOENHERR
letter to MaryAnn Kohl 2003

Peel away masked areas after painting. They will remain white and bold offering great contrast.

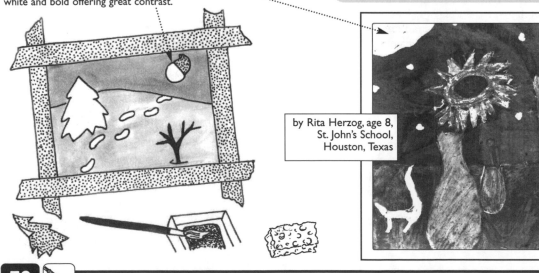

by Rita Herzog, age 8, St. John's School, Houston, Texas

Owl Moon • *Jane Yolen, author*

A little girl and her father search for owls late one winter night, sharing precious time together search.

CALDECOTT MEDAL 1988

Winter Night Stencil

Materials
watercolor paper or heavy white
    drawing paper
sponge dampened with water
pencil
black crayon
scissors
materials for masking white areas -
    contact paper
    masking tape
watercolor paints - blue and black
wide, soft paintbrush & other brushes
jar of water for mixing and rinsing
plate for mixing paint

Process
1. Tape all edges of the paper to the table with masking tape which will act as a border or frame. It will also keep the paper from curling. Brush the entire watercolor paper with the damp sponge. Then let it dry completely.
2. Lightly sketch a winter scene on the paper with a pencil. Try to make simple scenes, such as, bare trees and hills or ponds. Go over some of lines with a black crayon. Leave other lines in pencil.
3. Think about what areas in the drawing will stay white (unpainted). Cover those areas with pieces of masking tape or shapes cut from adhesive contact paper. Suggestions for areas left white are – footprints, moon, trees, clouds, ice.
4. Mix blue or gray paint with water on the plate. Experiment with color mixing on a scrap of white paper to see how the colors look. Then with a wide, soft brush, spread color across the paper to form sky, shadows, and darker areas of snow. Use light blue, dark blue, light gray, and dark gray.
5. Leave some of the painting white or unpainted. The watercolor paint will resist the black crayon marks, making them stand out. Let the painting dry.
6. Now for the fun part — the art surprise! Peel the masking tape (or contact paper shapes) away from the paper carefully. Peel the border of masking tape away too. Now, behold the wintry night snowscape framed in white with bold white shapes!

Variation
• While the watercolor paint is still wet, sprinkle a little table salt into the paint on the paper. This will form crystals that will look like mysterious snow beautifully crystallized.

Charles G. Shaw May 1, 1892 –1974

It Looked Like Spilt Milk • *Charles G. Shaw, author*

The delightful simple text shows white cloud shapes formed on a bright blue background. The clouds resemble everyday objects and animals, but who's to know? Is it a rabbit, a bird, or just spilt milk? Children are kept guessing until the surprise ending — and may be inspired to improvise a white design of their own.

Shaving cream is one of several choices of white art materials that allow for an interesting take-off on Charles G. Shaw's imaginative illustrations in this well-loved old classic.

Cream Clouds

Materials
white glue, 1/4 cup [60ml]
shaving cream, 1 cup [240ml]
bowl
spoon
dark paper

Process
1. Mix 1/4 cup [60ml] white glue with 1 cup [240ml] aerosol shaving cream in a bowl. Stir with a spoon.
2. Plop the mixture on dark blue paper.
3. Shape the fluffy thick mixture into clouds with fingers, a spoon, or a Popsicle stick. Make the clouds in interesting shapes like a rabbit, bird, balloon, or star. Use imagination and think up new ideas.
4. The mixture will dry puffy.

Variations
- Squeeze the mixture from a clean squeeze bottle onto paper or cardboard. Try writing words and letters, as well as making designs and shapes.
- Lie on the grass and look up at the cloudy sky, imagining what the shapes could be. Use those same shapes in art, cutting white paper into the the same shapes or objects that were seen.
- Paint white paint on blue paper. What could it be? Write the word on the paper. Staple several different paintings together to make a Spilt Milk booklet.

~ art idea generously contributed by
Linda Grenier, Marion, Indiana

by Laura Sanchez, age 9

"Much of my education that mattered, that stuck with me, was found and formed in the library of our house because my father and uncle had a very good library and all kinds of books to read. I started reading at an early age. I read a good deal even before going to school. In that process, I have thought often afterwards that there are [many] things that you never learn at school or in college. Never. A family is so important to the child. There are so many things schools cannot teach or assume that [children] should have been taught before."

- Charles G. Shaw
permission from artarchives.si.edu/askus.cfm
ArtArchives tape recorded interview 4/15/68,
Paul Cummings interviewer

Chris Van Allsburg · June 18, 1949

Imitate the snowy look of Chris Van Allsburg's illustrations. Paint an image of snow falling, with warm yellow light shining from night windows. Van Allsburg uses only paint, but adding a bit of cut & paste adds to the fun!

The Polar Express · Chris Van Allsburg, author

A magical train ride on Christmas Eve takes a boy to the North Pole. He travels through falling snow and sees lights that glow from windows of passing houses and buildings. CALDECOTT MEDAL 1986

by Sarah Wiley-Jones, age 14

"… as a successful author, every time the book is read, the book happens. I feel not a sense of power, but a sense of connectedness, I guess. Just to be able to make those books and have them out there, and to know that kids are going to take them home and actually have an experience, not identical with the one I had. But they're going to be, in a way, captives of my mind and their imagination."

- CHRIS VAN ALLSBURG
Lannon, Linnea. "The Van Allsburg Express,"
Sunday Magazine, Detroit Free Press, 10/22/95 p.7-9

Lights & Snow

Materials
large gray or blue drawing paper
tempera or watercolor paints
paintbrushes
water in jar for rinsing
cotton swab and white tempera paint
   in a dish
sheet of yellow paper
scissors
glue or tape

Process
1. Begin by painting any outdoor winter scene on the gray or blue paper. Include buildings and other night objects that could have light shining from their windows, like houses, barns, high rise office buildings, street lights, and churches. Then let the painting dry.
2. To create falling snow, dip a cotton swab into white paint, and dab white dots all over the dry painting. Let this dry too.
3. To make the warmly shining windows, cut little squares and rectangles in appropriate window areas in the painting. Cut as many windows (holes) as desired. Then tape or glue a sheet of bright yellow paper to the back of the painting, so the yellow paper will show through the cut out window holes.

Variations
• Cover the back of the painting with yellow cellophane or yellow art tissue. Then display the painting in a window so the light will shine through the yellow windows like stained glass.
• Spatter white paint on the painting to make a snowy look.

Storybook Art © 2003 Bright Ring Publishing, Inc.

Light • *retold by Sarah Waldman*

Neil Waldman and his author/teen-daughter, Sarah, tell the dramatic story of the first seven days of Biblical creation with simple words and colorful mosaic-like illustrations. *Light* is the first book for the father-daughter team.

Imitate the book cover's artistic design, *Light*, as seen on Neil Waldman's book. Cut the letters of a word from black paper. Then place the paper with its cut-out letters removed over a bright painting. Each letter will open a window to the colors beneath.

Window Letters

Materials
black construction paper (about 16"x24" [40cmx60cm])
pencil
pointed scissors
white drawing paper (same size as black paper)
paints and brushes
glue, tape, or stapler

Process
1. Think of a word to draw in bold letter shapes on the black paper. This word will be highlighted with a painting, explained in steps 4 and 5.
2. Sketch the letters of the word on black paper. Make them thick and large with no fine lines. All the lines should be broad and bold.
3. Gently and carefully poke the point of the scissors carefully into the first letter, and cut the letter out. It won't matter if the letter is cut into pieces, as it is the paper surrounding the letter that is important. Cut out each letter of the word. Discard scraps, or save in the scrap box. Set aside the black paper until the painting is done.
4. Paint a picture on the white paper that will peek through the cut out letters of the word. Some suggestions are:

If the word is –	Paint –
light	sunrise, stars
sky	clouds
cat	toy mouse
your name	yourself

5. When the painting is nearly dry, place the black paper with the cut out word over the painting. Match edges. Staple, tape, or glue the two pieces of paper together.
6. The painting will peek through the cut out word, looking brighter with the contrast to the black paper.

Variations
- Draw a word on black or dark blue paper with bright colored chalk dipped in water. Fill in each letter with colorful chalk designs.
- Cut out letters from black or any other colored paper, and glue them in a design onto a dry, bright painting.

by Nicholas Snydar, age 9

"There are difficulties in living the life I've chosen. Sometimes I struggle for weeks or months, searching for the soul of a story that continues to elude me. At other times I worry about the erratic work schedule and unsteady income. But the countless joys and thrills that tumble about me like autumn leaves make it clear that there is no other profession on earth that I would choose."

- NEIL WALDMAN
interview by MaryAnn Kohl 2003

Ellen Stoll Walsh September 2, 1942

Explore Stoll's color mixing idea as acted out by three white (briefly) mice. Print colorful mouse tracks with a plastic toy mouse dipped in paint. Imaginative mixing of colors is encouraged, like any good mouse would do!

by Hannah Robinson, age 9

"While I'm writing my stories, I begin to imagine what the characters who move through them look like, and I want to see them on paper. Drawing my characters helps establish their personalities and makes them and my stories come alive for me."

- ELLEN STOLL WALSH
Something About the Author®,
Vol.99, p.210
©2003 The Gale Group, Inc.

Mouse Paint • Ellen Stoll Walsh, author

While trying to outsmart a cat, three white mice come upon jars of red, blue and yellow paint. They dance, jump, and amaze themselves as they mix colors, discovering how to make purple and orange and green!

Mixing Mouse Tracks

Materials

plastic toy mice (used for party favors and around Halloween) Alternative idea: If plastic mice are not available, simply make a thumb or finger print, and pretend it is a mouse track! The eraser of pencil also makes a nice little track.

tempera paints in flat Styrofoam grocery trays

Process

1. Spread a thin layer of paint in a Styrofoam grocery tray, one color for each tray. Red, blue, and yellow primary colors are good choices and correlate with the story illustrations.
2. Press the feet of a plastic mouse into one color of paint, and then onto paper to make mouse tracks. Make many many tracks here, there, and everywhere!
3. Dip the toy mouse in a variety of paint colors so colored tracks can mix and combine, just like in the book. Try to make purple, green, and orange.

Variations

- On a warm, sunny day, go outside with bare feet. Walk in a tray of cool squishy paint, and then on paper, recreating the idea of mouse tracks. Repeat making tracks over and over. Walk through more than one color or walk through previously made footprints so colors will mix and create new colors.
- On the end of a wooden dowel, glue a mouse shaped track cut from the insole of a shoe or a stick-on toe pad. Let the glue dry. Make mouse track prints by pressing the track in paint and then on paper.
- Create painted foot prints directly on a blacktop or concrete playground, sidewalk, or driveway. Prints will eventually rinse away after many rainy days.

~ art ideas generously contributed by –
Nancy Yost, Indiana, Pennsylvania
Linda Grenier, Marion, Indiana
Lisa Brunick, Sioux Falls, South Dakota

Lynd Ward June 26, 1905 –1985

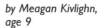

The Biggest Bear • Lynd Ward, author

Johnny Orchard brings home a playful bear cub that soon becomes a huge, tremendous challenge to his family and neighbors.

CALDECOTT MEDAL 1953

Lynd Ward's illustrations come to life through monochromatic color (shades of one color). Imitate the monochromatic range of browns using natural supplies on hand — tea, coffee, or mud.

Mono Color Painting

Materials
selection of materials to make brown
  monochromatic paints, such as —
    tea bags
    coffee grounds
    mud
    food coloring
    bark
    brown leaves
adult assistance
quart of water in a pot
stove
cups, one for each paint-making
  material
spoon, strainer if needed
paper
paintbrushes

Process
1. An adult can heat a pot of water to boiling to use for making the paints. A quart should be about right.
2. Sort each of the materials into separate cups.
3. An adult can carefully pour 1/4 cup [60ml] hot water into each cup, covering the paint-making materials. Let the cups sit for two hours or until the water has colored well. There should be variations of color from light to dark.
4. Remove the coffee, tea, and mud with a spoon or strainer.
5. Paint a picture using the monochromatic variety of colors.

Variation
• Experiment with other materials that can make other colors, such as cranberries for red, beets for pink, crepe paper scraps for bright red.

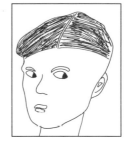

"It is said that Lynd Ward decided to be an artist when, in the first grade, he realized that "draw" was "Ward" spelled backwards."

- JIM VADEBONCOEUR, JR.
ABOUT LYND WARD,
Bud Plant Illustrated Books
www.bpib.com

by Meagan Kivlighn, age 9

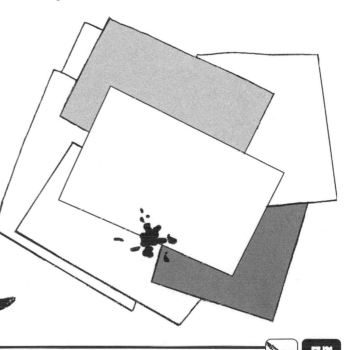

Taro Yashima's drawn and painted illustration style resembles a scratchy kind of painting on plaster called *fresco*, also similar to *scrimshaw* (etching designs in ivory or bone). Make a plaster tablet and etch designs into it with a pointed tool. Paint on the damp plaster to highlight the work with color.

Seashore Story • *Taro Yashima (Jun Atsushi Iwamatsu), author*

Children hear an old Japanese tale about a fisherman who rode under the sea on a turtle's back.

CALDECOTT HONOR 1968

Etch & Paint Plaster

by Abby Walters, age 9

From 1967 until 1970, I had the good fortune to have been a student of Taro's. "Paint what smiles at you," Taro Yashima told us — the founder and sole instructor at the Yashima Art Institute in Los Angeles. One phrase that stays in my mind is Taro saying "Nay", (sounded like nay, but drawn out and rising at the end as if to mean, "Oh, is that so?"). Sometimes he would follow up with a fast and energetic string of words. Other times, though, his "nay" would be soft and falling, part of a slow melancholy discussion, as if to say, "Oh, yes the world can break your heart."

- JOHN O'BRIEN,
former student of Taro Yashima,
writeman.homestead.com
letter to MaryAnn Kohl 2003

Materials
choice of container for the plaster
   mold (cardboard box, pie tin, or
   paper plate)
plaster of Paris
water in a container
stick or paint stir stick
etching tool, such as —
   cuticle stick
   opened paperclip
   ballpoint pen
watercolor or tempera paints
paintbrushes

Process
1. Mix the plaster of Paris in a container according to directions on the package until it is like a thick 'whipped cream' consistency. Pour the plaster into the selected mold. Smooth the top of the plaster with the flat side of a stick. Let the plaster harden slightly and set briefly. It should be damp, but not soft and wet.
   * DO NOT WASH PLASTER DOWN THE DRAIN. It will clog pipes and make for an unhappy day. Toss plaster scraps into the trash or crumble and sprinkle in the garden to help aerate the soil mix.
2. Gently remove the mold from around the plaster form. Work carefully so the form does not break. Turn the form over to the flat side. What was the top of the plaster form is now on the bottom.
3. Etch and scratch designs into the plaster form with a cuticle stick or other tool. An opened paperclip or closed ballpoint pen also work well. Make cross-hatchings, squiggles, or other designs to fill in or shade as if "drawing" with a pencil. Brush away the scrapings.
4. With a very dry brush, paint on the damp plaster etching with tempera or watercolor paints. The paint will brush over the design, leaving the etchings white and brushing color on the flat plaster.
5. The form should dry overnight.

Variation
• To display —
Insert a wire or paperclip into the plaster during the pouring stage. The wire will dry into the plaster and form a sturdy device to loop over a hook or nail in the wall.

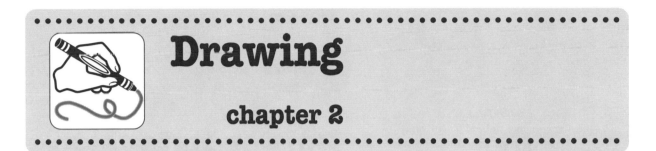

Drawing

chapter 2

Nap Doggie Dog by Erin McGill, age not given
based on
Where the Sidewalk Ends by Shel Silverstein

Off to Planet X by Megan Kohl, age 5 (1983)
based on
The Magic School Bus Lost in the Solar System
by illustrator Bruce Degen, author Joanna Cole

Diving Ducks by Valeria Quiroz-Nava, age 8
based on
The Story of Ping
by illustrator Kurt Wiese, author Margaret Wise Brown

Jim Arnosky September 1, 1956

Imitate one of Jim Arnosky's illustration techniques. Extend the drawing beyond its borders and into the surrounding frame.

by Sarah Wiley-Jones, age 14

"I am convinced that if you love the outdoors, natural places, and wildlife, you will grow into a person who will consider those factors no matter what work you do. My job is to foster an appreciation of nature and a curiosity about wildlife. I tell kids what I know and let them decide how to think about it. Hopefully they'll use that knowledge and make a difference."
- JIM ARNOSKY
interview by Lisa Horak,
reprinted with permission from
BookPage: America's Book Review
11/98 issue

The Empty Lot • Dale H. Fife, author

Harry inspects a partially wooded empty lot before selling it, but finds it is not empty at all! It is the home of birds, frogs, insects, and a place where children have built a tree-house. Harry makes an environmental decision. AMERICAN BOOKSELLER PICK OF THE LISTS • NCSS-CBC NOTABLE CHILDREN'S TRADE BOOK IN SOCIAL STUDIES • NSTA-CBC OUTSTANDING SCIENCE TRADE BOOK FOR CHILDREN

Border Extension

Materials
large drawing paper
rectangle or square to trace
pencil
colored pencils
permanent markers, optional

Process
1. Trace a rectangle or square in the middle of a piece of drawing paper. There should be no less than 2"-3" [5cm-8cm] around the traced shape giving a wide border.
2. Draw a picture in the square, drawing parts of the picture to extend beyond the border. For example, Arnosky draws a vine of ivy growing off of the picture, the beak of a bird extending beyond the border, and tree limbs reaching outside the border.
3. Color the illustrations with colored pencils.
4. If desired, highlight the outlines of the illustration with permanent markers.

Variation
• A famous painter, Georgia O'Keeffe, painted "larger than life" flowers that extended beyond the border of her canvas. Paint a huge flower to the edges of the paper, letting the rest of the flower disappear onto the table top. When the painting is done, wash the remaining paint from the table.

border of drawing

illustrations extend beyond the central drawing

Muriel Batherman 1926

The Alphabet Tale • Jan Garten, author

This rhyming alphabet book is a "tale of tails" presented within a guessing game and clues on each page. Readers look at the tail, hear the clue, and then guess which tail belongs to that animal.

> Imitate Muriel Batherman's scribbly illustration style. Create an animal or imaginary creature with a self-designed stencil, using markers for added color.

See Through Scribbles

Materials

very heavy paper (old file folders, thin posterboard, tagboard)
black marker or pencil
scissors
white drawing paper
tape
colored markers

Process

1. With a black marker or pencil, draw a simple animal or creature shape on the heavy paper. Do not worry about details. Draw a bold shape like drawings found in a coloring book.
2. To cut out the shape only, poke a little hole in the animal shape with the point of the scissors. Slip the point into the hole and begin cutting. Cut away the inside shape, leaving the surrounding paper intact. This will be the stencil. Only the outside shape will be needed; the inside shape can be added to the scrap box.
3. Place the stencil on top of a sheet of drawing paper. Tape down the corners of both to hold both sheets of paper to the table.
4. Begin scribbling inside the stencil shape with a marker. Make curly, scribbly marks to fill in the shape. No need to color it in completely.
5. Move the stencil and make another scribbly shape. Do this again and again, making as many scribbly stencil shapes as desired.
6. When done, remove the stencil.
7. Add other simple features to the stenciled shapes, such as eyes, noses, or smiles!

Variations

- Trace around the inside shape, adding this design to the scribbly ones from the stencil.
- Look at other books illustrated by Muriel Batherman, such as, *Before Columbus* (Houghton Mifflin, 1994).

Muriel Batherman was unavailable for a portrait sketch.
Morgan Van Slyke, age 7, has created a portrait sketch of Muriel Batherman from her imagination.

"I find being an author-illustrator wonderful. Not only do I have the pleasure of visualizing the complete book, I also have the job of sharing my interests with young people as well. I can think of nothing more rewarding."
— MURIEL BATHERMAN
Something About the Author®, Vol.125 p.67 ©2003 The Gale Group, Inc.

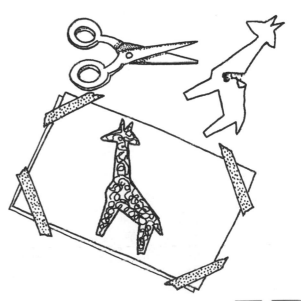

Patrick Benson January 5, 1956

With a black pen and white paper, imitate Patrick Benson's shaded cross-hatch technique. Draw objects or animals that are shaded on one side, appearing as if seen in the shadowy dark of night.

by Laura Sanchez, age 9

"I always had a pencil in my hand when I was a little boy and I drew and drew all the time. I like drawing from real life but I could not find any baby owls for this book so I had to imagine them. These are tawny owls . . . and where I live in Scotland, if I go out just as it is getting dark, I quite often hear them going "Twawitt . . . twawooh" in the woods behind the house . . . and there was one sitting on my garden fence just last week!"

- Patrick Benson
letter to MaryAnn Kohl 2003

Owl Babies • Martin Waddell, author

Three fluffy, wide-eyed and very worried owlets wait for their mother to return from her night flight.

Cross-Hatch & Stipple

Materials
paper
choice of drawing tools —
    black fine tipped marker
    pen

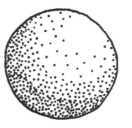

Process
1. Learning to cross-hatch takes some practice, and practice is an exciting experiment.
2. To begin, draw a simple bold shape on the paper, such as a square. Inside the square on one side, experiment with making lines that cross each other called "cross-hatching" (see illustrations). Cross-hatch means to make fine lines and then cross over those lines with more fine lines. Cross-hatching is a great way to make objects look like they are in the shade, or shaded on one side. The other side can be unshaded — perfect for a night drawing full of both dark shadows and moonlight.
3. Stippling is another form of shading that creates a feeling of shadows and light. Draw another shape, perhaps a circle this time. Experiment with stippling, a series of many dots on one side of the shape, some close together (very dark shading) and some father apart (lighter shading) or no stippling at all (bright light).
4. Practice cross-hatching and stippling on other shapes until the technique feels comfortable. Experiment with actual drawings of things like a house, mountain, tree, apple, or person's face. Imagine a bright flashlight is shining on part of the shape, and then cross-hatch or stipple the shaded part.
5. Ready for the real artwork? Draw a picture of something that is part of a dark night, and then cross-hatch and stipple the shadows and light into the picture. Baby owls might be fun to draw sitting on a branch, like in the book. Perhaps other night ideas would be interesting to draw.

Variation
• Benson works with a black background and white or colored lines in his illustrations. On black paper, draw with white chalk or white pencil, cross-hatching and stippling the shaded areas with white.

Marvin Bileck March 2, 1920

Rain Makes Applesauce • *Julian Scheer, author*

This 30 year old classic book of nonsense verse gives the reader a real story cleverly hidden in the illustrations. The colorful drawings change throughout the book, winding and jubilantly tumbling, squishing, and changing.

1965 CALDECOTT HONOR BOOK • 1965 ALA NOTABLE BOOK
• NEW YORK TIMES 10 BEST ILLUSTRATED BOOKS

To appreciate the imagination and design used in his lettering, imitate illustrator, Marvin Bileck. Draw words or names expressed through stylized lettering. The words *are* the art!

Fancy Words

Materials
pencil
colored pencils, crayons, markers
white drawing paper

©1978 Marvin Bileck By Trolley Past Thimbledon Bridge
The Wee Folk of Thimbledon are looking for a publisher (31 illustrations) by Marvin Bileck.

Process
1. Think of an interesting word. It can be a name or any word at all. Words that sound intriguing or look interesting are good choices. For example, the word "puffy" sounds like something that is soft, and when it is written, it has several round shaped letters that look puffy!
2. Draw a word or name lightly on the paper with a pencil. Make the shape of the letters doubled lines so they can be colored in or decorated. Draw it in a way that is unusual or special, like stretching it out very wide, or shrinking it up very tall and thin. Make it curl around in circles or change it into a box shape. Practice some ideas on scrap paper and then make the fancy word design.
3. When the design is complete, begin coloring and decorating it any way. Decorate all around the word too see illustrations).

Variation
• Write a sentence or several words in a row to illustrate a picture. Create the design of the words artfully to fit into, through, and around the picture.

by Weston Whitener, age 8

"I consider a body type as dynamic and functional a shapeform as any part of the illustration. I was delighted by the imagery and excited by the thought of my pictures (in this book) giving rise to such fantasies and how as they grew they implicated more and varied ramifications of these imaginings."
- MARVIN BILECK
Something About the Author®,
Vol.39 p.38, ©2003 The Gale Group, Inc. &
letter to MaryAnn Kohl

EMILY BILECK, *an award winning artist in her own right, says of her husband's talent, "Marvin is a fine artist who is also a fine illustrator."*
- EMILY BILECK
by telephone 2003

Storybook Art © 2003 Bright Ring Publishing, Inc.

 Chapter 3: Drawing • Bileck **43**

Jan Brett January 2, 1949

Jan Brett incorporates a technique called "sidebars" in her illustrations. Sidebars give the reader a peek at what is happening "behind-the-scene," often an unexpected twist to a familiar story. Draw a picture that tells a story and add a few "behind-the-scene" happenings in the side-bars.

by Karla Witte, age 10

"I remember the special quiet of rainy days when I felt that I could enter the pages of my beautiful picture books. Now I try to recreate that feeling of believing that the imaginary place I'm drawing really exists. The detail in my work helps to convince me, and I hope others as well, that such places might be real."

- JAN BRETT
letter to MaryAnn Kohl 2003 & Brett's website www.janbrett.com

Goldilocks and the Three Bears • *Jan Brett (adapted & illustrated by)*

Jan Brett retells her version of the timeless story about Goldilocks, the golden-haired uninvited little girl exploring the house of three bears, who are out walking in the forest.

Behind-the-Scene

Materials
large white drawing paper
pre-drawn side boxes, drawn simply
    with a straight edge (on the short
    side of the paper – see illustration)
ruler
choice of drawing tools –
    pencils
    crayons
    markers
    pens

Process
1. Think of any favorite story from a book, or imagine an entirely new one.
2. Illustrate one scene from the story in the main body of the drawing paper.
3. Illustrate what else might be occurring "behind the scene" in the side boxes. (See the example in the illustration: A cat is sitting with his eyes closed. He looks like he might be dozing. Now look at the sidebars to see what is going on behind the scene. He might be planning to do some kitty mischief, and perhaps a little mouse has plans for his own mischief!)

Variations
Other book-style ideas –
• Fold a paper in half to open and close like a book. Draw one part of the story on the front. Then open the paper and draw the "behind the scene" picture on the inside. Draw a final closing picture on the back.
• With an empty, clear plastic CD box, trace four squares of paper: 1 for the cover, two for the inside, and one for the back. On the first square, draw or write a "cover" for the "behind the scene" story and press into the CD cover. For the second square, draw a scene from the story. On the third square, draw a "behind the scene" picture. Press these into the center sections. For the fourth square, draw or write a "the end" picture. Display the CD drawings like an open book on a table.
• Read other books by Jan Brett, the author of many favorite books, including *The Mitten* (1989).

Inside boxes can either be pre-drawn, or folded ahead.

The cat and mouse are having a nice quiet rest.

But what are they really thinking? Are they dreaming, or are they remembering something that really happened?

Look at the sidebars to find out.

The cat is dreaming about catching a fish.

The mouse is dreaming about scaring the fishing cat by popping a balloon.

Does he want the cat to fall into the pond? Did it really happen?

~ art idea generously contributed by
Charlene Woodham Peace
Semmes, Alabama

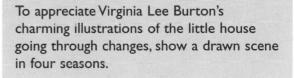

The Little House • *Virginia Lee Burton, author*

Virginia Lee Burton's classic story tells the happy-sad-happy-again story of a little pink house on a hill surrounded by apple trees, who contentedly watches the seasons go by. The surroundings of the little house begin to change in a sad turn of events, but instant happiness awaits with the perfect ending.

CALDECOTT MEDAL 1943

To appreciate Virginia Lee Burton's charming illustrations of the little house going through changes, show a drawn scene in four seasons.

Four Square Seasons

Materials
white drawing paper, folded into four squares
any drawing tools: crayons, markers, colored pencils, oil pastels, chalk, pastels (Consider a multi-mix combination of drawing tools)
ruler or straight edge

Process
1. Fold a sheet of drawing paper in half. Then fold it in half again to make four equal boxes (see illustration). Unfold. With a straight edge as a guide, draw a dividing line on the folds.
2. Think of an outdoor scene that will be drawn in four different seasons, such as a house, a tree, or something seen outdoors. The major subject of each of the four scenes will stay the same in each box (a house, a tree, a fence), but the colors and details of the seasons will change around it. For example, a tree would remain the same in each box, but the leaves would be gone in winter, and in summer, the tree would be bushy with leaves, in spring it would have buds, and in fall the leaves would be colorful and drifting down.
3. To create the four seasons, draw colors and objects in each box that are specifically symbolic of that particular season. Some suggestions are:
   - In the first box, draw summer colors and objects – sunshine, flowers in full bloom, green grass, summer fun.
   - In the second box, change the drawing to "fall" by drawing falling leaves, pumpkins, harvest, and fall colors, etc.
   - In the third box, work with white, blue, gray, snow and ice, or winter fun.
   - In the fourth box, "spring" arrives with bright green colors, buds, birds, and rain to make the flowers grow.

Variation
• Paint four seasons, one on each of four sheets of large paper. Display as a series or staple together as a four page book.

by Briley Ammons, age 12

"I literally draw my books first and write down the text after. . . I pin the sketched pages in sequence on the walls of my studio so I can see the books as a whole. Then I make a rough dummy and then the final drawings, and at last when I can put it off no longer, I type out the text and paste it in the dummy."
-VIRGINIA LEE BURTON
©University of Oregon Library System Bernard McTigue, Director, Division of Special Collections & University Archives
www.libweb.uoregon.edu

fold once
then fold again

Draw the same outdoor scene four times.
Decorate each scene with specific seasonal details.

Donald Crews August 30, 1938

What can be done with ten black dots? Count out black dot stickers, press them on drawing paper. With crayons, make them part of the drawing. Create a counting book, just like Donald Crews!

"To tell a story . . . to write so that people call you an author . . . it's very heady to be called an author and writer, to know that things you create could be useful. In the beginning you don't think in terms of these books in the library, in the card catalog with a list of works you've created. So it is kind of a heady thing to do."

— DONALD CREWS
interviewed by George Bodmer, Professor, Indiana University Northwest, ©1998 *African American Review*

by Molly Brandt, age 7

Black Dot Mouse, artist unknown

Caterpillar by Jazmin Mendoza, age 8

Ten Black Dots • Donald Crews, author

Each page of this rhyming counting book presents a number of inch-wide, counted black dots, and a picture of an object made from those dots.

Spot Dots

Materials
black dot stickers (optional: cut out 1"-2" [3cm-5cm] wide black circles, use glue, gluestick, or tape)
paper
crayons or markers

Apple Tree by Valeria Quiroz-Nava, age 8

Process
1. Count out and stick any number of black dots on the paper.
2. Draw and color with crayons or markers, integrating the black dots into a picture. For example, 2 dots might be the eyes of a puppy, 10 dots might be rocks on a beach, and 4 dots might be the ears of two mice. Imagination is the key.
3. Write a numeral on the black dot drawing telling how many black dots are counted and used.

Variations
• Create a "My Ten Dots" book, making 10 dot drawings starting with a picture made from one dot, another picture made from two dots, then three, and so on. Staple them into a counting book and write the numerals on each page.
• Create dot drawings with any colors of sticker-dots.
• Create a dot picture with very small - or very large - dots in multi-colors.
• Instead of using stickers, make thumbprint or fingerprint dots.
• Create a connect-the-dot drawing.
• Instead of "dots", create with squares, triangles, or even cut circular hoes in the paper.

The Magic School Bus Lost in the Solar System • *Joanna Cole, author*

Ms. Frizzle takes her third-grade class on a trip to the planetarium, but the magic bus has a better idea! It blasts off into space to show the children the real solar system.

BOSTON GLOBE-HORN BOOK AWARD

Draw a picture that imitates Degen's cartoon style. Incorporate "talking bubbles", "talk-outs", or "call-outs" — a common form of dialogue boxes in comics and cartoons.

Talking Bubbles

Bruce Degen has loved art ever since he was a child growing up in Brooklyn, New York. "In sixth grade, I had a wonderful teacher who would let me stand in the back of the room and paint all the time. Once I didn't even have to take a spelling test!"

- BRUCE DEGEN

by Courtney Shoemake, age 9

Scholastic Inc., Kids' Fun Online, The Magic Schoolbus™ ©2003-1996, www.scholastic.com/magicschoolbus/

Materials

poster board or drawing paper
pencil
any drawing materials
such as —
crayons
colored pencils
marking pens
oil pastels
mailing labels
scissors
fine point marking pen
(permanent is good)

Process

1. Look at Bruce Degen's illustrations and find a cartoon bubble called a "call-out" or a "talking bubble". These shapes indicate which character or object is talking. Th call-out technique is also seen in comic books or the Sunday funnies. Graphic lettering or printing in the bubbles will indicate if the character is very loud, quiet, or happy. The use of exclamation points ! ! ! makes what the characters say imperative (very important !).
2. Draw a picture using crayons, colored pencils or other choice of drawing tool. Create a picture that has action about which the characters want to talk or exclaim.
3. To make talking bubbles for the characters, spread a sheet of white lpell-off mailing labels on the table. Decide how many labels are needed — one for each talking bubble. Write the words of one character on one label, and the reply of the other character on another label. Use artistic printing to help communicate how the people are feeling or sounding. Bold letters, thin or small letters, and capitals, will show others how the characters sound and feels.
4. Draw a cloud or black outline around the words on the label. Then peel it off the sheet and press it next to the drawing of the talking character. Do this for all the talking bubbles.
5. More: To make the call-out clearly show which bubble belongs to the correct character, create a pointer for the bubble. Draw a triangle or "tail" shape on a label. One end will be pointed and one end will be wide. Cut the pointer out. Stick the wide end of the pointer so that it just touches the bubble, and the point towards the character who is talking.

Variation

• Fold a long piece of paper into three or four sections in a row. Draw a sequential cartoon, one part of the story in each box. Give the characters "talking bubbles" or "call-outs."

by Taylor VanDalen, age 8

Ed Emberley October 19, 1931

The Emberley couple's classic picture book won a Caldecott medal for its bright, bold illustrations. It is illustrated with colorful woodcuts. Young artists can imitate Ed Emberley's illustrations with marking pens and a special technique that looks a bit like stained glass.

"One of my guiding principles (I have many): Do what you like, hope for the best. It has worked so far. 40 years a children's book illustrator. 100 plus books. 71 years old."

- ED EMBERLEY
letter to MaryAnn Kohl 2002

by Jodi Drost,
age 15

Drummer Hoff • *adapted by Barbara Emberley*

This cumulative folk song tells the tale of seven soldiers who build a cannon and of how Drummer Hoff makes things happen! One of the soldiers, General Border, gives the order. Then Sergeant Chowder brings the powder. But it is Drummer Hoff who fires it off!   CALDECOTT MEDAL 1968

Bold Marking

Materials
wide black permanent marking pen
marking pens in many colors
heavy white paper or poster board

Drummer Hoff Style Tree with Flowers
by Adriana Mitchell, age 8

Process
1. Look at Ed Emberley's illustrations and notice how they look a little like stained glass - blockish thick black outlines filled in with bright colors, bold people, and bold objects.
2. Think of something to draw, perhaps soldiers like those in the book or think up another idea. Draw a scene, or simply draw one thing. As a basic example, draw a round sunshine with rays. Outline all the rays individually, outline the sun, outline every part of it, even a smiling face if desired.
3. Color inside the permanent black lines of the sun with other colors, even colors that the sun would not normally be. Using unusual colors is creative and fun to do.
4. Outline the drawing boldly first, add outline details, and then color in with more pens. Try to stay within the black lines.

Variation
• To experience the idea of making a "wood cut", scratch a design on a *flat* bar of soap, drawing the lines thick and wide. Then, with some adult help, cut away the parts of the design that are NOT lines, leaving the lines of the design raised. (These lines will be the same design style as the black outlines in the above project.) Paint black paint on the bar of carved soap, press it on paper to make a print, and the "soap cut" is complete.

Marie Hall Ets December 16, 1895 –1984

Gilberto and the Wind • Marie Hall Ets, author

A young boy named Gilberto finds a playmate with many moods - the wind! Gilberto becomes involved in the wind's frolics and enjoys an adventure playing and pretending with his new friend.

Imitate the drawing style of Marie Hall Ets, accenting the important elements of pencil drawings with brown and white chalk.

Accented Pencil

Materials
pencil
light green construction paper
   (or another chosen color)
brown chalk
white chalk
black colored pencil

Process
1. Look at the illustrations by Marie Hall Ets. Notice that she uses only a very few colors to highlight her pencil drawings.
2. Begin by sketching a drawing on the green paper with pencil. Make the drawing simple and large so it will be easy to color with chalk.
3. Next, accent parts of the drawing with white and brown chalk. Accent means to make some parts of the drawing more colorful or special, while other parts remain the same. Brown is useful for accenting skin tones, and white for accenting clothing, or think of other ideas. Perhaps accent one of the following suggestions:
   - the petals of a flower with white,
     and the grass with brown
   - a white cat with brown stripes,
     and a brown catnip mouse
   - white clouds in the sky,
     and a brown bird flying
4. Draw and color lightly with the chalk, blending chalk marks with a cotton swab or fingertip.
5. Add more accents with regular pencil, soft drawing pencil, or black colored pencil.

Variation
Accent colors with art materials other than chalk –
   • tempera paint
   • crayon
   • colored pencil
   • oil pastel

Daisy Accent
by Kayla Comstock, age 8

by Molly Brandt,
age 7

"The happiest memories of my childhood are of summers in the north woods of Wisconsin. I loved to run off by myself into the woods and watch for the deer with their fawns, and for porcupines, badgers, turtles, frogs and huge pine snakes and sometimes a bear or a copperhead or a skunk."

- MARIE HALL ETS
Contemporary Authors Online,
©The Gale Group 2000 www.gale.com
& letter from Gale Group 2003

Paul Goble · September 27, 1933

Goble's bright illustrations show the reflections of the wild horses in a creek — a visual concept worth exploring through this drawing experience.

The Girl Who Loved Wild Horses · Paul Goble

A young Native American girl devotes herself to caring for her tribe's horses. When a violent storm frightens the horses into a stampede, she meets a beautiful strong stallion and her life is changed forever.

CALDECOTT MEDAL 1979 · READING RAINBOW AUTHOR

"Coming from England, everyone had a very positive, if romantic, view of Native American people. Since living here, I'm amazed at what people don't know about the Native American culture. I suppose I am partly one to put that right. This country wants everyone to be the same. I like the differences."

- PAUL GOBLE
South Dakota State University
from Lynn Verschoor, interview,
director of the Art Museum
& South Dakota State University,
Honoring Paul Goble, 4/30/02, www.sdstate.edu

by Kate Propersi,
age 11

Mirror Reflection

Materials
fine point marker for
    outlining
2 sheets of white
    drawing paper
scissors
glue
pencil with eraser
colorful marking pens

Process
1. Fold a sheet of drawing paper in half the "hot dog" way (the long way). Place the folded side in line with the edge of the table (see illustration) and the open end towards the other side of the table.
2. With a fine point marker (or a pencil), draw a picture on the folded drawing paper with the base of the drawing touching the fold. Do not color it in yet. (What to draw? Draw a horse if imitating the illustrations in the book, but any subject matter will be fine. Consider drawing a simple picture instead of a detailed or complex picture because it will be easier for this first drawing experience.)
3. Now, cut the doubled drawing out just outside the lines, but do not cut anything on the fold. Then open the folded cut-out drawing.
4. Place the entire cut-out on another sheet of paper and glue it down. The shapes on the lower part of the folded paper will be like a reflection of the drawing on the upper half, but are not yet drawn.
5. Now begin to copy the exact drawing that is seen on the upper half onto the lower half. Use a pencil lightly, and be prepared to erase because it is challenging! When satisfied with the "reflection" drawing, trace the pencil lines with the fine point black marker. Then color the drawing with marking pens, making the top image and the upside down lower image twin reflections of each other. (Optional idea: Coloring-in a pond or lake on the lower image will make the drawing look like it is reflected in water.)
6. Add other details to the reflection art like trees, water, sky, and clouds.

Variation
• Hold a sheet of reflective Mylar or a medium sized mirror directly on the fold of a drawing. Tip it slightly to see an actual reflection of the drawing on the upper half of the paper.

2. reflection template cut & ready

1. preparing the reflection template

3. reflection template in place, further designed & colored

Crockett Johnson October 20, 1906 –1975

Harold & the Purple Crayon • David Johnson Leisk (Crockett Johnson), author

Harold draws a picture of himself with his purple crayon. He draws everything he needs for a very adventurous walk. His line drawing continues from page to page in purple and purple only.

Crockett Johnson's illustrations show Harold drawing one purple line that becomes his walking adventure. To experience the illustrator's representation, create a one-line design with many more drawing tools than just one purple crayon!

All in a Row, One-Line Design

Materials
roll of adding machine or calculator tape
newspaper to cover floor
tape
crayons, markers
roller paint bottle or sponge bottle (if paint bottles are not available, skip this step)
yarn (any color, one long piece)
glue
tape measure

Process
1. Tape a long piece of adding machine paper tape to the floor. Unroll it so that it is very long, as long as possible! (It might be a good idea to put newspaper under the paper to protect the floor.)
2. With a crayon or marker, begin by drawing one line that wiggles and loops across the narrow paper. Try not to lift the crayon from the paper, making it one very long uninterrupted line. Rest a moment. (Keep marks on the paper and not on the floor!)
3. Starting at the last point of the drawn line, continue with a new line of paint made with a roller ball bottle or sponge bottle. Keep going and going, trying not to lift the bottle tip from the paper, making one long uninterrupted line. Then rest again. (If no roller bottle of paint is handy, skip this step and go on to the next.)
4. Now begin working with yarn. Dip a long piece of yarn in glue and continue the one-line design, looping and squiggling the yarn. Add another long piece of yarn in a different color, changing colors whenever desired. Then change back to crayon or paint, just so the line goes on and on.
5. When the end of the design has been reached, sit back and look it over. For fun, measure the one-line design with a tape measure and see how long it is.

Variations
• Start a second or third design that interweaves and crosses through the first design. Use a contrasting color or art material.
• Experiment with other design additions continuing the one line design, such as ribbon, surveyor's tape, or chalk.
• Three sequels are: *Harold's Trip to the Sky* (1957); *Harold's Circus* (1959); *A Picture for Harold's Room* (1960).
• Imitate the illustrator (draw on gray paper) drawing with purple crayon or marker. Then add features with a black fine point marker. Next, glue a character's face into the picture.

"I draw people without hair because it's so much easier! Besides, to me, people with hair look funny."

- CROCKETT JOHNSON
Phil Nel ©1998-2003
Kansas State University
www.ksu.edu/english/nelp/purple

by Jennifer Reinstra, age 9

~ art idea generously contributed by Linda Grenier, Marion, Indiana

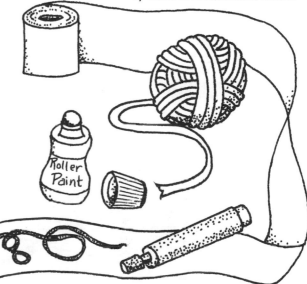

Beth Krommes January 6, 1956

Imitate Beth Krommes' scratchboard technique. Etch a colorful design on "easy to make at home" scratchboard.

by Elizabeth Kayser, age 11

"Although I knew I would be an artist, it took me a long time to figure out that I wanted to be a children's book illustrator. I found that I loved wood engraving with its tiny detail and bold line. Eventually I switched to scratchboard, which is faster but has the same look as wood engraving. Now that I am illustrating children's books, that's all I want to do!"

- BETH KROMMES
interview with & letter to
MaryAnn Kohl 2002

Grandmother Winter • *Phyllis Root, author*

Grandmother Winter shakes out her feather quilt after tending her geese and gathering their feathers.

Homemade Scratchboard

Materials
matboard or white poster board
crayons
bar of soap
masking tape
black tempera paint
paintbrush
un-bent paperclip or wooden cuticle stick for "scratching" (a gently sharpened pencil-sized dowel makes a great stylus)

Process
1. Tape off an area on the poster board or matboard with masking tape. Make the tape form a frame or border on all four sides. (See illustration.) Leave the tape on throughout the entire art activity.
2. Use brightly colored crayons to color within the framed area. Make any pattern from rainbows to blobs to stripes to zigzags. Wildly scribbled colors are also effective. Press very hard to make a thick layer of crayon all over the paper with very little white showing.
3. Rub a bar of soap over the crayon design so the paint will stick to it in the next step.
4. Brush black tempera paint over the colorful crayon layer. Choose to stay within the tape frame, or brush over it and outside its lines. Both ways have a nice artistic result. Then let the paint dry.
5. Scratch a design into the dried black paint with an opened paperclip, cuticle stick, or other scratching tool. The colors from the crayon layer will show through the scratched design.

Variations
• Paint over the crayon layer with white paint. Let dry. Scratch through it. Further draw with waterbased markers on the white paint after the scratching step.
• Purchase scratchboard (already coated with black, white, or other colors - including metallic style) from an art store or school supply store. Draw in the scratchboard with the scratching tool provided in the package.

Leo Lionni June 5, 1910 –1999

Fish is Fish • Leo Lionni

When Little Fish's tadpole friend becomes a frog and leaves the pond, Little Fish works up some ideas for doing the same.

Imitate the drawing style of Leo Lionni, combining two art techniques. Make a textured crayon rubbing background scene. Then glue fish cut-outs (or other creatures) onto the rubbing.

Rub & Cut Scene

Materials
large white drawing paper
scraps of paper with different
   textures —
      sandpaper
      corrugated cardboard
      paper with holes punched
      other papers
pencil and scissors
tape, optional
peeled crayons
   or peeled crayon stubs
colored paper
glue or paste

Process
1. Assemble some textured papers. Cut them into shapes for a picture design, such as these examples:
   seaweed and shells   underwater scene
   cactus and tumbleweed   desert scene
   clouds and rain   sky scene
2. Scatter the shapes on the table in a design or scene. Position the sheet of paper over the tops of the shape design, being careful not to disturb the lightweight pieces. Tape the corners down to hold the paper in place, or hold the paper in one hand while continuing the work. Rub the flat side of a crayon on the paper picture so part of the design beneath it appears. Continue until the picture scene is complete. Then set aside.
3. For the next technique, on colored paper draw the animal or objects that will be glued on top of the scene. In the book, the Lionni has glued fish on crayon rubbings.
4. Cut out the animal or object, and glue or paste it on the crayon rubbing background scene. Draw and cut out, then glue as many drawings as desired for the picture.

Variations
- First create a crayon rubbing with shapes, and then, glue the shapes on top of the rubbing. Shapes can be anything from geometric to wild-n-wacky.
a To create a brushed chalk design, trace around a cutout shape with soft pastel chalk. Before lifting or removing the shape, brush the line with tissue or a make-up pad. Then remove the shape. Make many traced and brushed shapes that overlap one another on the paper.

by Kenzi Robinson, age 9

Lionni wrote in My Children's Books that "a good children's book should appeal to all people who have not completely lost their original joy and wonder in life … I make them for that part of … myself and my friends … which is still a child."

- LEO LIONNI
Educational Paperback Association
www.edupaperback.org
originally: Junior Authors & Illustrators
©HW Wilson Co

Glue the cut-out fish shape in place on the crayon rubbing background scene.

Josephine Martin c. 1950

Imitate Josephine Martin's embossing style. Push designs into thick white paper with the rounded handle of a paintbrush.

The Snow Tree • Caroline Repchuk, author

Read about Little Bear's search for color in a white wintry world on pages bountifully embossed by Josephine Martin (that means they feel bumpy). Little Bear is chosen to guard the snow tree through the cold, white winter.

Ms. Martin was unavailable for a portrait sketch or quote.
Morgan Van Slyke, age 7, *Imaginary Portrait of Ms. Martin* (The portrait looks quite a bit like Morgan!)

"Josephine Martin studied Scientific Illustration at the Hornsey College of Art. The majority of her work is related to natural history. She has illustrated a wide variety of books, including: several children's natural history books; encyclopedias, dinosaur books and illustrated dictionaries; adult reference books on wild flowers, birds and garden plants; illustrations for packaging; and 200 special issue overseas stamps on various subjects. In her spare time she loves sailing. Josephine also plays the violin in two orchestras."

DAVID MACMILLAN,
ABOUT JOSEPHINE MARTIN,
Ms. Martin's former publisher,
Templar Publishing, UK books for children
letter to MaryAnn Kohl 2003

Embossed Drawing

Materials
working pad: thick pad of newspaper or paper towels, or a square of foam core board
handmade or purchased medium-weight paper in white or light colors (stationery, fancy letter-writing paper, or plain note cards work well)
removable tape
sponge, water (damp, not dripping wet)
stylus choices —
    rounded end of a paintbrush handle
    orange stick
    pencil, no point
    ballpoint pen, tip retracted
    dowel, end rounded
    bamboo skewer, end rounded
heavy background paper (matboard or poster board)
tape or glue

Process
1. Spread a thick pad of newspaper or paper towels on the table to be the working pad. Another alternative that works exceptionally well is a square of foam core board because it is an excellent cushion that allows for pressing-in designs without poking holes.
2. Place the medium-weight paper on the working pad and tape it down.
3. To soften the paper, pat and dab the paper with a damp sponge until it feels moist but not wet or soaked.
4. While the paper is damp, gently press a stylus into the paper, being careful not to poke holes. Draw a picture or make designs. Work slowly and press firmly but carefully.
5. When done, let the paper dry on the working pad for an hour or more. Then remove the tape and turn the paper over so the embossed design is raised (not indented). The paper may curl slightly, but can be taped down on all four edges to a background paper like matboard or poster board for permanent display.

Variations
Highlight areas of the embossed design with —
  • pastel chalks, then brushed with tissue to blend
  • waterbased marking pens used on damp paper will blur and blend
  • fingertips or a tissue pressed on a colored ink pad, then brushed on parts of the design

White Glue

Clare Turlay Newberry
April 10, 1903 –1970

Marshmallow • *Clare Turlay Newberry, author*

A baby rabbit named Marshmallow and an apartment cat named Oliver become close friends. Both the artwork and the story are gentle and charming.

CALDECOTT HONOR 1943

Imitate the illustration style of Clare Turlay Newberry through exploration of charcoal sketching.

Charcoal Sketch

Materials
charcoal drawing sticks (from art, hobby, or school supply stores) (Idea: An adult can make – or collect – pieces of charred wood from a campfire or fireplace, cool them, and place them in a cup for drawing use. If charcoal is not available, use black chalk or an extremely soft drawing pencil.)

white drawing paper or blank newsprint (very large paper allows for large arm action)

damp sponge for wiping fingers

hairspray (optional, with adult help) or clear hobby sealer

Process
1. Though charcoal sticks break easily and are very messy, marks wash off hands, fingers, and clothing with soap and water, Keep an old towel and an apron on hand. Place a damp sponge on the drawing table for wiping messy fingers.
2. First, practice making charcoal lines, marks, and drawings on scrap paper to find how charcoal acts on paper. Blend and smudge it with fingers or a tissue to see how it blends and shades. Charcoal has a soft look – not precise – so expect a simple light-handed drawing style to work best.
3. When ready, think about a simple idea to draw, such as these –
   fluffy rabbit   single flower in a pot
   trees in winter   sleeping cat
   Use imagination to think up a unique idea.
4. Hold a charcoal stick (or a broken smaller piece of charcoal) like a paintbrush (not like a pencil), and begin the drawing. Smudge and blend lines for shadows and shading with fingertips. Fewer lines drawn freely are more effective than drawing many lines or details, so work simply and lightly.
5. When the drawing is complete, pin or tape it to a display wall. (Do beware of magically appearing fingerprints on walls and doors!)
6. An adult can take the drawing outside or to a ventilated area and spray the drawing with hairspray or a clear hobby sealer to help protect it from further smudging. The drawing can also be rolled and stored, drawing side in facing inward.

Variation
- Explore drawing with a very soft drawing pencil, using an art eraser for smudging and blending.
- Explore painting with black watercolor paints, another technique used often by Clare Newberry.

by Abby Brandt, age 5

"People often ask me where I get my ideas for books. To tell the truth, almost all my stories are drawn from my own experience. I have usually acquired a pet, made studies of it for several months in pencil, pen and ink, charcoal and pastel, and then thought up a story based on actual incidents. The story of Marshmallow and his friendship with Oliver the cat is all true and the drawings done from life. I recall wondering, as I sketched Oliver with the bunny in his arms, if anyone would really believe me."

- CLARE TURLAY NEWBERRY

"The Unexpected Surrogate" *(House Rabbit Society)* by Diana Murphy, www.rabbit.org

by Morgan Van Slyke, age 7

Nancy Winslow Parker October 30, 1930

Imitate Nancy Winslow Parker and John Langstaff by making up verses to a song. Illustrate one or many verses in book style on white drawing paper with black line drawings filled in with softly crayoned colors.

by Molly Koker, age 9

"I knew from the time I was in kindergarten that I would be an artist when I grew up. Between that early thought and today's reality, many worlds have been explored. In addition to the local school curriculum, I was given lessons in dance, horseback riding, tennis, swimming and acting, and I had ten years of piano lessons. But what I really wanted were lessons in art."

- NANCY WINSLOW PARKER, letter to MaryAnn Kohl 2002 www.nwparker.com

Oh, A Hunting We Will Go • *John Langstaff, author*

"Oh, a-hunting we will go, A-hunting we will go; We'll catch a fox and put him in a box, And then we'll let him go!" chants one verse of this popular folksong, inviting children to make up their own rhyming verses. The author and illustrator have worked some old and new stanzas to fit this classic old favorite – to illustrate and sing (and giggle). Sheet music is included at the end of the book – everyone can sing along with guitar or piano.

Illustrated Music

Materials
choose a song! *(Oh, A Hunting We Will Go* is one idea, or choose another favorite) A few other songs that work well for creating new verses are –
    The Farmer in the Dell
    Old MacDonald Had A Farm
    Down by the Bay
    If You're Happy and You Know It
black fine-point marker
crayons
sheet music & photocopy machine, optional

Process
1. Choose a song and sing it out loud several times. While singing, think up new verses by changing the words and experimenting with rhyming. Imagine how the verses might look if illustrated in color.
2. Choose the first verse of the song (a new verse or the actual verse) and illustrate it on a sheet of white paper. Draw it with a black fine point marker, and then fill in softly with crayon. Try lightly coloring over one color of crayon with another color like the illustrations in the book.
3. Draw another version of the song – a second verse – on the second sheet of paper.
4. Continue to draw as many verses as desired.
5. Staple all the sheets together, and the song is now a song book! The lyrics are fresh and unique!
6. If a copy machine is available, and there is also the original music on paper, copy the music and tape it into the book too, just like in *Oh, A Hunting We Will Go.*

Variations
• Compose an original melody and make up words to go with it. Illustrate it, if desired.
• Fold a paper into four squares, and illustrate one verse in each square.

Storybook Art © 2003 Bright Ring Publishing, Inc.

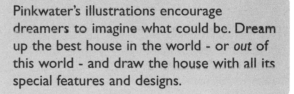
The Big Orange Splot • *Daniel Manus Pinkwater*

When a seagull drops a can of orange paint on Mr. Plumbean's neat house, Mr. Plumbean decides that a multicolored house would be a great idea. Little by little he influences each of his neighbors to decorate their own plain houses in new and daring ways.

Pinkwater's illustrations encourage dreamers to imagine what could be. Dream up the best house in the world - or *out* of this world - and draw the house with all its special features and designs.

Fantasy Architecture

Materials
crayons, colored pencils, marking pens
scraps of paper
several sheets of white drawing paper
scissors, and paste or glue

~ art ideas generously contributed by
Charlene Gowen, League City, Texas
and Margaret Poznick, La Crescenta, California

Process
1. Dream up the perfect imaginary house! Will the house have a kitchen and bedrooms, or is there another way to design a house with a different kind of living? Does the house need a landing port for a helicopter, or a moat to float the pirate ship? Perhaps this house will have a special room for indoor horses or an indoor tree for a family of kittens to climb. Maybe the house isn't a house at all, but is a tree with interesting ladders and crannies. Anything goes when it's time to fantasize about architecture!
2. Ready to draw? Draw how the fantasy house will look from the outside, using crayons and pencils for detail, and adding in color with marking pens.
3. For an additional feature, add scraps of paper cut into shapes and objects and glue these in place to enhance details.

Variations
- Draw a house plan for the perfect house showing rooms and walls, and where doors and windows could be, and adding exciting details like a rope swing and swimming pool. Take another piece of drawing paper and show the rendition of the outside of the imaginary house - windows, doors, where trees or plants will be, what kind of siding and roof it will have, and best of all, what colors it will be.
- Build a fantasy dream house in a shoebox or cardboard carton. Design, cut, assemble, and attach cardboard furniture, add wallpaper, draw pictures for the walls, and make curtains from fabric scraps. The choices are up to the designer!

by Lauren Kaemingk,
age 11

"I imagine a child. That child is me. I can reconstruct and vividly remember portions of my own childhood. I can see, taste, smell, feel, and hear them. Then what I do is, not write about that kid or about his world, but start to think of a book that would have pleased him."

- DANIEL PINKWATER
an interview by Marilyn Wann,
www.fatso.com
The Afterlife Diet, *Daniel Pinkwater*

Shiny Castle
by Carley Roddy, age 8

Patricia Polacco July 11, 1944

Imitate the drawing style of Patricia Polacco and draw with pencil. Only the key element of the drawing will have color — rich, vibrant, full color.

"I am lucky . . . so very lucky! I love my life. Can you imagine doing what you want to do every day? . . . My thoughts boil in my head. They catch the air and fly. The images and stories come back with fury and energy . . . My heart sings when I am drawing."

- PATRICIA POLACCO
Firetalking,
Richard C. Owen, 1994

by Kailey Olson,
age 9

The Keeping Quilt • *Patricia Polacco, author*

A basket of old clothes - Anna's babushka, Uncle Vladimir's shirt, Aunt Havalah's nightdress and Aunt Natasha's apron - become *The Keeping Quilt*. The quilt is passed along from mother to daughter for almost a century and four generations. It is used as a Sabbath tablecloth, a wedding canopy, and a blanket that warms new babies in the family, holding the immigrant Jewish family together.

ASSOCIATION OF JEWISH LIBRARIES SYDNEY TAYLOR AWARD

Key Element Color

Materials
soft drawing pencil (any pencil is fine)
eraser
white paper
choice of drawing tools -
   crayons
   marking pens
   colored pencils

Process
1. Look at Patricia Polacco's illustrations, and notice that the only color she uses focuses attention on a "key element" in the story - the keeping quilt. All other elements of the illustrations are drawn in soft pencil. Her illustrations appear as if someone turned a colorful light on the most important part of the picture, and everything else remains in shadow.
2. Think of a picture to draw, and decide what the "key element" of the drawing will be. Some suggestions follow:
   - an important soccer game — key element: the star player in uniform making a goal
   - under the sea scene — key element: one bright tropical fish among seaweed
   - birthday party — key element: a specially wrapped secretive gift
3. Draw an entire picture in pencil.
4. Now the key element is ready for color. Fill in the key element with colorful crayons, marking pens, or colored pencils. Make bright, vibrant, rich colors to that focus attention on the key element.
5. Add outlines or other features with a black fine point permanent marking pen to make the key element even more central.

Variation
• Add glitter or metallic gold or silver marking pen to focus attention on the key element in the drawing.

Maurice Sendak June 10, 1928

Where the Wild Things Are • *Maurice Sendak, author*

When Max dons his wolf suit and becomes a little too wild, he is sent to his room without his supper. He embarks on a magical boat ride that sails to where the Wild Things are, and Max is made King of All the Wild Things. King Max and the Wild Things enjoy a wild rumpus. Then Max sails home again, where his dinner is waiting.

CALDECOTT MEDAL 1964

Scratchboard Watercolor

Materials
large white paper and pencil
ballpoint pen
black scratchboard,
  oversized, approximately
  12"x19" [30cmx50cm] (art
  store, hobby, or craft
  store)
tape
scratching tool, with adult
  help if needed
      (tools with points -
      scissors, paperclip,
      knife, screwdriver, nail)
Note about tools -
With *adult supervision for
older kids,* an X-acto knife
with a supply of "nibs"
(points) can be used. Nibs
are the best scratching
tool of all, but only with
supervision.
scrap of scratchboard for
  practice
watercolor paints & brushes
  (waterbased markers
  may be used instead)

Process
1. With a pencil, draw a picture on the white paper. A wild thing or monster is one drawing subject, or think of something new. Draw the subject large and clear with some details, but no cross-hatching is necessary at this point.
2. Now place the drawing on top of the scratchboard and tape down the corners. Trace over the drawing with a ballpoint pen, pushing into the drawing to dent the scratchboard. Use firm pressure. Every now and then, peek under the tracing to see if the pen is denting the scratchboard sufficiently. When done, remove the white paper.
3. Begin the scratching step. Explore different scratching tools on the scrap scratchboard to see how they work. Then scratch on the dents to "draw" through the black and expose the white underneath. Do not brush the scraping away with hands; instead, tap the board on the table and the scrapings will fall away.
4. When the main drawing is done, begin adding cross-hatching (see the book's illustrations) to shade and give design to the drawing.
5. Paint watercolor lightly on the scratches. Then apply more, adding layers of color that will become stronger without soaking the scratchboard. Let the artwork dry.

Variations - Wild Thing Wild Rumpus Masks:
- Create an easy 'wild thing mask' from a paper plate, with elastic threaded through holes on each side of the plate to hold the mask in place. Cut holes for nose, mouth, eyes, or whatever features desired (do this with the plate removed from the face). Decorate with yarn, crayons, stickers, and so on into a very wild mask.
- Roll the open end of a brown paper grocery bag three or four times, and place the bag over one's head. Feel where the eyes will go, remove the sack, and cut eye holes. Then decorate the bag as a very wild thing. Let the wild rumpus begin!!

by Karla Witte, age 10

"The point of my books has always been to ask how children cope with a monumental problem that happened instantly and changed their lives forever, but they have to go on living . . . These are difficult times for children. Children have to be brave to survive what the world does to them."

- MAURICE SENDAK
"Maurice Sendak", Factmonster
©2002 Family Education Network 2/1/03
www.factmonster.com/ipka/A0801320.html

Dragon Wild Thing by Morgan Van Slyke, age 7

Shel Silverstein September 25, 1930 –1999

Imitate the humorous drawing style of Shel Silverstein. Draw funny pictures using black ink on white paper. The 'color' will come from laughter, not from crayons or paint.

Where the Sidewalk Ends • Shel Silverstein, author

Silverstein's humorous poetry is beloved by many for its clever use of silly words and simple pen-and-ink drawings. Poems with titles like "Dancing Pants" and "The Dirtiest Man in the World" are full of fun!

by Jennifer Reinstra, age 9

"When I was a kid – 12, 14, around there – I would much rather have been a good baseball player or a hit with the girls. But I couldn't play ball, I couldn't dance. Luckily, the girls didn't want me; not much I could do about that. So, I started to draw and to write. I was also lucky that I didn't have anybody to copy, be impressed by. I had developed my own style . . . By the time I got to where I was attracting girls, I was already into work, and it was more important to me."

- SHEL SILVERSTEIN
Publishers Weekly, 2/24/75,
Jean F. Mercier. "Shel Silverstein,"
www.nassio.com

Pen & Ink Humor

Materials
choice of black ink pen -
   fine-tip roller ball
   felt-tip pen
   ball-point pen
stack of white drawing paper

Process
1. Look at Shel Silverstein's drawings. See how he draws with simple black lines, similar to the outlining in a coloring book:
   • no color is used
   • people look unusual, not like real people
   • eyes are tiny dots or extra large like saucers.
   • hair sticks out, drawn with wiggly lines
   • nothing looks realistic
2. Experiment with drawing something very simple, like a smiling sun or a cat. Try to make it look "funny" or silly, not realistic. Use Silverstein's style of tiny dot eyes, or wiggly lines for hair. Try several different ideas, working on the sun or cat each time.
3. Think up an idea to draw. Draw the idea on a fresh sheet of paper. Make up a poem about the drawing, Silverstein-style.

Variations
• Draw humorous cartoons or drawings with chalk on a sidewalk. (Ask permission first.)
• Write a funny poem and illustrate it with humorous cartoon drawings. Put together an entire book of original poems and illustrations.
  "My dog's name is Spot,
  Of which he has a lot."
   ~ poem by Marty Faubion, age 8

Spot Dog
by Casey Collins,
age 11

Marc Simont November 23, 1915

A Tree is Nice • Janice M. Udry, author

Many enjoyable delights are described – in a tree, under a tree, or with a tree – including picking apples, raking leaves, swinging, or sitting quietly in the shade.
CALDECOTT MEDAL WINNER 1957

Extend appreciation of Marc Simont's illustrations of trees through the fun of collection and crayon rubbings. Collect leaves, pine needles, fir needles, twigs, and other fallen materials from trees. Make a crayon rubbing in a unique tree design that is indeed "nice".

Assembled Tree Rubbings

Materials
basket, bag or box for collecting
   fallen material from trees
peeled crayons
big sheet of paper
tape
scissors

basket for collecting

Process
1. Bring the collected items back to the work area and spread them out. Look over their shapes and colors. Choose items to assemble the shape of a tree on the table. This is like drawing with objects. With a short piece of tape, make a loop to stick the items to the table, keeping them from being blown off the table by drafts.
2. When the design is assembled in a tree shape, gently place a large sheet of paper over the "tree". Tape the corners to keep the paper stable.
3. Using the side of a peeled crayon, rub the paper to reveal the tree design. Use natural colors, or use wild and unusual colors. Selecting colors is part of the fun!
4. When the rubbing is complete, carefully remove the taped corners and lift the paper.
5. Make another rubbing with the same design. Perhaps choose to change colors or try the same technique with colored pencils, markers, or oil pastels. Consider adding more items to the same design.

Variations
• Select collage items or scraps of paper or yarn to enhance the nature item rubbing design.
• Create rubbing assemblages of flowers or plants.
• Add further illustrations to the tree rubbing with fine point markers.

"The child in me must make contact with other children. I may miss it by ten miles, but if I am going to hit, it is because of the child in me."

- MARC SIMONT
Books Are by People: Interviews with 104 Authors and Illustrators of Books for Young Children,
Lee Bennett Hopkins.
Citation Press, 1969

by Laura Sanchez, age 9

Louis Slobodkin
February 19, 1903 –1975

The *New Yorker* once commented, "The lovely, squiggly illustrations in color are exactly right." Imitate Louis Slobodkin's light and airy illustrations using colored pencils on white paper. Display the sketch in a homemade magnetic frame on any metallic surface, like the fridge or washer and dryer.

by Lindsey Harkness, age 12

My father was convinced that all young children can draw, sing, dance, and write poetry and that these abilities can be destroyed in elementary school in almost all of them. He also once said, "We, the children's authors and illustrators of America, cannot cater to that small esoteric clique in our audience who can read!"
— LAWRENCE B. SLOBODKIN, remembering his father, LOUIS SLOBODKIN letter to MaryAnn Kohl 2003

Many Moons • *Louis Slobodkin, author*

Lenore is ill from eating too many tarts. She believes possessing the moon will cure her. Lenore is quite used to getting whatever she desires, and a troubled chain reaction spreads through her father's kingdom.
CALDECOTT MEDAL 1944

Lightly Sketch

Materials
colored pencils
white drawing paper
black matboard (scrap from framing shop)
magnetic strips, self-stick variety if possible (from hobby or craft store)
glue & scissors, if needed

Process
1. Imagine a subject to sketch, using only colored pencils. Lightly sketch the idea, keeping details to a minimum, using light, airy, squiggly lines.
2. When the sketch is complete, use a variety of colored pencils to highlight parts of the drawing. Keep a light hand and gentle pressure on the pencils while drawing to get a smooth, free effect like Louis Slobodkin's sketches.
3. To display the finished colored pencil drawing, make a simple magnetic frame for the fridge or other metallic backing (file cabinet, washer or dryer, metal door). Simply glue pieces of magnetic strips to the back of a matboard from a frame shop (or peel backing from self-stick magnetic strips).
4. Position the sketch on the refrigerator door (or any metallic surface), and slip the magnetic frame over the illustration. The magnets will hold the sketch and frame it at the same time; no additional tape or glue is needed.

Variation
• Look at other books illustrated by Louis Slobodkin, such as *Mr. Mushroom* and *The Moffats*.

William Steig  *November 14, 1907*

Sylvester & The Magic Pebble • *William Steig*

Sylvester Duncan is a young donkey who finds a magic pebble that grants his wishes. In a moment of fright, he wishes himself to be a rock. How Sylvester finds his way back home is another magical wish with a happy ending.

Imitate the classic illustration style of William Steig. Draw a picture and then paint in the drawing with thinned tempera paints.

Classic Illustrating

Materials
white drawing paper
black crayon or black pencil
tempera paints, in a variety of colors,
   (thinned with water in individual
   cups)
paintbrushes, variety of sizes
jar of water
masking tape

Process
1. Tape the drawing paper to the table.
2. Draw a picture that has a main character and tells a simple story or has action in it. Draw with black pencil or black crayon. Draw the outlines and some details, but do not color in with the pencil or crayon.
3. Paint some of the picture with the thinned tempera paints. Paint within the lines of the drawing. Let paint dry briefly before painting adjacent areas so they do not smear or bleed into one another. Try to keep the painted areas separate.
4. Finish painting the entire picture. Let dry again.
5. Add any further details to the dry painting.

Variations
• Produce a play of the story of Sylvester with dialogue and props from the book.
• Color a picture with colored pencils or markers.
• Use watercolor paints instead of tempera.
• Read William Steig's award-winning book, *The Amazing Bone.*

by Kenzi Robinson, age 9

"I went to art school because I was given my choice whether to get to work or go to school. What I had in mind at the time was to go to sea when I got the chance – at least for a while. But my father went broke in the [stock market] crash of `29 . . . So it devolved on me to find some way to support my family."

- WILLIAM STEIG
Washington Post Book World,
5/11/80, Patrick Hearn

Fishing at Sunrise by Maurice Woodley, age 13 (1998), *Arts&Activities* magazine, 2/98

Kurt Wiese April 22, 1887 –1974

There is an old saying, "Get your ducks in a row." Little Ping is one of many ducks in a long row of duck cousins, aunts, uncles, & many many relatives. So many ducks can take a long time to draw! Imitate Wiese's simple duck drawings using a nifty little drawing trick called "pattern repeat".

by Sonia Baranek, age 8

"Drawings for children have to be very correct because if something doesn't look right, if there is a mistake, I can always be assured of getting a letter from one of my young readers . . . Animals are the most delightful subject to me and they are what I do best.. There is not a zoo in the East which I have not visited and sketched at."
- KURT WIESE
Delaware Valley News, 1/12/73
courtesy of Hunterdon County Library,
Reference Department, Flemington, New Jersey

Ducks in a Row
by Hannah Robinson, age 9

The Story About Ping • *Marjorie Flack, author*

A young duck named Ping lives on a fishing boat on the Yangtze River with his many cousins and other hard-working relatives. Ping heads out on a river adventure, but does not return to the boat on time as he was told he must. Ping must face the consequences.

Pattern Repeat

Materials
heavy paper (old file folder)
pencil
scissors
drawing paper for background
crayons

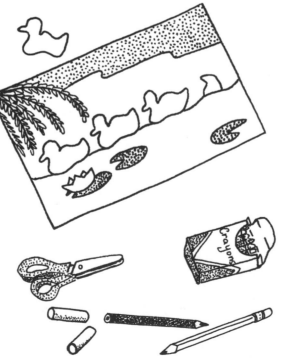

Process
1. Decide on a main character for the drawing. It can be a duck like Ping, another animal like a cat or dog, or even an imaginary creature. This main character will be traced over and over forming a long line of identical shapes.
2. Draw a simple bold character on the heavy paper keeping details to a minimum. Cut the character out with scissors. This cut-out will be the template to make a repeating pattern of the same character.
3. Start at one side of the drawing paper, and trace the character template. Then move it beside that tracing, and trace another. Trace as many across the paper as will fit. This makes a repeating pattern where all the shapes are the same. Overlapping the tracings is sometimes fun, or turning them back and forth to face right, left, upside down, or backwards.
4. Color the pattern of repeating characters, making them all look identical or perhaps, if desired, very different. Add other details to the drawing in any way.

Variation
- Trace the same cut-out pattern on drawing paper, and then trace another to overlap the first. Keep tracing the pattern until the paper is filled with overlapping patterns in a wild design. Color each crossed-over section in a different way. The original shape will be integrated into the sections of color and will not be plainly seen – a truly abstract experience!

Cut & Collage

chapter 3

Snowy Watercolor Collage
by Jazmin Mendoza,
age 8
based on
The Snowy Day by Ezra Jack Keats

Flower Frame Collage
by Kayla Comstock,
age 8
based on
Veggie Soup by Dorothy Donohue

Barbara Cooney June 9, 1917 –2000

Imitate the beautiful lupines in Barbara Cooney's illustrations with realistic "stand-out" art. Paint with a variety of tools, and then cut-and-glue the lupine paintings to a "stand-out" scene.

by Eleanor Davis
age 12

"[My mother] gave me all the art materials I could wish for and then left me alone, didn't smother me with instruction. Not that I ever took instruction very easily. My favorite days were when I had a cold and could stay home from school and draw all day long."
-BARBARA COONEY
Denise Ortakales ©1999-2002
www.ortakales.com/illustrators
& letters to Denise Ortakales

~ art idea generously contributed by
Pat Fournier, Bellingham, Washington

Miss Rumphius • *Barbara Cooney*

Follow a girl's life as she discovers what she will give to the world, ultimately deciding she will beautify it by planting the seeds of the lovely lupine.   AMERICAN BOOK AWARD

Realistic Lupine

Materials
choice of tools for making lupine dots—
    fingertips
    dowel end
    pencil eraser
    carrot cut in half
lupines, if possible
watercolor paints, brush, water
heavy white drawing paper, 2 sheets
scissors
brown and black crayons
paper scraps
blue, purple, pink, and green
    tempera paints in shallow dishes
glue, tape

Process
1. Look at real lupines, if possible, and note the mixed colors and shapes. A book of flowers is another resource for viewing lovely lupines.
2. Draw long stems with the brown crayon on one sheet of white drawing paper. Make as many stems as desired.
3. Dip a finger or other tool into paint. Print "dots" up and down the crayon stems. Experiment with combining tools and colors on one flower. Fill the lupine stems with painted blossoms. Then set aside to dry.
4. Tape the second sheet of drawing paper to the table. Freely draw a background meadow or grassy field with the black crayon. Brush water over the crayon drawing. Then brush watercolors over the wet paper so that the colors blur and blend. Let dry.
5. Cut the paintings of lupines out with scissors. Set aside.
6. Cut scraps of paper into strips about 1"x3" [3cmx8cm], two for each lupine flower. Make each strip into a loop using tape or glue to hold. Tape or glue two loops on the back of each lupine.
7. When the watercolor background is dry, tape or glue the loops of the painted lupines to the background scene. The lupines will "stand-out" from the background, giving a realistic look to the flowers.
8. Carefully peel away the masking tape holding the background paper in place, and the realistic lupine artwork is complete.

Variation
• Make the world more beautiful - plant flowers, paint a fence, or sweep the sidewalk. Miss Rumphius would appreciate the effort!

Smoky Night • *Eve Bunting, author*

When Los Angeles riots break out in the neighborhood, a young boy and his mother learn the value of getting along with others. CALDECOTT MEDAL 1995 • WEST VIRGINIA CHILDREN'S BOOK AWARD NOMINEE 1998 • CALIFORNIA BOOK AWARD 1995 • BEST BOOKS FOR CHILDREN 1999

David Diaz uses collage materials to illustrate important events in *Smoky Night*. In his collage scene showing the looting of a grocery store, Diaz uses breakfast cereal to express food spilling. Imitating Diaz, collage becomes an art experience to illustrate and express one's own story.

Mixed Collage Story

Materials
assorted collage materials
   (see step 1 for collage themes)
   leaves   cotton balls
   sequins   sand
   shells   pebbles
   buttons   beads
   see the index for more collage ideas
paper
white glue
tape or glue
scissors
cardboard
marking pens

Process
1. Think of a story or scene to create that will relate to collected collage materials. For example, a story about —
   – a walk in the woods with real leaves or fir needles glued into the drawing
   – a princess with a gown decorated with sequins
   – a beach trip with real sand
2. Draw a picture on the paper that tells a story. Then glue or tape the paper to the cardboard backing.
3. Glue collage items onto the picture to add to the details of the picture. Let it dry.
4. Tell the story of the picture aloud, or write the story on the back of the cardboard or on a separate sheet of paper.

Variations
• Cut out pictures from a magazine or catalog that represent one theme, and glue them with edges over-lapping on drawing paper.
   Some theme suggestions are —
      happiness   pets
      pretty colors   babies
      toys I love   good to eat
      things that go   things that grow
• Add collage materials to a magazine collage —
   – dry pet food in a "pet collage"
   – bits of toys in a "toy collage"
   – leaves, seeds, and flower petals in a "things that grow collage"

by Lauren Olson age 10

"*I realized I wanted to be an artist when I was in first grade. I was working on a vowel worksheet, and was doing the word* **NOSE**. *The sheet said* **N_SE**. *I filled the* **O** *in, and then I drew a face in it. And that's when I realized I wanted to be an artist.*"

-DAVID DIAZ

Scholastic Inc.™ /© 2003–1996, "Celebrate Hispanic Heritage: Meet Famous Latinos", interview by Scholastic students, teacher.scholastic.com/activities/hispanic/diaz.htm & communication with Jean Potter

Dorothy Donohue September 15, 1952

Imitate Dorothy Donohue's collage illustrations using a variety of textures and papers.

by Meagan VanBerkum, age 8

by Eleanor Davis, age 12

"I grew up in a small town in Wisconsin. I attended Catholic schools and had very few art classes. One summer I remember reading Alice in Wonderland *and looking at the wonderful illustrations though I don't think I even knew the word illustrations or illustrator. I decided I wanted to create my own pictures for the story and took the back side of wall paper and drew and painted on it. It was so much fun to think of how I would picture the Mad Hatter or Alice. Looking back, I think this was probably when I began dreaming of being a picture book illustrator. But you need to know I didn't have much talent. It was lots of years of drawing and work before my dream ever happened."*
- DOROTHY DONOHUE
letter to MaryAnn Kohl 2002 &
www.author-illustr-source.com/
DotDonohue.htm

by Caitlyn Woods, age 8

Veggie Soup • *Dorothy Donohue , author*

Miss Bun begins making her grandmother's veggie soup for a dinner party. As her guests arrive, they each contribute food to the soup with terrible results! Miss Bun finds a way to remake the soup strictly following her grandmother's recipe with a happy delicious outcome.

cover art permission Dorothy Donohue

Thick Paper Collage

Materials
decorative edge scissors (Fiscars™·pinking shears with fancy edges, scrapbook scissors)
textured papers, thick & decorative
drawing paper
glue
pencil
straight edge scissors
tracing paper
construction paper (12"x18" [30cmx45cm])

Process
1. To make a fancy frame for the collage, cut the edges of the large sheet of construction paper with the decorative edge scissors. Glue another sheet of paper in the center of the frame where the collage work will be done.
2. Think of a picture or design to construct with the papers. Some ideas are:

familiar landscape	geometric shapes
bowl of fruit	abstract design
favorite animal	sky (clouds, sun, birds)

3. Draw a design or object on tracing paper. Notice sections of the object that can be cut, each from a different paper, to make a collage picture. For example, a bunny's ears might have a long white section and another section cut from pink. Or a worm might be constructed with a green section for the body and some wiggly strips added for stripes. Decide which decorative papers would be best for each section of the collage.
4. Trace the sections on the choices of decorative papers for each part of the object. Then glue them in place on the paper. For example, if making bunny ears, glue the white ears in place first and then glue the pink inner section. (Think through each item and its placement before gluing it on the collage.)

Variation
• Explore using fabric scraps, felt scraps, or foam paper scraps instead of paper.

Lois Ehlert November 9, 1934

Fish Eyes: A Book You Can Count On • *Lois Ehlert, author*

A child imagines what she would see if she were a fish, through rhymes, counting, and bright colors. Count spectacular fish from one to ten as they swim through pages of deep blue. One fish cleverly predicts the next number in the counting sequence.

Imitate Lois Ehlert's dazzling fluorescent collage style. Cut and paste bright colored papers into shapes. Embellish the shapes with dots made with a hole punch.

Count on Cut-Outs

Materials
brightly colored papers (florescent
    colored papers are perfect for this
    project)
choice of drawing tools —
    pencil, marker, pen, or crayon
scissors
glue
paper punch (hole punch)
    Craft stores sell square squeeze-
    style punches with fancy punch
    shapes

Process
1. Think of a simple bold object to draw, such as a fish, mouse, bird, flower, bug, or a silvery snowflake! Draw it on the colored paper using no details other than shape. Cut it out with scissors.
2. With the paper punch, add punched holes — or make paper punch dots to glue on the paper shape. This will embellish the work with color and design. Here are a few suggestions: two hole punches become a rabbit's round eyes, five hole punches become the seeds in a cut apple, ten hole punches become the freckles on someone's nose.
3. Glue the object on a contrasting fluorescent color paper background. (The color of the background paper will show through any punched holes.)
4. Continue to create and add more designs and details with cut-outs made from the colored paper scraps and hole punches.

Variations
• To imitate the dazzling look of Ehlert's art —
    – paint with Liquid Watercolors™ (see Index) on white paper
    – draw with bright pastel chalks on deep blue paper
    – draw with marking pens on water dampened glossy paper

by Eleanor Davis, age 12

"I think being creative is a part of a person's makeup. It's something I feel very lucky about. I've worked hard to make this gift as fine as I can make it, but I still think I was born with certain ideas and feelings just waiting to burst out!"
    -LOIS EHLERT
    Something About the Author®,
    Vol.128 ©2003 The Gale Group, Inc.

Lois Ehlert November 9, 1934

Imitate Lois Ehlert's bright, bold illustration technique. Incorporate alphabet letters into drawings. Cut letters from catalogs or magazines. Create a picture where the letters are important elements in the design — a blue sky filled with bird **W**'s, fluffy cloud **B**'s, and a sun that is a round flaming **O**!

Chicka Chicka Boom Boom • *Bill Martin, Jr., & John Archambault, co-authors*

Recite the familiar words of this alphabet chant about what A told B, and the coconut tree. The illustrated letters of the alphabet boogie and bop through a series of bouncy, rhythmic, colorful chanting sprees. Everyone likes when the letters climb up a coconut tree, and then go Chicka Chicka Boom Boom! BOSTON GLOBE-HORN BOOK AWARD NOMINEE 1990 • BLUEGRASS AWARD 1991

Letter Collé

" [writing and illustrating] is like being a grandmother, in a way — setting down something that might, if I'm lucky, be remembered after I'm gone. And also to communicate what I think is important. Look for those birds! Plant a garden or a tree! They are very homely, ordinary subjects — yet spiritual."
- LOIS EHLERT
Something About the Author®,
Vol.128 ©2003 The Gale Group, Inc.

by Abby Brandt, age 5

Materials
magazines or catalogs for
   clipping, cutting
paste or glue
border paper: pink, orange, or
   other colors of paper
scissors
white or colored paper for
   background
crayons or markers

Process
1. Collé: a collage where pieces represent objects or pictures (see illustration). To make a collé, cut letters of different sizes and colors from old magazines or catalogs. Try to find a wide variety of style and pattern.
2. Combine 2 or more letters to create a scene or a design. A few suggestions of letters used to represent an object or animals are —

W = flying bird	S = snake, vine
O = mouth, eye, sun, wheel	T = table, telephone pole
H = window, chair	U = cup, nose

3. Arrange the letters in a scene or design, and when satisfied, glue them to the background paper. Add other details with crayons or markers.
4. To make a border similar to the one in the book, cut 2" [5cm] wide strips of pink paper (or another color choice). Glue these to the background paper as a border or frame on all four sides. Then cut out orange polka-dots (or other color choice) and glue them to the pink border. (Press-on sticker dots also work well.)

Variations
- Cut out one big letter of the alphabet and incorporate it into the whole picture . . .like an A could be a clown hat or a B could be a pair of glasses.
- Draw a letter of the alphabet, and continue drawing the letter, changing it into some new object.
- Draw numerals or other shapes and create new objects.
- Roll coconuts (an important component of the book's illustrations) through paint — like bowling — down a long sheet of paper in an outdoor area or on the grass.

~ art idea generously contributed by Tina Nichols, Manchester, Missouri

Steve Jenkins March 31, 1952

Looking Down • *Steve Jenkins, author*

A landscape on Earth is seen in a progression of views from outer space . . . from very far away, to closer, and closer, and closer.

Imitate the collage style of Steve Jenkins' planet Earth design. Create an imaginary planet from colored paper, tissue paper soaked with thin glue, and assembled on a black-as-the-universe backing.

View of My Planet

Materials
selection of papers –
   facial tissue (Kleenex™)
   construction paper scraps
   colored paper scraps
   wrapping tissue
   colored art tissue
   paper towels
   wax paper
   clear plastic wrap
   newsprint, newspaper
   construction paper scraps
   other choices of papers
scissors
pencil
mixing bowl or other big circular
   shape to trace
very watery glue (medium bowl)
paintbrush to spread glue
colored construction paper
black background paper or
   poster board
watercolor paints & brush

Process
1. Imagine a planet with features, such as – swirling colors, clouds, vapors, land forms, moons and other possibilities. Picture it as if looking down on it from very far out in space.
2. Begin creating an imaginary planet. Choose a sheet of colored construction paper for the main part of the planet. Trace a large circle using a mixing bowl or other round template. Cut it out and place it on the table (protect the table with newspaper, if needed). This circle will be the base for the planet collage.
3. To make features and details for the planet, tear scraps of paper. Cutting scraps into shapes also works. Soak cut or torn paper scraps in glue. Press the scraps on the circular planet paper by hand. Keep a damp sponge handy for wiping fingers.
4. Additional ideas for paper and glue collage techniques are –

   – tear Kleenex or toilet tissue and press into wet glue brushed on the planet background
   – crinkle glue-soaked papers in a ball, uncrinkle, and press on the planet background
   – drip watercolor paints directly on the wet papers glued to the planet background
   – cut papers into unusual shapes, soak in glue, and press onto planet background

5. Let the planet dry. When dry, trim any ragged edges with scissors
6. Glue the planet to a sheet of black or dark blue paper (the background universe). Add any other features with more paper to the black universe or the planet. Does the planet have a name?

Variation
• Add a universe full of stars, moons, suns, nebulas, comets, meteors, and galaxies with a metallic marking pen or bits of foil glued in place.

by Weston Whitener, age 8

"I think that's one of the appeals of this kind of art for kids, that they are filling in part of the information. So not only is it satisfying for me to find a piece of paper that is at the same time a hippopotamus' skin, but I think kids get the same satisfaction from filling in the details and making it into a hippo as well as a piece of paper. My son Alec was the model for the little boy with the magnifying glass at the end of Looking Down."

- STEVE JENKINS
20th Anniversary Children's Literature Conference
Ohio State University, interview by Ken & Sylvia Marantz
Children's Literature (www.childrenslit.com),
www.jenkinspage.com & letter to MaryAnn Kohl 2002

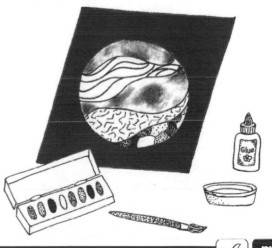

Marthe Jocelyn February 24, 1956

To imitate the style of Jocelyn's collage illustrations, incorporate cloth, paper, and found objects set against a patterned background.

Collection Collage • *Marthe Jocelyn, author*

As part of Hannah's school assignment, she must bring a collection to share with the class. Hannah collects buttons, Popsicle sticks, shells, leaves, feathers, barrettes, dolls, leather purses, and much more. She must find a solution for how to share one collection.

by Monika Baranek, age 11

"In her previous vocational life, Marthe Jocelyn was a toy designer, among other things, and uses this talent brilliantly to illustrate her own picture books about a little girl named Hannah. Hannah is quite the collector. Whatever it is she has gathered is depicted through cloth collages, causing the pages to appear 3-dimensional. It is hard to believe that given the amount of books she has written, and the diversity of the situations in each book, that Jocelyn has only been writing for 5 years!"
- about MARTHE JOCELYN
from a school visit to Trevor Day School
www.trevornet.org

Collection Collage

Materials
collection of collage items, such as —

buttons	pebbles
bottle caps	wooden beads
stamps	shoe laces
small toys	balls
dominoes	stickers
seeds	broken jewelry

sheets of patterned fabric scraps
cardboard
glue
scissors

Process
1. Spread the collected items on the table and decide which ones will be used for the collage.
2. Cut a background shape from a piece of patterned fabric to match the same shape as one of the collections. For example, cut a circle if gluing a collection of buttons (circles); cut a rectangular shape if gluing items like dominoes (rectangles); cut a jewel or gem shape if gluing broken jewelry. Cut a matching shape for each type of collection in the collage.
3. Glue all of the patterned fabric shapes onto the cut shape of cardboard. Try to cover the entire cardboard piece.
4. Glue each collection on its matching patterned shape. For example, glue buttons on the circle covered with fabric, dominoes on the rectangle covered with fabric, and jewelry pieces on the gem shaped cardboard covered with fabric. Glue the pieces on in any style or arrangement.
5. The collage will be heavy and wet with glue. Let it dry several days.

Variation
• Glue a variety of collection pieces onto one square of cardboard, making a design or collage with a mosaic style.

Buttons (circle shaped) are glued on a circle of cardboard which is first covered with fabric.

Stephen T. Johnson June 20, 1964

Alphabet City • *Stephen T. Johnson, author*

Paintings of objects in an urban setting show the letters of the alphabet in unexpected places

CALDECOTT HONOR 1996 • YOUNG HOOSIER BOOK AWARD-HONOR 1997

Imitate Stephen T. Johnson's realistic alphabet illustrations. Find hidden capital letters in everyday objects around the neighborhood, school, or home. Photograph the letters, and assemble the prints in an alphabetical photo-book.

Photo Finish

Materials
camera (chose instamatic with film, or digital with printer)
photo album (staple sheets of paper together to make a homemade album)
tape and permanent marking pen, optional

Process
1. Look around the neighborhood, school, and house for things that have a capital letter naturally designed or formed into their structure. For example, a stoplight is shaped like the letter **E** from the side. A window in a house looks like an **H**. The wheel of a car looks like an **O**. Try to find as many of the letters of the alphabet as possible. Some are easy to find, and some are very difficult.
2. Take close up pictures of all the letters in their natural settings.
3. When the film is processed and pictures are ready, assemble the pictures in alphabetical order. Arrange them in a small photo-display album, or tape them into a homemade book made from paper stapled together. Label them with handwritten alphabet letters, if desired.

Variation
• 1950's Family Game: Play a game while traveling in the car. See how many letters of the alphabet can be discovered in signs, license plates, and billboards. To make the game more challenging, find alphabet capital letters hidden in objects, like the letter **C** in the spots on a cow or the letter **H** in a window frame.

by Lauren Kaemingk, age 11

"*I hope that my paintings will inspire children and adults to look at their surroundings in a fresh and playful way. In doing so, they will discover for themselves juxtaposition of scale, harmonies of shadows, rhythms, colorful patterns in surface textures, and joy in the most somber aspects of a city, by transcending the mundane and unearthing its hidden beauty.*"
- STEPHEN T. JOHNSON
K-State Media Relations & Marketing
www.mediarelations.ksu.edu
www.stephenjohnson.com

Ann Jonas January 28, 1932

Like the special quilt written about in Ann Jonas' book, *The Quilt,* design a memory quilt wall-hanging. Incorporate scraps from favorite old clothes and papers that hold memory and special meaning.

by Chelsea Whitener, age 11

"I grew up in a family that attached great importance to knowing how to do as many things as possible, from skating to skiing to cabinet-making to repairing the family car. Everyone always had several projects going at the same time, and drawing was considered an incidental skill, a tool for planning a project rather than an end in itself."

– ANN JONAS
National Center for Children's Illustrated Literature
www.nccil.org/artists/txt_tcf.html

The Quilt • *Ann Jonas, author*

A young girl's new patchwork quilt is made from her old pajamas, curtains, and her first crib sheet. She recalls memories associated with the quilting scraps and that bring her bedtime adventure.

AN ALA NOTABLE CHILDREN'S BOOK

Memory Wall Quilt

Materials
old clothes, blankets or scrap material (family and personal clothing with associated memories)
other papers, napkins, wrappings, or greeting cards
white fabric or baby sheet for the background (white fabric should be cut to baby sheet size or desired size)
pencil
fabric markers
scissors
wooden dowel (same width as quilt, plus 2" [5cm])
fabric glue
stapler or needle & thread
yarn or string

Process
1. Think of a wonderful time that has been shared with family, such as these –
   - picnic — holiday
   - birthday — camping trip
2. Draw the special event on the white sheet with a pencil. Make the sections of the picture very large and clear like a coloring book. Draw the people and objects very large so that the picture can be "colored-in" with the fabric scraps later on.
3. Outline the drawing with a fabric marker. Color-in some of the shapes completely like coloring a picture. Leave other shapes open for fabric work.
4. Look at the fabric pieces. Cut the fabrics to fit into parts of the drawing and glue them in place. Fabric can be used as clothing, hair, shoes, skin, hats, pet's fur, and so on.
5. Fill in the quilt drawings with scraps that hold memories. Then let the quilt dry.
6. When dry, roll the top edge of the quilt around a dowel, and staple or sew it in place to hold. Then hang the memory quilt from the dowel on a hook in the wall. The memory quilt will be a reminder of happy memories.

Variation
• Make a real quilt by first gluing fabric scraps to a bed sheet or large piece of fabric as the backing. Then stitch over the edges of each piece with a sewing machine set on narrow zig-zag to bind the raw edges. Sew another fluffy, soft backing to the quilt.

Ezra Jack Keats March 11, 1916 –1983

The Snowy Day • *Ezra Jack Keats, author*

Little Peter wakes up to discover that snow has fallen during the night. He celebrates the snowy day making footprints and snow angels - an ageless childhood experience. According to Horn Book magazine, *The Snowy Day* was "the very first full-color picture book to feature a small black hero".

CALDECOTT MEDAL 1963

Imitate Ezra Jack Keat's snowy illustration style using cut-out construction paper, watercolors, and a scene-building collage technique.

Watercolor Snow Collage

Materials
construction paper
(including the speckled or flecked variety)
white drawing paper
watercolor paints
paintbrush
jar of water
scissors
glue
choice of collage base –
poster board, heavy paper, cardboard, matboard

Process
1. Assemble supplies including paper scraps and watercolor paints to make a snowy collage.
2. Some of the paper for the collage can be painted ahead of time. Paint on white construction paper with watercolor paints, experimenting with different painting effects –

sprinkle from a brush	smudge with tissues
swirl with a wet brush	splatter from a very wet brush
blur on wet paper	drip tiny drops on paper
speckle by shaking a brush lightly	

3. Paint and cover several sheets of paper in different ways. When dried briefly, these self-painted papers will add to the supply of papers that can be cut for the collage.
4. Cut some of the painted paper into curving shapes that resemble Keat's piles of deep snow. Arrange them on the base paper and glue in place. Note: The beauty of the watercolor paper is that snow does not have to be white to look like snow. The color adds depth, shadow and light.
5. Cut or tear other papers to form more of the snowy scene, such as these suggestions –

tall building	stoplight	dog
tree	snow fort	footprints, snow angels
house	footprints	snowballs
bundled up child	cat	sled

Think up ideas and add them to the collage too.
6. Continue until the base paper is filled with paper collage shapes and cut-outs that form a snowy scene.

Variations
Create a snowy collage of –
• torn papers only (not cut), for a softer look
• magazine and newspaper cut-outs

by Jordan Drost, age 16

"Then began an experience that turned my life around – working on a book with a black kid as hero. None of the manuscripts I'd been illustrating featured any black kids – except for token blacks in the background. My book would have him there simply because he should have been there all along. Years before, I had cut from a magazine a strip of photos of a little black boy. I often put them on my studio wall before I'd begun to illustrate children's books. I just loved looking at him. This was the child who would be the hero of my book."

- EZRA JACK KEATS
letter from Ezra Jack Keats Foundation & deGrummond Children's Literature Collection, University of Southern Mississippi, Hattiesburg
www.lib.usm.edu/~degrum/html/ collectionhl/Keats/biography.shtml

Christopher Knight *January 10, 1943*

Imitate Christopher Knight's photography and take real-life pictures with a camera. Let the pictures tell their own story. Then present the photo story in a simple homemade book.

Sugaring Time • *Kathryn Lasky, author*

Making syrup from sap has changed little over the years. Through real-life black-and-white photographs, see all the aspects of sugaring time. Though this is a non-fiction book, it reads like a great story.

NEWBERY HONOR 1984 • ALA NOTABLE CHILDREN'S BOOK • HORN BOOK FANFARE LIST

by Jennifer Reinstra, age 9

"I went to drawing classes when I was 11, and envied the students who could draw things the way they really looked. I wanted to draw boats, but could never get them right, so a camera appealed to me. My parents gave me one, and I never went back to drawing until I studied architecture. I still like taking photos of boats."

- CHRIS KNIGHT, PHOTOGRAPHER
letter to MaryAnn Kohl 2002 &
www.newfilmco.com

Photo Story

Materials
camera and black and white film
    or digital camera and printer
    (color film is also acceptable)
heavy paper, cardboard, tag board,
    old file folders
stapler
tape or glue
pen, optional

Process
Taking the pictures -
1. After looking at the pictures in *Sugaring Time,* think about an event or series of incidents to photograph and to tell its story in pictures. Here are a few ideas –
    – photograph a series of pet's antics
    – photograph a soccer game from beginning to end
    – go to work with a parent and photograph the business happenings
    – capture a special holiday or celebration with its own story
2. When all the pictures have been snapped, take the film to be developed (or print them on on a printer). Waiting is the hardest part! Spread all the pictures on the table. Arrange them in story order. Keep pictures that tell the story best, and set the other aside.

Making the book -
3. Fold sheets of heavy paper in half to make a book, allowing for one blank page for each picture in the story. Then staple the pages together to form a simple book.
4. Tape or glue the pictures in order, one per page, into the book. Remember a picture for the cover!
5. When done, turn the pages and tell the story aloud. "Read" the book to friends and family.

Variations
• Write the photo story directly on the pages of the photo book. Use the same words as if telling the story aloud.
• Create a special photo story for a special occasion, such as Father's Day, Mother's Day, a birthday, or wedding.

Suse MacDonald March 3, 1940

Sea Shapes • *Suse MacDonald, author*

This bold and colorful picture book follows Suse MacDonald's unique graphic style. She shows how the shapes of sea creatures can begin with a simple geometric shape. A star becomes a starfish, a circle becomes the eye of a whale, a semi-circle becomes a jelly fish, and a square becomes a sea ray – a total of 12 creatures in collage, each beginning with a simple geometric shape. Facts about each creature are also given at the end of the book.

Imitate the collage style of Suse MacDonald's bright illustrations. Begin with a cut paper geometric shape and transform it into a collage sea animal.

by Sonia Baranek, age 8

"*I love the process of writing and illustrating children's books. There is great pleasure in encouraging my readers to go beyond their usual stopping points and make their own artistic discoveries. Children are inventors. They just need situations that bring out that quality of inventiveness. In my books I create those opportunities.*"

– SUSE MACDONALD

from Suse MacDonald's website - www.create4kids.com
& letter to MaryAnn Kohl 2002

See Shapes

Materials
colored paper scraps
pencil
scissors
glue
poster board for the base
marker

Process
1. Think of a creature or animal to create in cut-out collage style. Some ideas in addition sea creatures are listed. Think about the animal and decide what the basic shape of the animal is, or what basic shapes make up a part of the animal. Here are some ideas:

bat – triangle wings	parrot – tear drop body
bear – circle body	pig – oval body, circle head
cat – circle head, body	rabbit – oval ears, circle body
dog – rectangle	seal – triangle fins
eagle – fan wings	sheep – oval body
lion – triangle teeth	yourself – circle head, oval body

2. Using the basic shape chosen, cut out the shape from colored paper and glue it on the background paper.
3. Add more details to the animal from cut paper scraps and glue them in place. Some ideas are eyes, mouth, feathers, scales, stripes, fuzzy hair, and whiskers.
4. Add environmental details in cut paper, such as trees, leaves, grass, flowers, sun, clouds, and so on.
5. Let the collage picture dry completely.
6. If desired, trace the beginning shape with a marker to show where the design began.

Variation
• Read other books by Suse MacDonald such as *Alphabatics* (Caldecott Winner); *Nanta's Lion; Peck, Slither and Slide; Numblers; Puzzlers; Who Says a Dog Goes Bow-Wow?;* and *Elephants On Board.* Create art in the style of any of these MacDonald favorites.

Sheila McGraw June 12, 1949

Sheila McGraw illustrates with a lovely glow of delicate pastel drawings, which brings the feeling of love to Robert Munsch's story. Capture the feeling of family love with a collage of magazine clippings mixed with family photographs.

"Sheila McGraw has managed to turn an avocation into a profession, channeling her interest in crafting, sewing, renovating, decorating, and painting into the creation of numerous craft books for both adult and juvenile audiences."
    - FIREFLY BOOKS, PUBLISHER
    www.fireflybooks.com
permission by letter to MaryAnn Kohl 2002

by Jodi Drost,
age 15

Love You Forever • *Robert Munsch, author*

A mother sings the same song to her child throughout his life as he grows to an adult. Then, as she grows older, a poignant change of caring and singing takes place. CHILDREN's ABBY NOMINEE 1993

Loving Family Photo Collage

Materials
old magazines
scissors
glue, paste, tape
construction paper background
photographs of family that can be cut up and used in collage
piece of cardboard and clear contact paper, optional

Process
1. Look through old magazines for pictures showing places a family might live or pictures of families doing things together. This might include pictures of a house, a room, a castle, or an apartment building. Other pictures might be a dad and son making cookies, a grandmother reading a book, or a dog playing in the yard. Cut these pictures out and glue them to the construction paper as a background. Try to cover the entire construction paper with magazine pictures that show families in some way.
2. Now look through the collection of family photographs. Select some for the collage. Cut out important parts of the photographs and arrange them on the collage background. Include family pets, relatives, activities, and anything that shows family love.
3. When satisfied with the arrangement, glue them on the background and let dry.
4. For a more permanent collage, glue the completed collage on a piece of cardboard about the same size as the paper. Then cover the collage with clear contact paper. Wrap the contact paper over the edges to the back of the cardboard. Rub the contact paper with the back of a spoon or the straightedge of a ruler to make the pictures more visible and remove bubbles. If any bubbles remain, prick the bubble with a safety pin and press out the air.

Variation
• Make a "loving family photo album" of family pictures. Represent and express the love felt for one's family. Label pictures with memories or feelings.

Family Collage by Morgan Van Slyke, age 7

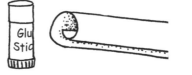

Hush! A Thai Lullaby • *Minfong Ho, author*

In a remote Thai village, a mother tries to hush the green frog and other noisy animals while the baby sleeps. The noisy animals finally respect the mother's wishes and Mother and Baby share a special smile.

CHILDREN'S BOOK AWARD (NORTH CAROLINA) NOMINEE 1998 •
CALDECOTT HONOR 1997 • CHILDREN'S PICTURE STORYBOOK AWARD NOMINEE 1999

Imitate the outlining style of Holly Meade. Outline important parts of a drawing with red, and then cut and glue paper scraps to fit in the spaces of the drawing.

Outline Focus

Materials
white drawing paper
pencil
colored papers, wide variety of scraps
scissors
glue
permanent red marking pen
permanent black marking pen
colored marking pens, optional

Process
1. Draw a simple picture on the drawing paper with a pencil. Draw the picture as an outline, much like a coloring book, using no colors yet. Outline drawings of trees, a house, a vase of flowers, or even a pet sleeping on a bed. Use very little detail. There can be more than one object in the drawing or scene. Each should be a simple outline.
2. Go over all the pencil lines with a black marker, again, like a simply drawn coloring book.
3. Choose a few important parts of the drawing for the collage focus. For example, if there is a tree in the drawing, select some collage papers to cut and then fill-in the tree shape. Use whole pieces, or cut many small pieces to fill-in. Glue the pieces in place. Select one part of the drawing to fill-in with collage papers, or fill in several parts with collage papers.
4. When the collage fill-ins are complete, outline them with red marking pen, like Holly Meade's illustrations.
5. The rest of the outlines can be left uncolored or filled in with colored markers.

Variation
• Draw a simple picture using the bold outlining technique. Leave the picture uncolored. Cut the picture out, just outside the edge of the outline. Glue this cut-out on a background of collage magazine pictures, fabric pieces, wrapping paper scraps, or other paper background. Glue more cut-outs to the background paper as desired.

by Jordon Drost, age 16

"[My mind] feels its way along [as I begin working with colored paper]. I find it difficult, but more like serious play than serious work. The shape I cut off and around from the shape I wanted ends up being the most interesting . . . that odd shape on the floor discarded two days ago leads me to a new idea I hadn't thought of."

- HOLLY MEADE
Education Place,
www.eduplace.com/kids/hmr/mtai/meade.html
©2000 Houghton Mifflin Company

Yaroslava Mills June 11, 1925

Yaroslava Mills creates charming illustrations with clear winter colors. Imitate her style, creating an impression of winter with color and cut-outs. Draw a winter scene on colored paper with a black marker, adding cut paper snowflakes. Then add a paper mitten that can open and close to reveal the crowd of creatures inside.

by Molly Brandt, age 7

During a vacation to Europe, Mills discovered a folk art form called 'reverse glass' painting which she has since incorporated into her artwork. "My palette has acquired the bright 'folk art' colors and my illustrations have a 'sophisticated primitive' look to them. I feel so much at home with my style that I'm really a 'folk artist' at heart'."

- YAROSLAVA MILLS
Something About the Author®,
Vol.35 p.171 ©2003 The Gale Group, Inc.
& packet to MaryAnn Kohl 2002

The Mitten: An Old Ukrainian Folk Tale • *Alvin R. Tresselt, author*

A boy's lost mitten becomes a refuge from the cold for one animal after another until the delightfully explosive ending. There is a new version of this story, but the older classic version should not be missed.

ALA NOTABLE BOOK

Peek-a-Boo Mitten

Materials
scissors
black fine tip marking pen
paste or glue, tape
aqua or blue construction paper
colored paper scraps
crayons, markers, or colored pencils
white paper for snowflakes (or large white shipping labels make short work of the glue step!)

Process
1. With a black marker, draw a winter scene including a wooded background of bare trees. Leave space for a big mitten and forest animals. Because so much is covered by snow in the winter, many things do not need to be drawn because they are hidden!
2. Cut small snowflakes from folded pieces of thin white paper and glue them to the picture. (If large white shipping labels are handy, fold and cut these, peel the backing and stick to the picture for an easy alternative.)
3. Trace a hand on a sheet of colored paper to make a mitten shape. Go around the hand, and then go around the thumb. Cut this out. If a little animal is going to peek out of the thumb, also cut a "hole" off the end of the thumb. Then cut the mitten in half. Glue the two mitten pieces at the outside edges to the winter picture (see the illustration). Make two flaps that open like a window. Then fold the flaps open and press open.
4. On scraps of paper, draw animals that will take refuge in the mitten. Color them and cut them out. Tuck them into the mitten and glue or tape them in place. Fill the mitten with animals. Glue them to the scenery around the mitten if the mitten is full. Let the glue dry briefly, and then press the mitten closed.
5. Open the flaps of the mitten — peek inside to see the animals, then close up the door again. (Is that a little mouse peeking out the thumb hole?) Open & close, open & close!

Variations
• Mitten ideas:
  – staple an old mitten to the artwork instead of the paper version
  – make a mitten print and then glue on cut-outs of animals
• Read *The Old Man and the Tiger* and *It's Time Now!*, both by Alvin R. Tresselt.

Crocodile Beat • *Gail Jorgensen, author*

While lively animals dance and sing by the edge of the river, the crocodile sleeps. King Lion leads the foot-stomping fun. When the napping croc wakes, King Lion must protect his friends. Readers can clap the jungle beat while the crocodile hunts for his dinner.

Imitate Patricia Mullins' appealing tissue paper collage with the basic technique of overlapping tissue paper pieces on the background paper. Then glue them in place.

Tissue Exposé

Materials
art tissue, bright and pastel colors (art stores, hobby stores, gift stores)
background paper, white drawing paper
extra piece of practice paper
scissors
thinned white glue (or liquid starch) in a dish with a soft paintbrush

Process
1. Think of an illustration to create on white paper with colorful tissue scraps and glue.
2. Instead of drawing the illustration, experiment with cutting shapes freehand.
3. For practice (not required): Cut shapes and arrange them on the practice paper without glue. When satisfied with the arrangement, glue the shapes on the background paper.
4. To do this, brush a little glue on the background paper where the tissue will be placed, and lightly press the tissue to the glue. Paint over this with a little more glue to seal the edges to the paper. Add more pieces, overlapping edges of tissue so colors will blend and form new colors. Construct the collage piece by piece until complete.
5. Let the collage dry overnight, or until the tissue is crisp and clear.

Variations
- Work with tissue and glue (or liquid starch), brushing the pieces of tissue onto the white drawing paper. But instead of letting them remain there, peel them off. The color from the tissue will be left, creating an abstract watercolor-look.
- For a transparent collage that displays well in a sunny window, work with tissue on wax paper or clear plastic wrap.

by Sarah Wiley-Jones, age 14

Patricia and her family live in Melbourne, Australia, and share their house with a dog, a family of rabbits, a terracotta dragon, a community of budgies, and various toys and wooden horses, all of whom provide inspiration for her illustrations. Patricia's favorite pastimes include toy-making, soft sculpture, and restoring old rocking horses.

- ABOUT PATRICIA MULLINS
Scholastic Inc. Australia
www.scholastic.com.au
©1997-2002 Scholastic Australia Pty Ltd

Crocodile Beat is out of print but is available in libraries.

Marcus Pfister July 30, 1960

Create a one-of-a-kind tropical fish in the style of Marcus Pfister's *Rainbow Fish*. Include glittery scales made from foil, metallic paper, or other shiny materials.

by Jodi Drost
age 15

"For me, there is one major criterion in determining the value of a book: If it brings adults and children together and makes them interact intensely, then it has achieved its purpose. A good book acts as a bridge between a child and an adult, sparking lots of questions, and expanding the imagination of the child."

- MARCUS PFISTER
Something About the Author®,
Vol.83 p.168 ©2003 The Gale Group, Inc.

The Rainbow Fish • *Marcus Pfister, author*

The most beautiful fish in the ocean discovers the real value of friendship and personal beauty. Glittery foil stamps on each page makes the little fish, its story, and its appearance impossible to forget.

CHILDREN'S ABBY AWARD 1995 • BOLOGNA BOOK FAIR CRITICI IN ERBA PRIZE • CHRISTOPHER AWARD • IRA-CBC CHILDREN'S CHOICE • NORTH CAROLINA CHILDREN'S BOOK AWARD

Glittery Pieces

Materials
choices of glittery materials —
  foil
  metallic paper
  Mylar scraps
  stamping glitter (powdery)
  glitter
  glitter pens
  sequins, faux jewels
  crystal glitter (looks like snow)
white glue in squeeze bottle
watercolor paints & brush, jar of water
white drawing paper for background
pencil, eraser
scissors

Process
1. Lightly sketch a tropical fish, real or imaginary, on the paper.
2. Add other undersea details like seaweed, starfish, sand, bubbles, treasure chest, and shells.
3. Paint the drawing with watercolor paints, and let dry.
4. When dry, add glittery materials to the painting. Cut scales to place on the fish. Add glitter to seaweed and shells.
5. Then let the glittery painting collage dry overnight.

Variations
• Design other creatures and imaginary folk that are glittery, like space aliens, princesses and royalty, magical castles and dream buildings, or stars and planets in the universe.
• Draw any picture with marking pens or crayons, and then add the glittery materials with glue.

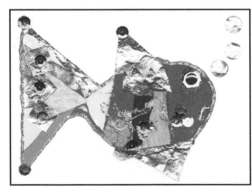

Sparkle Fish by Henry Dotson III, age 8
with embellishments by Eleanor Davis, age 12

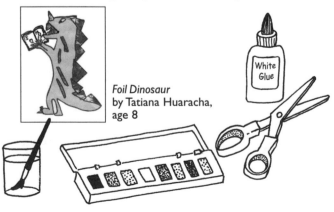

Foil Dinosaur
by Tatiana Huaracha,
age 8

Mira Reisberg March 1, 1955

Baby Rattlesnake • Te Ata (told by); Lynn Morona (adapted by)

In this Native American fable, Baby Rattlesnake wants his rattle even though he's not old enough to know how to use it. Like most babies, he throws a tantrum to get it. When his parents give in, the story really begins!

Mira Reisberg's artwork is a great motivator for children to try their own hands at designing snakes. Wallpaper scraps make fancy, wild patterns for baby rattlesnakes.

Snakeskin Patterns

Materials
old wallpaper books or wallpaper scraps
large sheet of craft paper
   or butcher paper
bright sheet of additional background
   paper, optional
scissors
glue
drawing tools (optional, like a black
   permanent marking pen)

Process
1. Select some wallpaper samples from an old wallpaper book to use for creating an imaginative snakeskin collage. Don't be afraid to use unusual patterns that would never be found on a real snake!
2. Cut shapes from the samples.
3. Cover the entire large background paper with wallpaper scraps. Glue in place.
4. Draw a snake shape on the wallpaper scraps. Then cut the snake out on the drawn line.
5. If desired, outline the snake further, or add details with a permanent black marking pen.
6. The snake can be glued to a bright background paper, or displayed in its wiggly cut-out form.

Variations
- For a great decoration, cut out the snake and display it on a window, along the base of the wall near the floor, on a door, or climbing over a window. Have a parade of art snakes that circles the entire room!
- With crayons, color different kinds of patterns on a snake shape. Color hard with firm control, making the marks shiny. Then spray a bright color of paint on the drawing from a hand spray bottle. Before the paint dries, scrape the paint away with a spatula or other straight edge for an unusual crayon resist effect.
- Make a snakeskin pattern collage with stickers, aluminum foil, scraps of fabric, art tissue, or scraps of wrapping paper.

by Tabitha Silva, age 9

by Eleanor Davis, age 12

"Growing up in Australia, I was filled with a love of eccentric animals and light drenched landscapes. Aboriginal art with its bold colors and patterns influenced me as a young artist and still inspires me as an older artist today. I drew constantly, sometimes using my drawings to make sense of things that were difficult and other times to just make my own beautiful world that I could escape into. I could be a mermaid or a kangaroo if I wanted to. I loved books with a passion (as did everyone in my family. I am available for school visits and presentations, and enjoy inspiring children and teachers."

- Mira Reisberg
from the website of Mira Reisberg
www.mirareisberg.com ©2000 Mira Reisberg
& letter to MaryAnn Kohl 2002

~ art idea generously contributed by
Teri Mason, Hutto, Texas

Faith Ringgold October 8, 1930

Explore Faith Ringgold's fabric technique described as "tankas" – painting on cloth and making border frames of fabric.

by Shon Gorsuch, age 7

"When I was a little girl growing up in Harlem, I was always encouraged to value who I was and to go after what I wanted. Ever since I was young, I've always had a need to express my ideas through art. Being an artist and a writer of children's books is a fulfillment of my lifelong ambition. My books are ... about children having dreams, and instilling in them a belief that they can change things. All good things start with a dream."   - FAITH RINGGOLD

permission to MaryAnn Kohl 2002, www.faithringgold.com &
We Flew Over the Bridge:
The Memories of Faith Ringgold, Little Brown, 1995

Tar Beach • *Faith Ringgold, author*

While Cassie sits on her quilt, she flies off to places she feels free to go. Eight-year-old Cassie states that she is free to go wherever she wants for the rest of her life. Sleeping on a tar beach is a magical experience for Cassie. A tar beach, an *island in the sky*, is really a flat roof in the city that is covered with tar.

CALDECOTT HONOR 1992 • PARENTS CHOICE AWARD 1991

Tankas

Materials
length of plain, smooth fabric like canvas or muslin (1 yd. [1m])
piece of cardboard (approximately 30"x30" [1m x 1m])
duct tape
scissors
scraps of fabric to collect in a variety of patterns and textures (approximately 2"-3" [5cm-8cm] square):

cotton	silk
wool	chintz
denim	felt
burlap	jersey
brocade	taffeta

Hint: fabric scraps can be found in clearance bins at fabric stores, collected from garage sales, or recycled from old clothes and worn or used materials around the house.
fabric paints and brushes (substitute marking pens if fabric paints are not available)
fabric glue (Tacky Glue works well)

~ art idea generously contributed by Teri Mason, Hutto, Texas

Process
To stretch the fabric over the cardboard –
1. Spread out the fabric on the table. Place the cardboard square in the center of the fabric.
2. Fold one edge of fabric over the edge of the cardboard, and tape it. Stretch the other side of the fabric tight, fold it over the edge of the cardboard, and tape it in the same way. Do the same with the remaining two edges. All of the fabric will be tightly taped to the back of the cardboard. Turn it over (fabric side up, ready to create.

The Tankas –
1. Paint (or draw with markers) a picture in the center of the stretched fabric. Leave a border area untouched, perhaps 2"-3" [5cm-8cm] all the way around the big square. If painting, let dry. If using markers, proceed to the next step.
2. Choose squares of fabric that add to the design and color of the picture in the center of the fabric. Spread them around the border of the picture, moving and reorganizing them in a pattern that is appealing.
3. When ready, glue each square down, one next to the other, creating a border of fabric color and design surrounding the picture. Pat down the edges with fingers. (Keep a damp sponge handy for cleaning sticky fingers.) When the glue is dry, check for loose edges of fabric squares that may need a little more glue touch up.
4. The finished artwork will resemble a quilt. Quilting is a major inspiration for Faith Ringgold's work.

Variation
• Sew fabric scraps on an electric sewing machine to make a composite of scraps for the art border. Sewing over the scraps gives them a quilted look.

Susan L. Roth February 29, 1944

How Thunder and Lightning Came to Be • *Beatrice Orcutt Harrell (retold by)*

Two very large and silly birds are chosen to warn the Choctaw people of coming rainstorms. They accidentally create thunder and lightning as a bright noisy warning which entertains and pleases the Great Sun Father.

Imitate the feathery component of Susan L. Roth's collage technique. Create birds with feathers and glue.

Fine Feather Collage

Materials
craft feathers (available in large bags from hobby or school supply stores)
scissors, tweezers, toothpicks
matboard or poster board
bowls for holding feathers
pencil
glue in a dish
variety of scrap papers (interesting colors, textures)
damp sponge for wiping tools
marking pens, optional

Process
1. Look at the birds in the book and see how Susan L. Roth has constructed them from paper cut to look like real feathers. See how they overlap like shingles on a roof? For this collage experience, actual feathers will be used instead of paper! Paper will be used for adding other details.
2. Lightly sketch a bird shape on the matboard background with pencil. This will be a guide for the collage.
3. Snip feathers into smaller pieces. Keep the feathers in bowls or trays so they won't blow away. Fill the bowls with feathers.
4. With tweezers, pick up a feather piece, dip it in glue, and place it on the design. Continue adding feathers, letting them overlap, forming the shape of a bird. If the tweezers tips become "gluey", wipe them on the damp sponge to clean. Toothpicks work well for placing drops of glue directly on the collage. Press the feather piece into the drop of glue with the tweezers.
5. When the bird is formed, add other details with scraps of paper, like –

legs	feet	beak
eyes	toes	top-knot

6. Make more than one bird, if desired.
7. Add more details to the collage with paper scraps, or leave the bird collage in a simple format. Let dry completely. If any feathers come loose, re-glue at any time.

Variations
- Other books illustrated by Susan L. Roth are *Fire Came to the Earth People* (New York Times Best Illustrated Book/written by S.L. Roth); *Pass the Fritters, Critters*; *The Great Ball Game*; *Ishi's Tale of Lizard*.
- Cut, snip, and fringe paper scraps to look like feathers. Glue in a collage design in Roth's style.

by Lauren Olson, age 9

"When I finished the art for this book, the publisher sent it to the author for fact checking. It turned out that I had made a big mistake and only had men and boys dancing for the harvest celebration. The Chocktaw women were permitted and invited to partake in all dancing celebrations.
   Fortunately, I used a rice and water based glue from Japan. With a small, hot wet towel, I soaked the pages, one at a time. When the collage was almost saturated, slowly and carefully, with my skinny, sharp and precise tweezers, I peeled off half the boys' headdresses and pants. Then I attached girl's hair and dresses to these figures with a little more glue. If I remember correctly, they even have ribbons for their braids. This is one of the things that I love about the collage medium: if you're careful, you can change your mind without ruining anything."

-*Susan L. Roth*
letter to Jean Potter 2002
& letter to MaryAnn Kohl 2003

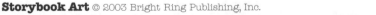

Synthia Saint James February 11, 1949

Synthia Saint James' painting technique in this snowy book authored by Cheryl Chapman is applying oil paint on canvas. The paintings have a bold, simple look, almost like collage. Most children do not have oil paints or canvas on hand, so can imitate the bold shapes of Synthia Saint James' work using a collage technique. Cut bold paper kids and glue them on vast paper cut-outs of snow.

"I'm a self-taught artist and writer who has learned, and is still learning, through trial and error."
- SYNTHIA SAINT JAMES
www.authorsden.com
synthiasaintjames.com
& letter to MaryAnn Kohl 2003

by Jordan Drost, age 16

Snow on Snow on Snow • *Cheryl Chapman, author*

A boy and his dog wake up on a snowy day under warm blankets. Mama fills the boy's plate with food. Then he pulls on his snow clothes. With his longhaired dog, he sleds with his friends. When the dog becomes lost, all the children search behind trees and around bushes. When the dog is found, they all live happily ever after.

Cut & Paste Scene

Materials
colorful construction paper scraps, including whites, light blues, and grays
pencil
scissors
glue or paste
sheet of white or colored background paper

Process
1. Imagine a snowy scene.
2. On construction paper scraps, draw bold shapes and characters (boys, girls, dogs, cats) for the scene. Cut them out and spread them on the table.
3. Cut big pillowy shapes of snow from white, gray, and light blue paper. Spread these on the table.
4. Now begin assembling the scraps into a scene on the background paper. Move them around until satisfied with the arrangement. Glue them in place.
5. Add more shapes and designs if needed to finish the scene.

Variation
- Create abstract shapes from free-hand cutting and glue them into a collage on paper.
- Make a collage of a different kind of scene, such as a colorful autumn walk in the woods, a fun day at the seashore, or the universe and all its planets, suns, and stars.

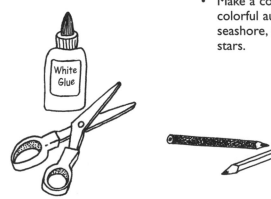

Jerome Wexler February 6, 1923

Everyday Mysteries • Jerome Wexler, author

Everyday things become mysteries by the way they are viewed. Enlarged photographs that show only parts of objects make this book a guessing game.

Imitate Wexler's photographic mystery style. Enlarge common household items on a photocopy machine. Create an interactive collage guessing game.

Mystery Clips

Materials

photocopy machine
  with enlargement
  feature
selection of household
  items with a flat
  surface –
  sliced open green
    pepper
  salt in a plastic bag
  tea bag
  eraser
  telephone cord
  nail file
  domino
  unusual envelope
magazine pictures
large piece of
  cardboard for the
  collage base
glue, tape, scissors
marking pens
highlight pens
large envelope
index cards, tag board,
  or heavy paper

Process

1. Look around the house and find interesting objects that will be enlarged and copied on a photocopy machine. They should be fairly flat or have one flat surface. Find these same objects in magazine or catalog. (Keep in mind the goal of the project is to conceal the true identity of the object so others must guess what it is.)
2. The copies: Place each object, one at a time, on the photocopy machine (color copies are a nice option). Then ENLARGE and press copy. Choose to copy unusual parts of objects such as the bottom of a ketchup bottle, a coiled or twisted telephone cord, or a green pepper sliced open.
3. Glue the copies to a large piece of cardboard, eventually covering the entire background. Allowing edges to overlap slightly works well. Glue the edges of each copy down so the collage is flat. Then dry.
4. To add color:
   – with markers, outline the shapes of the enlarged copies
   – use highlight pens to color the copies
   – paint a little thin watercolor paint on each copy
5. Tape a heavy envelope to the back of the collage. Then let the collage dry.
6. To make matching game cards, find magazine clippings to match each item. Cut out and glue each magazine picture to an index card or heavy paper square. Let dry.
7. Spread the picture cards on the table, and ask friends and family to match them with the copies on the mystery collageboard that they represent. For example, match a picture of a domino to the copy of the domino; match a picture of a doll to the copy of a doll's arm; match a picture of a telephone with the copy of the coiled telephone cord.
8. When play is done, store the picture cards in the envelope taped to the back of the collage.

Variation

• Make flip-up picture cards. tape them picture side down over the matching copy on the collage. First guess what the photocopy is. Then flip up the picture card to confirm!

by Jennifer Reinstra,
age 9

"In my science books, I write about ideas, rather than just the facts. I try to ask a question, such as how do scientists guess what dinosaurs were like? Then I try to answer the question as I write the book. Writing is hard work, but it's the greatest fun in the world."
- JEROME WEXLER
*Morning Record, 1/20/78,
"Photographer Studies Life,
Then Teaches Kids About It,"
Wallingford, CT, James M. Gaffey,
article courtesy of Wallingford Public Library*

Guess what the parts of these familiar objects really are.

Candace Whitman · February 8

Candace Whitman first paints damp rice paper with watercolor patterns, letting colors absorb, spread, and blend. She tears the shapes to precisely fit & fill the picture, creating soft edging with fibers showing. Next, she glues the shapes onto the background paper, creating a fuzzy-looking, soft collage picture.

by Jennifer Reinstra, age 9

"Warm and fuzzy – beautiful – delightful – spiritual – are the words I hear people use to describe my picture books. Readers say it comes through the color, the language, the texture in my collage art. These comments are very gratifying since I want to touch children in memorable ways, especially very young ones. A child's first impression of books matters."

— CANDACE WHITMAN
*letter to MaryAnn Kohl 2002 &
www.candacewhitman.com*

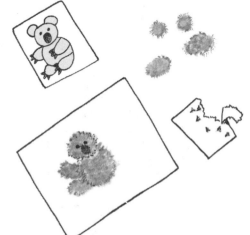

Zoo-Looking · *Mem Fox, author*

In this rhyming book of softly painted and torn collage illustrations, Flora visits the zoo with her father. Not only does Flora look at the animals, but some of them look back at her!

Fuzzy Collage

Materials
large sheet of rice paper (Any highly absorbent paper – desk blotter – will work, but rice paper is the best with its fibers and textures – from hobby or art supply stores.)
fingers/hands for tearing paper
watercolor paints, paintbrushes
water
glue
scissors
large sheet of background paper
cardboard or matboard (a little smaller than the background paper)

Process
1. Think about a collage illustration to create, and the colors and shapes needed. Then sketch it on a plain piece of paper. Use this as a guide for the next steps.
2. Spread a piece of absorbent rice paper on the work table. Dampen it with water from a sponge or under a faucet. Pat down on the table to flatten.
3. Paint designs and patterns on the rice paper that go along with the sketch plan, letting colors soak and blur. Paint one kind of design in one space, and another in a different space. Then let the paper dry.
4. Look at the sketch again. Think of what sizes and shapes will be needed. Loosely cut the big paper apart between painted areas to make it easier to handle. Then, begin tearing one painted area to make the planned collage design. Do the larger shapes first, and then move on to more detailed shapes.
5. Arrange the shapes on the background paper, but do not glue yet. Arrange and rearrange until satisfied with the arrangement. Start adding more detailed pieces. When everything is in place, it's time to glue.
6. Glue the pieces in place. This may take a long time, so work in an area that can be left undisturbed.
7. Finish gluing all the pieces in place. The effect will be soft and gentle torn pieces with fuzzy fibers showing at the edges.

Variations
• Paint shapes and designs on wet paper. Let it dry. Then cut them out with scissors instead of tearing. Glue them on a background paper. Matboard works very well.
• Paint on dry paper, tear or cut out the pieces, and glue on a background paper.
• Work with art tissue, torn into shapes, and pressed onto a wet background paper. Paint over the entire collage with liquid starch or white glue thinned with water.

Storybook Art © 2003 Bright Ring Publishing, Inc.

David Wiesner February 5, 1956

Tuesday • David Wiesner, author

Frogs ride their magic lily pad carpets through suburbia, surprising those below. *Tuesday* has few words, but holds a story through unusual events and surreal illustrations.   CALDECOTT MEDAL 1992

Imitate the surreal art style of David Wiesner (surreal simply means *not real*, strange, or imaginary). Enlarge or reduce magazine cutouts on a photocopy machine to create a surreal illustration.

Surreal Illusion

Materials
magazine picture of an animal, person, or inanimate object
photocopy machine
scissors
choice of drawing tools –
    crayons, marking pens, colored pencils, highlight pens
glue or paste
white drawing paper

Process
1. Select a magazine picture of something that will be the main focus of the surreal art, similar to the frogs or pigs in David Wiesner's book. Cut around its shape with scissors.
2. Place the picture on a photocopy machine, and reproduce numerous images *reduced* several times, and *enlarged* several times. A total of five to ten images works well, but any number is fine.
3. Cut all the images out and set aside.
4. Draw the background scenery on the drawing paper for the image. Draw a choice of rooftops, buildings, landscapes, or seascapes for the images to fly over.
5. Spread the images on the background scenery. Try different configurations - some overlapping, some appearing far away, some closer. When a satisfying arrangement is in place, glue or paste them to the background.
6. Leave the images in black and white, or color them with a choice of drawing tools.

Variations
• Create a surreal impossible collage with a variety of magazine picture images. Draw a background, or work on blank paper.
• Explore humor in surreal work. Imagine a baseball picture as the head of a person, a bowl of fruit as the hair on a lovely actress, or a bowl full of yummy puppy-pasta!

by Monika Baranek, age 11

"Art has always been a part of my life: I can't pinpoint the exact time when I began drawing; it was something I was always doing, and it became part of how I was perceived. It also defined my personality to a certain extent: clearly when relatives were aware of my interest in art, I would get various art supplies for Christmas and birthdays, and a lot of hand - me - downs: boxes of pastels, watercolors from Carol, my older sister, and George my brother, who are both pretty artistically inclined. I loved to watch them draw things."

- DAVID WIESNER
Something About the Author®,
Vol.117 p.197 ©2003 The Gale Group, Inc.

Penguin Collage by Morgan Van Slyke, age 7

Ed Young November 28, 1931

Explore the technique of composing a replication pattern similar to that in Ed Young's illustrations. Begin by cutting seven identical shapes in seven different colors. Present the replications – or *clones* – in a creative arrangement on a black paper background.

"Be open to inspiration. Inspiration leads to creativity. Be open to play. In play we see mistakes as stepping-stones to fulfillment. Be open to challenges. Challenges offer us a chance to grow. Be open to work. It is in the willingness of labor that we mature and find excellence."

– Ed Young
National Center for Children's Illustrated Literature, www.nccil.org
& letter from McIntosh & Otis, Inc.

by Morgan Van Slyke, age 7

Seven Blind Mice (adapted from The Blind Men and the Elephant) • Ed Young, author

An Indian fable recounts the experiences of seven blind men. Colorful paper mice in Young's version discover different parts of an elephant and squabble over their conflicting observations. The brightly colored nearly identically shaped mice discover color, days of the week, and that wisdom comes from 'seeing the whole'.

Clone Collage

Materials

seven squares of
   construction paper in
   different colors
   (6"x6" [15cm x 15cm])
pencil
black background paper
   or poster board
sharp scissors
white construction
   paper square
   (6"x6" [15cm x 15cm])
glue or paste
stapler
paper hole punches for
   clone features

Process

1. To imitate Ed Young's mice collage illustrations, choose an animal, shape, or simple object for this colorful collage. Make seven that will all be the same shape, or *clones*. Some suggestions of shapes are –

apple	rabbit	cat	leaf
circle	triangle	daisy	sun
pig	heart	ball	dinosaur

2. Staple the seven squares of paper together (one staple at each corner) to wiggly paper during the cutting step.
3. With pencil, draw the basic clone design on the white square. Make it chubby and round with large details (no tiny details).
4. When satisfied with the basic clone, cut it out. Place it on top of the stack of 7 stapled colored squares and trace it. Then remove. Cut all seven colors out at the same time. When done, the finished shapes should all be quite nearly identical clones of the basic shape. (Make more clones with more stacks of colored paper, if desired, but seven is about as thick as can be cut successfully by hand.)
5. Arrange them on the black background in any pattern or design. Some can be turned over, or upside down, or all of them can be identical in their positions. When satisfied with the arrangement, glue them in place.
6. Add hole punches for eyes or other details such as –

nose	polka-dots	ears	buttons

Variations

- seven (or more!) squares of thin art tissue is very easy to cut
- paint on the colored paper before cutting to create texture and depth
- cut shapes from contact paper in 7 different patterns, and self-stick to a background
- make clones from felt and tell a flannel-board story

Five Dancers
by Megan Kohl, age 7 (1985)

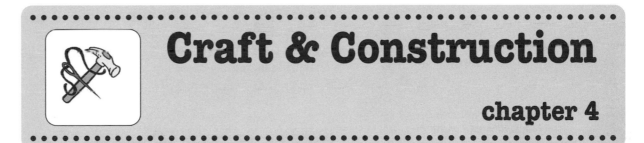

Craft & Construction

chapter 4

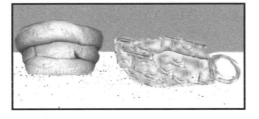

Tea Party Pottery by Hannah Kohl, age 6 (1981)
based on
Miss Spider's Tea Party by David Kirk

Shoe Art by students of Paula Guhin, art teacher
Aberdeen, South Dakota
based on
Alligator Shoes by Arthur Dorros

* image permission *SchoolArts* magazine
12/98, "Rococo Redux", p.19.

Clay Bird with Flower
by Kayla Comstock, age 8
based on
Have You Seen Birds? by Barbara Reid

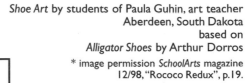

Little Miss Spider by Kelsey Switzer, age 7
based on
Miss Spider's Tea Party by David Kirk

Clare Beaton April 20, 1947

Imitate Clare Beaton's illustration style featuring stitched felt shapes in farmyard scenes comprised of yarn and sewing trims.

"I enjoy recycling otherwise forgotten scraps and giving them a new lease on life. I'm a tremendous hoarder and collector of everything from old craft books to fabrics, buttons, jewelry, postcards and toys."

- CLARE BEATON
Barefoot Books,
www.barefoot-books.com
publisher letter to MaryAnn Kohl 2002

by Abby Brandt,
age 5

How Big is a Pig? • *Stella Blackstone, author*

Follow the story path of animal opposites through the appliqué farmyard. Who is the biggest pig of all?

Stitching Time

Materials
felt scraps
pencil or fine-tip marker
scissors
materials to stitch into the design –
    yarn
    sequins
    braid
    fabric scraps
    sewing trim
    beads
    faux jewels
    embroidery floss
    buttons
background fabric (burlap, canvas or other loose weave fabric), about 15"x15" [40cmx40cm] or larger
square of cardboard, about 12"x12" [30cmx30cm] or larger
fabric glue (Tacky Glue works well)
needle and embroidery floss (optional)
stapler, tape, paperclips, rubber bands, duct tape, other glue (if needed)

Process
1. Look at the stitched felt designs in Clare Beaton's book. Notice how trims, fabric, and stitching are used. Think about an individual design to work on, perhaps a farm theme, or any other idea. Hint: Bold felt shapes are easier to work with than fine or narrow shapes.
2. Draw some shapes or designs on felt pieces, and cut them out.
3. Next, assemble the shapes on the burlap, moving them around until satisfied with the arrangement. Leave about a 3" [8cm] margin around the entire edge of the burlap.
4. Decide to attach the shapes by one of two methods: stitching or gluing. Stitching has the most lasting and artistic style, but gluing is faster.
5. Continue adding stitched or glued items. Glue will need to dry overnight or several hours to hold.
6. When all is done, place the stitching face down on the table. Then place the cardboard square in the center. Tape all the edges of the stitching to the back of the cardboard, pulling it tight.
7. Turn the artwork over, and the stitching will be ready to display.

Variations
- Sew two embroidery floss loops on the back of the stitching so that it can hang from nails or hooks.
- Make a cloth book with big squares of felt. Sew or glue felt scraps onto each page of the book. Cut the scraps into shapes or characters. Sew all the "pages" of felt together with a zig-zag stitch on a sewing machine (or sew by hand).

3" [8cm] border around the stitching area

Barnyard Stitched Collage
by Sara, grade 2

Harvey Potter's Balloon Farm • *Jerdine Nolen Harold, author*

Harvey Potter owns a balloon farm where he grows balloons to order, a most unusual crop! A young girl ventures out in the night, determined to discover the secret of Harvey Potter's specialty farm.

Extend appreciation of Mark Buehner's balloon illustrations. Create a balloon sculpture with double-sided tape and bunches of bright balloons.

Balloon Sculpture

Materials
balloons
double-sided tape
tape, string, rubber bands for
    reinforcement
square of cardboard, or other base

Process
1. Blow up a balloon, and knot the end. An adult will need to help and supervise. (Young children should not blow up balloons.)
2. Stick a small piece of double-sided tape on the balloon.
3. Blow up as many balloons as desired (without getting dizzy). Tie knots in balloons, and stick a little piece of double-sided tape to each one.
4. Make a bright and colorful balloon sculpture by touching the balloons one against another. Align the tape against another balloon. They will all stick together in a bright, cheerful sculpture. Additional tape, string or rubber bands may be needed for reinforcement.
5. To display, tape the base balloon to the table, floor, a piece of cardboard, or tie to a fence!

Variations
- Rub a balloon on a volunteer's hair, on a sweater, or on a carpet. Then roll the balloon in sugar, salt, confetti, sand, sequins, glitter or other tiny sprinkly items. Place the balloons on a party table for glittery decoration. The sprinkles will hold for a long time.
- Blow up a huge bunch of balloons. Tie each one to a long string, about 3"-5" [8cm×13cm] apart. Hang the string across a room for a fun party decoration, like a garland of balloons!

by Jennifer Reinstra, age 9

"The ideas for some of my books came up at our own family dinner table."

- MARK BUEHNER
*Virginia Center for Children's Books
VCCB ©2001
Curry School of Education
curry.edschool.virginia.edu/
go/tempo/VCCB/Authorsets2/
buehner/AuthorsetsBuehner.html*

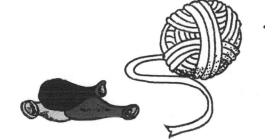

David A. Carter · March 4, 1957

Create a three-dimensional, touchable bug inspired by David Carter's illustrations.

by Eleanor Davis, age 12

"I cannot explain the creative process that goes on in my mind, but discovering that link between my childhood curiosities and thrills and my books has something to do with where the ideas come from. My goal in creating a book is to engage in this natural curiosity,, to entertain with surprise and silliness, and whenever possible to educate, because for me the end result is curiosity in learning."
- DAVID A. CARTER
letter to MaryAnn Kohl 2003 &
www.popupbooks.com

Feely Bugs: To Touch and Feel · David A. Carter, author

Never wanted to touch a bug? Think again! Each touch-and-feel bug presents an interesting assortment of textures for that exact purpose. There are bugs of all kinds - fuzzy, feathery, glittery, sticky, puffy, and even crinkly! *Feely Bugs* joins Carter's other long list of enjoyable bug books.

Feely Bug *art compliments of David A. Carter*

3-D Feelie Bugs

Materials
choice of textured fabrics –
    corduroy
    leather
    lace
    satin
    burlap
    felt
choices of decorative items –
    beads
    clear plastic wrap
    glitter
    plastic bags
    buttons
    colored wire
    paper scraps
    sequins
    cellophane
    craft eyes
    pipe cleaners
Styrofoam balls
white glue (glue-gun, with adult assistance)
scissors
jar lids for drying areas
optional reinforcement -
    pins, tape, rubber bands, string

Process
1. Arrange a selection of materials on the table to use for creating a "feelie bug".
2. Styrofoam balls are used in this craft idea, but any ideas for creating bugs are fine. Spread white glue all over a Styrofoam ball for the bug's body. Wrap a scrap of textured fabric around the ball. (The fabric may need sewing pins, tape, string, or rubber bands to help hold the fabric in place while drying.) Set aside to dry on a jar lid. Tuck in any loose edges of fabric and add more glue to those areas.
3. Spread white glue on a smaller Styrofoam ball for the head, and cover it with textured fabric (the same fabric or a different one). Use pins, etc. to hold if needed. Set aside to dry on a jar lid.
4. Join the two balls together with glue reinforced with pins or other holding materials. A squeeze from a glue-gun (with adult help) holds exceptionally well.
5. Design features for the feelie bug. Add pipe cleaners (legs, wings, antennae), sequins (eyes), buttons (eyes), or googly craft eyes. Clear plastic wrap or plastic bags make great wings!
6. There is no right or wrong way to make a feelie bug! Enjoy making a one-of-a-kind creation.

Variation
• Make a collage bug with similar materials glued to a Styrofoam grocery tray (no Styrofoam balls needed).

Alligator Shoes • *Arthur Dorros, author*

An alligator tries on many kinds of shoes, until a woman wants to try on his alligator feet!

Arthur Dorros inspires this shoe-decorating activity with his brilliant drawings of shoes. Create a unique, special, one-of-a-kind, wearable work of art! An old pair of shoes is the perfect canvas.

One-of-a-Kind Artsy Shoes

Materials
old pair of sneakers or tennie runners
paints or markers
fabric paints, if available
miscellaneous scraps & sewing trims –
    fabric scraps
    ribbons
    lace
    rick-rack
    felt scraps
    buttons, beads
    sequins
    sewing braid
scissors
fabric glue (Tacky Glue)
stapler, optional

Process
1. Select an old pair of shoes (with permission) for decorating into a one-of-a-kind work of art. Plain white tennie-runners are the perfect canvas!
2. Choose scraps to decorate the shoes. Paints or markers can add character and color.
   Note: Fabric glue will make most things stick to the shoes. If some items won't stick well, ask an adult to help with a little hand-stitching (challenging work, but some kids can do it).
3. Glue should dry overnight before wearing.
4. Wear shoes to school or out to play. Like any great work of art, shoes can be displayed for all to see on a shelf, table, or hung from a hook or nail in the wall.

Variations
- Read another book by the author/illustrator– *Abuela*.
- The same shoe-decorating ideas can be used to decorate mittens, gloves, hats, and old T-shirts.

"I believe everyone has stories to tell and can create great artwork, each in our own way — have fun creating yours!"
"Like Alvin in the story, I have an interest in various types of footwear, and I once got locked in a store!"

- ARTHUR DORROS
letter to MaryAnn Kohl 2002 &
www.arthurdorros.com

by Lauren Kaemingk, age 11

Shoe Art by a middle school student, Paula Guhin - art teacher, Aberdeen, South Dakota
    images by permission
    SchoolArts magazine,
    "Rococo Redux", p.19, 12/98

Roger Duvoisin November 28, 1904 –1980

Feel inspired by Roger Duvoisin's snowy illustrations. Create a blizzard of delicate snowflakes made from glue-stiffened crochet thread.

White Snow, Bright Snow • Alvin R. Tresselt, author

When it begins to look, feel, and smell like snow, everyone prepares for a blizzard.

CALDECOTT MEDAL 1948

"When Roger Duvoisin was a child, he showed talent and interest in art, music, and books. He grew up to create more than forty books and illustrate more than 140 books for children as well as illustrating covers for the New Yorker magazine. He is best known for his books featuring Petunia, the silly goose, and Veronica, the conspicuous hippopotamus."

by Jennifer Reinstra, age 9

— ABOUT ROGER DUVOISIN
FROM DEGRUMMOND COLLECTION
McCain Library & Archives, University Libraries,
University of Southern Mississippi, Haittisberg
avatar.lib.usm.edu/~degrum/findaids/duvoisin.htm

Crystal Snowflake

Materials
heavy white crochet thread
   (heaviest possible)
white glue in a shallow dish
wax paper
hanging device —
   tape, thread, or paperclip

Process
1. Prepare to make snowflakes for an art blizzard! Look at pictures of snowflakes to see the variety of designs possible for snowflakes, all with six points each.
2. For each snowflake, soak any number of 6" [15cm] long pieces of very heavy crochet thread in a dish of white glue. When removing the thread from the glue, pull between two fingers held against the edge of the dish, wringing out the excess glue.
3. Place the thread on the waxed paper forming the shape of a six-pointed snowflake. Add more sections of thread and pat with fingers and hands, adding more thread sections to the ones already in place. Continue adding sections of thread until the snowflake is complete. Pat the top of the snowflake again to help it stick together. Then let it dry for several days or until crispy-clear and hard.
4. Peel the snowflakes gently from the waxed paper, and hang by a thread, tape, or unbent paperclip wherever desired.

Variations
- Make a snowflake from one very long piece of thread, possibly 2'-3' [1m] in length.
- Poke six pushpins into a block of Styrofoam in a circle, evenly spacing them around the circle. Dip a long piece of string into glue, squeeze-wring it out, and then wrap the string from pin to pin in a snowflake design. This will resemble a "spirograph" design. Let dry until completely hard. Pull out the pins, and remove the snowflake from the Styrofoam.

Mama's Best Wax Paper

White Glue

Arthur Geisert September 20, 1941

Pigs From A to Z • *Arthur Geisert*

Seven piglets play through a landscape of hidden letters as they build a tree house. The clever illustrations employ the use of supple sticks to form the ABC's.

Arthur Geisert draws sticks formed into different letters hidden within the drawings. Young artists take another look at making sticks into letters by soaking narrow, supple branches in water and then bending them into shapes or letters.

ABC Sticks

"My main interest is illustration. I'm trying to combine a classic etching style inspired by Piranesi, Rembrandt, and Callot with humor and narrative."

- ARTHUR GEISERT
Something About the Author®,
Vol.133 p.72 ©2003 The Gale Group
& letter to MaryAnn Kohl 2002.

by Lauren Kaemingk, age 11

Materials
freshly fallen slender branches (supple and pliable)
bucket of water (or bathtub)
raffia
supplies for display –
   hammer & nails
   push-pins
   string
   board

Process
1. Look over the collected branches to determine if any look like a letter of the alphabet. It will be easy to find a letter **Y** or **K** but not so easy to find a letter **B** or **R**. Set any that resemble letters aside. The hard work is already complete for those branches!
2. Next, take several small branches and place them in the bucket of water. If the bucket isn't big enough, use the bathtub with permission. Soak the branches overnight.
3. The next day, bend the softened branches into letter shapes, such as the letters of a name. Experiment with easy capital letters like **O, C, P, S, D**. Once bending letters seems easier, try more challenging letters like **R, M, N,** or **B**.
4. Wrap raffia around the stick letters to hold them in their shapes. The raffia will also add color and design.
5. Let the branches dry for several days. Leave the raffia in place to help hold the letter shape.
6. To display: Nail ABC sticks to a board to spell a word or name; hang letters from push-pins; lean letters on a shelf; or hang letters individually from strings.

Variation
• For a bright alternative, explore wrapping soaked branches with long strips of crepe paper. Crepe paper acts like strong watercolor paint when wet. It will stain fingers or clothing but washes off fingers after a few soapy bathtimes.

Denise Fleming January 31, 1950

Experiment with the author-illustrator Denise Fleming's papermaking technique with this exciting project. Denise has given Storybook Art her papermaking directions from her website: www.denisefleming.com

"Papermaking for me is cathartic. Part of its appeal is that it's very physical - toting buckets of water, beating large quantities of pulp, hand-mixing huge vats of color. It's different from the Bob Cratchit-like existence that my former finely detailed style required - hunched over my drawing board with electric pencil sharpener close at hand. What other medium requires that you be up to your elbows in brilliant color? It's wet, messy, and wonderful - I haven't picked up a brush or a colored pencil since I discovered papermaking."

by Eleanor Davis, age 12

- *DENISE FLEMING*
letter to MaryAnn Kohl 2002 &
www.denisefleming.com

* *text and art reprinted with permission from ©Denise Fleming 2003*

Denise's video, *A Visit with Denise Fleming,* is available for loan from Henry Holt & Co., and shows her papermaking process. Borrow for up to 2 weeks. Photocopying permitted (but not for resale). Arrange, call: **212-886-9200.**

Cotton rag fiber is used to make Denise's paper and aqueous dispersed pigments to color the cotton. Supply source:
  Twinrocker Papermaking Supplies
  PO Box 413
  Brookston, IN 47923
  800-757-8946

Barnyard Banter • *Denise Fleming, author*

All the farm animals are where they should be, making their noises, except the goose who waddles here and there throughout the farm.

Denise Fleming's **Handmade Paper**
Beginning Pulp Painting

TO MAKE SQUARE OR RECTANGULAR PAPER

Materials
- Two canvas/needlework stretcher frames (same size)
- One piece fiberglass window screen cut 2" [5cm] bigger than the frame
- Stapler or tacks, hammer
- Duct tape
- Scissors

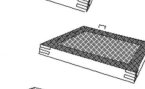

MOLD/SCREEN
- Stretch screen over one of the frames.
- Staple or tack screen in place.
- Trim excess screen.
- Tape over staples/tacks and frame edges with duct tape. This is the **mold/screen.**

DECKLE/FRAME
- The other frame is the **deckle.** The deckle sits on top of the **mold/screen** to hold pulp in place.

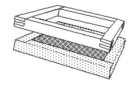

TO MAKE PULP

Materials
- Construction paper scraps, torn into small pieces & divided by color
- Blender
- Water – lots of it!
- Large containers, one for each color of pulp

MAKING PULP
- Place 1/3 cup [80ml] firmly packed torn paper in the blender.
- Fill the blender 2/3 full of water.
- Blend for 40 to 60 seconds.
- Pulp should be *slurry* consistency.
- More water should be added to the pulp when using squeeze bottles.

TO POUR PAPER

Materials • Cups for pouring pulp - yogurt containers work well.
• Dishpan - bigger than frames or hoops, or deep-dish foil pie pans.
• Two sticks - to support **mold and deckle** above the dishpan.
• Large waste-water bucket - to empty water from dishpan/pie pan.
• Extras - squeeze bottles, plastic spoons, cookie cutters, foam meat trays, craft knife to cut shapes in foam trays.

POURING PULP

• Place **mold and deckle** on sticks over dishpan. **Mold/screen** should be screen side up with **deckle/frame** on top.
• Pour pulp, using small cups, as evenly as possible over **mold/screen.** Pulp should be at least $1/8$" [.5cm] thick. This is the **base sheet.**
• Spoon different colors of pulp on the wet **base sheet** to create designs.
• Use plastic squeeze bottles filled with pulp to create different patterns and shapes. Squeeze pulp on the wet **base sheet.**
• Cookie cutters can be used as stencils, or cut stencils from the centers of a foam grocery trays.
• Place a stencil on the wet **base sheet.**
• Fill stencil shape with pulp using a spoon or squeeze bottle.
• Remove stencil carefully.

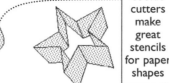

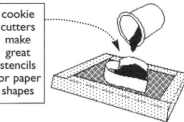

cookie cutters make great stencils for paper shapes

TO REMOVE WET PAPER FROM MOLD-COUCHING

Materials • Sponge
• Newspaper, bath towel, or old blanket
• Two synthetic dish clothes (HandiWipes™), or two pieces non-woven interfacing fabric bigger than **mold/screen.**

COUCHING

• Place dampened dishcloth/interfacing on a pile of newspaper/bath towel/or old blanket. This is the **couching pile.**
• Remove **deckle/frame.**
• Flip **mold/screen,** pulp side down, onto the **couching pile.**
• With a rocking motion, carefully remove the **mold/screen,** starting at the edge.
• Place the second damp dishcloth/interfacing on top of the handmade paper. Press with a damp sponge to remove excess water. Wring out excess water between pressing.
• Hold edges of top and bottom cloths. Flip over. Carefully peel off cloth. Ta-dah! **A pulp painting!**

TO DRY PAPER

Materials • Two sheets of plain white paper (typing paper) or manila paper
• Newspaper
• Heavy objects (books or bricks) to act as weights

DRYING PAPER

• Place handmade paper between two sheets of plain paper.
• Sandwich paper/handmade paper between layers of newspaper.
• Weight down with heavy objects.
• Change newspaper daily for several days, until dry.
* See www.denisefleming.com for more fun pulp painting and handmade paper ideas.

Experiment

• Blend ONE COLOR of paper until smooth then add PIECES OF ANOTHER COLOR and blend for a short time. The result is FLECKED PAPER.
• Add tiny bits of COLORED EMBROIDERY FLOSS to pulp.
• Add GLITTER to pulp, or cut up a clean foil margarine wrapper and blend with pulp to create glittery paper.
• Use COOKIE CUTTERS to make shaped paper.
• Add DRIED FLOWERS or DRIED HERBS to pulp for

Mort Gerberg March 11

To further enjoy cartoonist, Mort Gerberg's, illustrations of spaghetti, dip into sticky spaghetti art-fun. Soak strands of cooked spaghetti in glue, and make a silly spaghetti hanging decoration. Minnie the monkey would adore it! Even if Silly Spaghetti has no cartooning to do, Mort Gerberg approves of such silly spaghetti fun!

More Spaghetti I Say • Rita Golden Gelman, author

Minnie the Monkey is much too busy eating spaghetti in many different ways to play with her friend Freddie.

art compliments of
Mort Gerberg

by Megan
VanBerkum,
age 8

"When I was a kid, I was always drawing. I made pictures on drawing paper, but I also drew in my books and on my homework and on newspapers and shopping bags. I used pens and crayons and pencils and chalk. Drawing was always fun for me because I could make anything up that I wanted to. The only difference between when I was a kid and now that I'm a grownup is that sometimes people pay me to make drawings of things they want. Most of the time that's fun, but it's always the most fun when I create my own things. I had more fun drawing More Spaghetti I Say than illustrating any other book. If you love what you do, whatever it is, life is lots of fun."

- MORT GERBERG
letter to MaryAnn Kohl 2003

~ art idea generously contributed by
Linda Grenier, Marion, Indiana

Silly Spaghetti

Materials
cooked spaghetti (or white strands of
   heavy string)
glue, white or colored
bowl, and old fork for mixing
additions to decorate the spaghetti –
   small pieces of yarn
   confetti
   chopped paper scraps
   sequins
   glitter
   hole-punch dots
plastic wrap or aluminum foil
string

Process
1. Mix several strands of spaghetti and glue in a bowl. There is no exact count, so begin with five strands. (Artists who prefer not to use food for art can substitute cut lengths of heavy white string for the spaghetti.)
2. Add sequins, confetti, small pieces of yarn, or other small decorative items to the glue and spaghetti. Mix in with hands, a stick, or an old fork.
3. Spread the spaghetti mixture on a big piece of aluminum foil or plastic wrap. Let stand until dry to the touch. This may take overnight or several days.
4. Peel the spaghetti design from the foil. Turn it over to continue drying for a few days.
5. When dry and hard, attach a string to the silly spaghetti thing and hang it from the ceiling.

Variations
• Form the glue-soaked strands of spaghetti or string into shapes, letters, words, or designs. Let dry until crisp and hard.
• Dip yarn in glue and then form yarn into colorful shapes on cardboard. Leave it on the cardboard to dry and display.

Twelve Hats for Lena - A Book of Months • *Karen Katz, author*

Lena (Karen Katz's daughter's real name is Lena) imagines what makes each month special. She pastes and decorates an original hat for each month, packed with decorations and materials. The end of the book presents a hat of large proportions and fun. The book includes hat directions.

OPPENHEIM TOY PORTFOLIO GOLD AWARD 2002

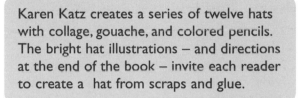

Karen Katz creates a series of twelve hats with collage, gouache, and colored pencils. The bright hat illustrations — and directions at the end of the book — invite each reader to create a hat from scraps and glue.

Calendar Hat

Materials
To make a cylinder hat
poster board rectangle
measuring tape or string
pencil
scissors
glue, tape, glue stick, stapler
collage, decorating & art materials —

greeting cards	doilies
pom-poms	paint
band-aids	paintbrushes
leaves, twigs	stickers
seeds, beans	fabric scraps
ribbons, bows	paper scraps
colored pencils	string, yarn
magazine pictures	small flag
photos	party favors
sewing trim	toothpicks
rick-rack	glitter
crayons	sequins
markers	faux jewels
stamps & pad	plastic flowers
crepe paper	wrapping paper

Process
1. An adult can help measure around the child's head with a measuring tape or string. Stretch the measuring tape on a flat rectangular piece of poster board. Then the adult can cut the poster board 1" (3cm) longer than the child's head. Make the posterboard as tall as the hat will be, from short to VERY tall.
2. Bend the rectangle into a cylinder. Tape or staple to hold. If using staples, tape over the staples so no points are sticking out.
3. Begin decorating! The hat can represent one special month of the year, a birthday month, or a hat that encompasses all twelve months into one, just like Lena's special hat at the end of the book. Glue, tape, or affix bits of this and that to the hat form until it is decorated as desired.
4. Wear the hat for a celebration, a party, pretending, or parading. Make a hat for someone special while the supplies are set-up. Then two can have fun together with calendar hats!

Variations
• Read Karen Katz's colorful award-winning titles — *Where is Baby's Belly Button?, Where is Baby's Mommy?,* and *Counting Kisses.*
• Experiment with other hat design bases, such as —

top hat	crown
head band	cone shape
plastic bowl with rim	paper plate

by Abby Asplund age 8

"When I was a kid my mother gave me the bathroom to use as an art studio. I made a really big mess with paint and glue and lots of stuff. The bathroom was my studio and it stayed like that for months. Thanks Mom. Now I'm grown up and have my own studio to mess up with paint and pencils and glue and stuff. I'm pretty lucky because even though I'm grown up, I still get to make a mess like a kid."

*- KAREN KATZ
letter to MaryAnn Kohl 2003
interview by MaryAnn Kohl 2003*

Clement Hurd
January 12, 1908 -1988

The gentle illustrations lull us along with the little bunny to quietly welcome sleep. Capture the mood of Clement Hurd's bunny bedroom by constructing a shoebox bedroom similar to the one we all know so well in *Goodnight, Moon*.

"When illustrating a children's book, use any style or art materials that express the story. Don't worry about what has been done before. Be yourself."

-CLEMENT HURD
*letter to aspiring writer,
MaryAnn Kohl, 1971*

*by Christina Duim,
age 11*

Good Night, Moon • *Margaret Wise Brown, author*

In a great green room, tucked away in his little bed, a bunny must bid goodnight to everything in his little world. He chants goodnight to his room and to familiar things in his softly lit room. The illustrations show a gentle progression of time moving through increasing darkness, moving clock hands, rising moon, and slowing movement, quietly headed towards sleep. CALDECOTT HONOR 1944

Shoebox Bedroom

Materials
shoebox and lid (large sturdy variety)
scissors
materials to help stick, hold, and
   assemble the box bedroom —

glue (all kinds)	rubber bands
brads	masking tape
regular tape	duct tape
mailing labels	paperclips
string	yarn

scraps, odds-&-ends for decorating the
   box bedroom —

scrap paper	contact paper
wallpaper	paperboard
cardboard	tagboard
fabric	ribbon
photographs	sewing trims
carpet	spools
match box	small toys
magazine clips	stamps
stickers	labels
pizza box "plastic support"	
doll furniture	

paints, brushes, markers

Process
1. Turn a large sturdy shoebox on its side and place it in the lid (see illustration). The box will look like a stage ready for scenery facing towards viewers.
2. Decide how to decorate the box to look like the bunny's bedroom in the book, or design an altogether new room.
3. Begin by covering walls and floor with choices of materials or paint. Let dry briefly while preparing other additions to the bedroom.
4. Construct the basic furnishings for the room. A few suggestions are —

bed	end table
lamp	rocker
books	toys
rug	pictures on the wall
story characters	fireplace

5. The design and décor of the room may take several sittings to complete because glue and paint must dry between times. Detailed construction takes time.
6. Tell a unique, imagined story to go with the bedroom box, or retell familiar *Good Night, Moon*.

Variation
• Read other books written by Brown or illustrated by Clement Hurd. A few are — *Runaway Bunny, Johnny Lion,* and *The Noisy Book.*

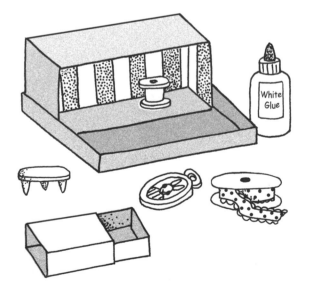

David Kirk April 25, 1955

Miss Spider's Tea Party • David Kirk, author

Miss Spider is lonely, so she decides to host a tea party. The other insects refuse to come for fear of being eaten!

CHILDREN'S ABBY AWARD NOMINEE 1995 & 1996

Be inspired by David Kirk's illustrations and story. Create a miniature tea set with sculpting clay and have a tea party for special dolls, friends, and toys. Don't forget to invite Miss Spider!

Clay Tea Set

Materials
any play clay (Crayola Model Magic™, Fimo™, or Sculpey™ work well and can be baked to a lasting hard consistency)
small cookie cutters
tools for working with clays & doughs, such as —
  rolling pin
  small knife
  fork
  paperclip
  toothpick
  hammer

Process
1. Soften clay by hand.
2. Make coils of clay. Form cups by stacking the coils round and round. Then smooth the coils. Add a rolled coil handle and press into the side of the cup. Use a toothpick to help press the handle to the cup to make it adhere.
3. Press a small circle cookie cutter into a flat slab of clay for dishes. Decorate the dishes with bugs or other designs. Designs can be carved or cut in clay, or pressed on.
4. The dishes can be baked to permanent hardness according to the product's directions.
5. Have a play tea party and invite all the toys!

Variations
• Make a tea set from found items like acorn caps, buttons, thimbles, bottle caps, jar lids, or other odds and ends.
• Make napkins and a tablecloth from fabric scraps.
• Make a vase for the tea party from a tiny thimble or the cap from a bottle. Put a teeny fresh flower in it.

~ art idea generously contributed by
  Dianna Mammone,
  Rochelle Park, New Jersey

by Karla Witte, age 10

"Whatever I do next, I know I love making stories. I think the life of a children's book author is bliss."
- DAVID KIRK
letter to MaryAnn Kohl 2002

Hello, I hope you will come to my tea party!

Little Miss Spider by Kelsey Switzer

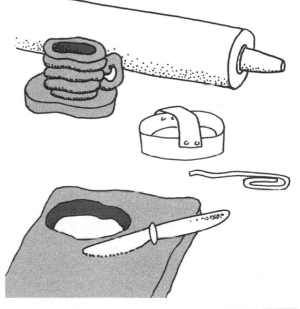

Leo Lionni June 5, 1910

Extend enjoyment of Leo Lionni's unique illustration style. Create inchworms with a special dough squeezed from a pastry bag.

"Since the picture book seems to be the door that leads into the complexities of literacy, it is surprising that it has been given so little attention."

– LEO LIONNI
profile of Leo Lionni
©HW Wilson Company,
www.edupaperback.org

by Kenzi Robinson,
age 9

Inch by Inch • Leo Lionni, author

One day a hungry robin sees a delicious looking green worm on a tree. Just as he is about to eat it, the inchworm explains his personal value in hopes of saving his own life — and measuring becomes the adventure.

CALDECOTT HONOR 1961

Squeezy Inchworms

Materials
Squeezy Dough Recipe
1 cup [240ml] flour
1 cup [240ml] water
1 cup [240ml] table salt
food coloring
    or tempera paints, optional
fork or spoon for stirring
bowl
pastry bag (hand-squeezing style
    with large opening)
aluminum foil
acrylic paints (or tempera paint)
small point paintbrush
marking pens, optional
green paper or green fabric
scissors

Process
1. Mix all of the ingredients in a bowl with a fork or spoon. Form a thick icing-like dough. This recipe can be increased — simply keep the measurements equal. For example, 4 cups flour (500g), 4 cups [1l] water, 4 cups (500g) salt.
    Optional Color Step: To make colorful inchworms, mix food coloring or tempera paints into the wet mixture. Stir well. Go to step 2.
2. Scoop the mixture into a pastry bag that has a large opening.
3. Roll the open end of the pastry bag closed, holding it closed with the *non-drawing hand*. Support the tip of the pastry bag with the *drawing hand*. Slowly squeeze the dough out of the bag. Direct the inchworms onto a sheet of aluminum foil. Pinch off each inchworm with the pasty bag point as it comes out of the bag.
4. Make as many inchworms as mixture supply allows. Make more mixture at any time, if needed.
5. Let the inchworms dry for several days on the aluminum foil. Turn them over each day so they dry evenly.
6. When completely dry, paint worm features like stripes, dots, fuzz, and eyes on the inchworms. Marking pens are a good option for coloring features on squeezy dough inchworms.
7. Display the inchworms on a large green leaf shape cut from green paper or green fabric.
8. Line them up in a row and read Leo Lionni's book to them. Be sure they can see the pictures!

Variations
• Make animals, creatures, or any designs with the pastry bag dough. Snail Suggestion: Snails are simple spiral constructions and easy to make.
• Decorate a make-believe playdough cake or cookie with this dough.

Wendell Minor   March 17, 1944

The Seashore Book • *Charlotte Zolotow, author*

A mother helps her child imagine the seashore, running in the surf, the "smooth pearly pink" of a shell, sea birds, the sun's warmth and the wave's chill.

Make a lasting sand sculpture to help remember seashore experiences and to appreciate the delights of Wendell Minor's illustrations of all aspects of the seashore.

Sand Sculpture

Materials
Sand Dough
 I cup [240ml] sand
 I cup [240ml] water
 I cup [240ml] cornstarch
saucepan & stove
measuring spoons
board for kneading
materials for decorating
 (press into the sand
 sculpture) –
   shells
   beads
   pebbles
   buttons
   stones
   dry pasta, beans, rice
   faux jewels
   leaves, twigs, seeds
   toy flag
   plastic party favors
   toothpicks
   sequins
   plastic flowers

Process
1. Mix together in a saucepan: I cup [240ml] sand, I cup [240ml] water, and I cup [240ml] cornstarch. Ingredients may be doubled or tripled for larger sculptures.
2. An adult should heat the mixture on a med low stove setting, stirring until it thickens and holds together. Set the pan aside and let it cool a bit. Then place the dough on a board – knead until smooth.
3. Now the mixture is ready to mold into shapes, figures, or even a sand castle!
4. Press decorations into the sand sculpture before it dries. Small shells, beads, pebbles, and buttons will hold well.
5. Let the sculpture dry well. Thicker sculptures will take longer than small ones. More decorations can be added with glue after the sculpture dries, if desired. This sand sculpture will last and last.

Variation
• Place shells and beach pebbles in a small pie pan. Sprinkle with sand. Press the dough into the pie pan. Let dry. Remove, and turn over to see the pressed-in design.

by Torie Lee, age 10

"A picture invites the viewer into it and offers a sense of mystery ... the viewer becomes part of the process. A good picture, like a good story, is timeless." Wendell Minor brings the scenes of the natural world to children.

- WENDELL MINOR letter to MaryAnn Kohl 2002 & www.minorart.com

Beni Montresor
March 31, 1926 –2001

Extend the enjoyment of Beni Montresor's jewel-like artwork. Make a special friendship stick to celebrate the fun of having a very good friend.

May I Bring a Friend? • *Beatrice Schenk De Regniers, author*

A small boy receives a very special invitation to join the King and the Queen for tea. He accepts under one condition – that he may bring a friend. Of course the King and Queen agree. The King and Queen have not imagined the kind of tea party that is about to begin!

CALDECOTT MEDAL 1965

by Jodi Drost, age 15

"Italian artist Beni Montresor will be treasured for having communicated his childhood fantasies in design and print. He was praised as a costume and set designer for the stage and motion pictures and as an illustrator and author of children's books. Throughout his career, Beni Montresor's illustrations have stimulated children's imaginations with their "dream-like imagery" and "great sense of richness and depth."

- ABOUT BENI MONTRESOR
University of Minnesota Libraries ©1999 Regents, University of Minnesota, Twin Cities, and University Libraries, special.lib.umn.edu/findaid/html/clrc/clrc0167.html

Friendship Stick

Materials
one 1'-2' [.5m-1m] stick from outdoors
    or a wooden dowel
with a very special friend, save and trade
    a collection of possessions, objects,
    and meaningful items –
        buttons
        jewelry
        hair bow
        sports cards
        ball
        compact disk (CD)
        hair clip
        key chain
        small toy
        party favor
ribbons
marking pens

Process
1. Find a stick (or wooden dowel) about 1'-2' [.5m-1m] long. Give it a general clean up, peeling away bark if needed.
2. Next, wrap ribbons the length of the stick. The ribbons may be wrapped in a tight style with no space between wrappings, or loosely wrapped, leaving spaces.
3. Tie the special traded objects to a piece of ribbon about 10"-15" [26cmx38cm] long or longer. Tie one end of the ribbon to one end of the friendship stick.
4. Wrap and fill the stick with the special memorabilia on one, or on *many* attached ribbons.
5. Writing the names of the special friend on the stick with markers to identify it very special artwork.
6. Add more designs and words with markers, if desired.

Variations
• Attach pictures of friends to the ends of ribbons or yarn, and then tie them to the stick.
• Attach an eye-hook to the end of a dowel, tie friendship objects to ribbons, and then through the eye-hook.
• Weave tidbits and collectibles into a friendship stick tightly wrapped with ribbons, crepe paper strips, or torn strips of fabric. (Idea: cut an old T-shirt starting at the hem. Follow a spiral cut that continues the entire body of the shirt, making one long strip.

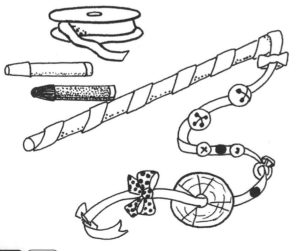

Strega Nona: An Old Tale • Tomie dePaola, author

Strega Nona leaves Big Anthony alone with her magic pasta pot. Anthony cooks up more enchanted spaghetti than he can handle, causing considerable spaghetti trouble!

CALDECOTT HONOR 1976

To enjoy Tomie dePaola's enchanting concept of spaghetti, construct a free-form pasta assemblage with uncooked pastas (including spaghetti) and glue.

Assembled Noodles

Materials
food coloring
rubbing alcohol, adult help required
   (alcohol helps the pasta dry
   quickly and stay very bright)
one bowl for each color of pasta
different types of pasta, including –
     regular spaghetti
     shells
     bows
     rigatoni
     manicotti
     rotini
     fettuccini
     macaroni
     pre-colored pasta (from craft
     and hobby stores)
spoons
paper towels, newspaper
   (cookie sheets, optional)
wide-sheet lasagna noodles
   for base of the assemblage
white glue
   (glue-gun with adult supervision)
toothpicks, coffee stir sticks,
   bamboo skewers, straws, cocktail
   straws

Process
To make colored pasta or noodles (adult help) –
1. Put 2–4 drops of food coloring in a bowl, one for each color. Add 3–5 tablespoons [45ml–75ml] of rubbing alcohol per bowl. Mix well with a spoon. Add a handful of pasta to each bowl and stir to coat with color. After all of the pasta is thoroughly colored, spoon it out on paper towels spread on newspaper (on cookie sheets is an option), and let dry several hours.

To construct the assemblage –
1. After all of the pasta is dry, look over all the colors and shapes of pasta. Imagine the assemblage they might become!
2. Place a wide-sheet lasagna noodle (or noodles) on some protective newspaper. The lasagna noodle will be the base of the assemblage.
3. Begin adding pasta pieces with glue (or a glue-gun with adult help) to build an abstract structure. Slip some toothpicks or other suggested "sticks" through pasta noodles to help reinforce the sculpture and quickly increase size and shape.
4. Build and build! Some drying time may be needed to keep the assemblage strong.

Variation
- **Spaghetti Hanging**: Cook 10-20 pieces of long, plain white spaghetti until limp but not soggy. Strain in a colander. Do not rinse with water, so it will stay nice and sticky. Pull spaghetti strands from the colander and drop them on a paper plate in any shape or wiggly tangled design. Sprinkle with glitter, tiny bits of colored paper, or dab with glitter-glue. No glue is necessary. Spaghetti is naturally sticky. Dry overnight. Hang the spaghetti sculpture from a string tied to a hook in the ceiling or from a window frame.

"Fall in love with reading and with books. They can be your best friends!"

- TOMIE DEPAOLA
BookPage Online, BookPage: America's Book Review, *www.bookpage.com*

by Jordan Drost, age 16

White Glue

Barbara Reid November 16, 1957

Imitate Barbara Reid's cheerful, pressed clay illustration technique. Pinch pieces of bright plasticine (modeling clay) and press them on poster board. Create art with the color and texture of the colorful clay.

by Briley Ammons, age 12

"I loved books [when I was a child]. When I came to the end of a good story, I hated saying goodbye to characters that had become friends. So I would draw them and keep the story going. My artwork with Plasticine is silly and funny".
-BARBARA REID
letter to MaryAnn Kohl 2002 & from National Library of Canada, biography 6/24/96, www.nlc-bnc.ca

Have You Seen Birds? • *Joanne Oppenheim, author*

This lovely book offers a simple description of birds, how they sound, and what they do. The illustrations are formed by pressed clay – with unusual perspectives and views.

Pressed Clay Illustration

Materials
Plasticine™ or other colorful clay
    material (any non-bake play clay or
    modeling clay in bright colors
    works well, available in school
    supply areas of variety stores, hobby
    & craft stores, art stores)
poster board or matboard
tools to press into clay, optional

Process
1. Warm up and soften the plasticine by kneading it by hand for ten minutes or so.
2. Pull pieces from the balls of plasticine and press them onto the background board in a design or picture. The plasticine will stick to the board easily. No glue or tape is necessary.
3. Colors can be mixed on the board or in the hand.
4. Create a picture, scene, or a design.
5. This clay will not dry out. When the art is done it will remain soft and bright for years!

Variations
• On the finished design, press waxed paper or clear plastic wrap over the design and roll it with a rolling pin. Then peel away the paper or plastic for a new flatter but blended version of the original.
• Work with the plasticine on a sheet of Plexiglas™. For additional fun, press a second sheet of Plexiglas™ onto the first, sandwiching the clay design between, and smashing it into a flat color-mixture.

Pressed Clay Bird
by Kayla Comstock, age 8

Robert Sabuda · March 8, 1965

T'was the Night Before Christmas · Robert Sabuda, author

Clement Clarke Moore's classic tale of *The Night Before Christmas* is brought back in an imaginative pop-up book.

Robert Sabuda is known for his detailed crafted pop-up books. Construct a pop-up scene with a story in the style of Robert Sabuda.

Pop-Up Scene

Materials
sheet of white drawing paper
choice of drawing tools -
   crayons
   markers
   colored pencils
   pencil, pen
   watercolor paints & brush
scissors
glue
sheet of construction paper
extra sheet of drawing paper

These campers are glued to tabs that pop-out from the background outdoor camping scenery.

Watercolor Pop-Up
Barbara Valenta, art teacher,
SchoolArts magazine, 12/97, p. 14

Process
The Background Scenery
1. Draw background scenery on the white drawing paper. Draw it centered in the sheet of paper. Some ideas are –
rolling grass hills and sky	ocean or lake
garden	alien planet surface
   * This scenery can be drawn with any drawing tools or paints.
2. Fold the scenery paper in half (see illustration). The scene will appear somewhat like the backdrop for a play with a stage floor.
3. Decide where the pop-up (and main part of the picture) will go. Cut a rectangular notch in the scenery, and push the notch inside out to the *front* of the scenery (see illustration).
4. Next, glue the scenery onto a piece of construction paper to help stiffen and strengthen the pop-up scenery.

The Pop-Up
5. To make the actual pop-up, think of something important to the picture story that will stand out from the scene. Draw a picture of that idea, and glue it on the popped-out notch.
   Some suggestions are –
      galloping horse (background scenery: rolling grass hills)
      boat sailing (background scenery: ocean or lake)
      butterfly (background scenery: flower in a garden)
      alien creature (background scenery: planet surface)
6. Tell a story about the pop-up scene.

Variations
- Make a book of several pop-up scenes stapled together.
- Make pop-up greeting cards.

by Lauren Olson, age 10

"I work in my studio in New York City that I share with my partner, children's book creator Matthew Reinhart. We love making books. It's hard work, but the best part is not having to worry about making a mess. When being an artist is your job, you can make as many messes as you like!"

- ROBERT SABUDA
letters to MaryAnn Kohl 2002 & 2003
www.robertsabuda.com

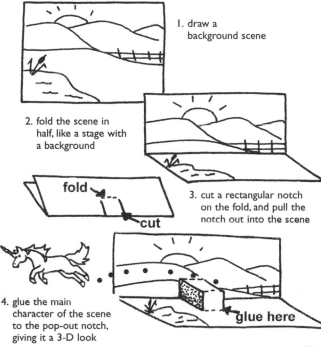

1. draw a background scene

2. fold the scene in half, like a stage with a background

fold ➤
cut

3. cut a rectangular notch on the fold, and pull the notch out into the scene

4. glue the main character of the scene to the pop-out notch, giving it a 3-D look
glue here

Allen Say August 28, 1937

"When the characters I'm drawing become real to me, then the story starts to take shape."

– ALLEN SAY

Children's Literature, College of Education University of Nebraska at Omaha, Allen Say: Author / Illustrator, prepared by Theresa A. Valish

by Geneva Faulkner, age 14

Grandfather's Journey • *Allen Say, author*

Allen Say tells the story of his own grandfather born in Japan. Say's grandfather raised a family in California and then returned to Japan where Allen Say was born. Because of World War II, his grandfather could never return to his beloved California. Later, Allen Say moves to California and shares in his grandfather's journey.

CALDECOTT MEDAL 1994

Rozan-Ji Garden

Materials
large baking pan or tray with sides
pencil
cardboard to fit into pan or tray
white glue in a dish
scissors
paintbrush
supplies for creating the garden –
    clean sand
    small rocks, pebbles, gravel
    small evergreen branches
    small bare twigs
    small twigs with leaves
    small mirror
    small square tiles, scrap
    green sand (see sand-
        coloring directions)

Process
1. Fit a plain piece of cardboard into the baking pan or tray. Use scissors to trim.
2. Design the shape of the garden with a pencil, drawing curving stone pathways through grass or moss areas (see illustrations).
3. Glue square tiles in a pattern throughout the grassy areas as stepping stones.
4. To make trees in the grassy areas, poke holes in the cardboard with the scissors points, and stick small evergreen branches and twigs into the holes. Add a little glue around the base of the trees to help hold.
5. To make a pond, place (or glue) the small mirror on the cardboard.
6. Spread white glue on the remaining grassy areas. Carefully sprinkle green sand on the wet glue to look like grass or moss. Brush away stray sand particles. Glue down more rocks or pebbles on the green grass to add to the garden design. Add more glue and green sand to the edges of the pond.
7. For the pathways, glue gravel or plain sand to the cardboard.
8. Add further details and designs of choice to complete the design. For example, place a small toy or figure in the garden to resemble a person or story character.

Variation
• **How to Color Sand Green:** Pour clean sand into a plastic mixing bowl. Stir in a few tablespoons of water deeply pre-colored with green food coloring. Mix the color into the sand with a spoon. Add more food coloring for a brighter green. Spread the colored sand in a thin layer on a pad of newspaper to dry overnight. When dry, use as an art material.

Dr. Seuss March 2, 1904 –1991

The Cat in the Hat • Dr. Seuss (Theodor Geisel), author

Among Dr. Seuss' most famous books is *The Cat in the Hat*, a story about two children who find themselves home alone with a playful, mischievous hat-wearing cat.

Dr. Seuss illustrated a bright red and white hat that is tall and floppy for the well-known Cat to wear. Artists construct a similar hat with two (or more) brown paper grocery bags, paper, and glue.

Kid in the Hat

Materials
two large white paper bakery bags
   (purchase several from a bakery,
   from a restaurant supply store, or
   wholesale chain store like Costco
   and PriceClub)
scissors
glue
tape
stapler
choice of decorative materials and
   supplies, such as –
      red paper (wrapping paper,
         craft paper, or construction
         paper)
      white paper
      black paper
      wide red tape
      wide black tape

Process
Any creative, unique, indivualized hat design can be made from the bakery bags, or, choose to follow these specific directions:
1. Cut the bottom from one bag. Fold or roll the edge of this bag down to form a rolled brim.
2. Insert this bag into the second bag, overlapping the edges slightly. This will make a very tall hat. Tape, glue, or staple the overlapping bags together.
3. Think about how to decorate the very tall hat. To imitate The Cat in the Hat's striped hat, wrap wide red paper strips around the tall hat, using glue to hold. Wide red tape or red paint could also be used.
4. Add a black head band at the base of the bag to resemble the cat's hat. Make the head band from any black paper or black tape.
5. Wear the hat for pretending, parading, or playing.

Variations
• Wear hats for a special "hat day" on Dr. Seuss' birthday March 2nd (1904). Have a Parade of Hats.
• Enjoy other books by Dr Seuss, such as, *The Cat in the Hat Comes Back, Green Eggs and Ham, Horton Hatches the Egg, Horton Hears a Who!, How the Grinch Stole Christmas, The Lorax, And To Think That I Saw It on Mulberry Street, The 500 Hats of Bartholomew Cubbins*, and *Oh, the Places You'll Go.*

~ art idea generously contributed by
   Roberta Williams, Correy, Pennsylvania

"I like nonsense, it wakes up the brain cells!"
   - Dr. Seuss (Theodor Geisel)
Seuss' quote is found in hundreds of sources, including: Borgna Brunner, Seuss Biography, Infoplease.com
©2002 Family Education Network. 2/5/03
www.infoplease.com/spot/seuss1.html

by Courtney Shoemake, age 9

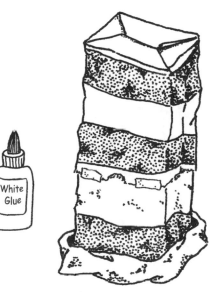

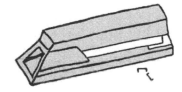

Uri Shulevitz February 27, 1935

Imitate Uri Shulevitz's adaptation of snow piling up on the title's letters on the book cover, the town, and the trees. Create a snowy transparency that will cover the drawing in just the right places with a thick layer of falling snow.

"A picture book is not a silly little plaything. It is much more. Sometimes it can be everything to a child . . . a messenger of hope from the outside world. A picture book does not have to be deep, but it does have to be alive — whether it offers pleasure, joy , or sadness."

by Taylor Niemi, age 11

- URI SHULEVITZ
The Illustrator's Notebook, edited by Lee Klinghman, Horn Book, 1978

Snow • *Uri Shulevitz, author*

Only a boy and his dog believe the snowfall will amount to anything. And they are right!

CALDECOTT HONOR BOOK 1999 • SCHOOL LIBRARY JOURNAL BEST BOOK OF THE YEAR • BOOKLIST EDITORS' CHOICE • PUBLISHERS WEEKLY BEST BOOK OF THE YEAR

Snowy Layers

Materials
9"x12" [22cmx30cm] gray or light blue colored paper (construction paper)
masking tape
pencil
crayons or colored pencils
blank overhead transparency sheet (acetate sheet)
markers and correction fluid —
- non-toxic correction fluid, with brush *Wite Out® PLUS Water Base Correction Fluid*
- non-toxic liquid correction fluid in pen style, *Fluid Bic Wite-Out Plus Waterbase™*
- waterbased presentation or transparency markers: *Stabilo OH Pen Marker™ or Vis-a-Vis™*

Process
1. Tape the corners of the gray or blue paper to the table with masking tape.
2. Draw a scene that will soon be covered with snow. Suggestions include a town, school yard, park, and house. Leave room for block letters that will title the picture.
3. Print or write the title of the picture in thick block letters. The title can be SNOW or any other word that goes with the picture, like FRIENDS, FUN, FLUFFY, or WINTER. Choose one.
4. Color in the drawing and the title, but do not draw or color any snow. That step will come later.
5. When the picture is complete, place a clear transparency sheet over the drawing. Then tape the top two corners only, so the transparency can flip up.
6. With the white-out correction fluid, make dots of white on the transparency to look like snow falling. Continue the dots in places where the snow might pile up - on the block letters, on a rooftop, on someone's hat. Draw more snow with the white-out. Snow, snow everywhere!
7. Make the snowfall stop by lifting the transparency. To see the snow cover everything, lower the transparency.
8. To display the snowy picture, tape the picture and transparency together at the top two corners, so the transparency will flip up. Tape or pin to a wall or bulletin board.

Variations
- Enjoy other books written and illustrated by Shulevitz: *Dawn* (ALA Notable), *Rain, Rain Rivers, The Secret Room* (New York Times Book of the Year), *The Treasure* (Caldecott Honor Book).
- Spatter paint over a drawn picture using a hand-misting bottle filled with slightly thinned white tempera paint.

Joan Steiner October 10

Look-Alikes Jr. • Joan Steiner, author

Simple verses challenge readers to identify everyday objects in 3D scenes made with everything from shells to empty soda cans.

Look-Alike Assemblage

Imitate the remarkable style of Joan Steiner. Build an assemblage using a wonderful variety of collected materials. Form a scene filled with interesting textural and symbolic effects. The first *Look-Alikes* won the *1999 Caldecott Medal*.

by Kailey Olson, age 9

"My projects take me to all different kinds of stores including hardware stores, party stores, thrift shops, brickyards, and art supply stores. I may spend ten minutes carefully looking at a mousetrap, turning it from side to side and upside down, thinking about whether it's something I can use."

— JOAN STEINER
letter to Jean Potter 2002 &
Time Warner Bookmark ©2002
www.twbookmark.com

Materials

collect odds and ends, items, & "stuff" to transform into a "look alike", such as —

bottle caps	dry beans
stamps	checkers
cereals	fruit netting
cookies	berry basket
puzzle pieces	marker lids
buttons	soda can flip tops
pennies	shells
crayons	carpet scrap
birthday candles	foil stars
dry pasta	marshmallows

glue, push pins, tape, stapler, string, anything to help hold the assemblage together

cardboard for a base

scissors

Process

1. Study Joan Steiner's amazing illustrations and see why she chose the objects and materials that she did. For example, she makes — a sofa from gloves; a fence from crayons; a tree from broccoli; a picture on the wall from a postage stamp; a rocket ship from a thermos bottle.
2. Look at the collection of things for "look-alike" materials. Think of a scene that would be fun to do any of these suggestions:

classroom	park
playground	doctor's office
library	bakery
kitchen	baby's room
toy store	factory
baseball game	fairy tale scene

3. Assemble the pieces and parts that will work best; adding more later is fine too. Start by deciding what the covering of the cardboard base will be. It might be a napkin, fabric, paint, magazine picture, or any variety of materials. Glue the covering to the cardboard.
4. Start building the scene with the collected materials, imagining what the simple items might represent.
5. Let the assemblage dry between stages. The project can take several days to finish.

Variations

• Create a collage using collected materials to build a different scene.

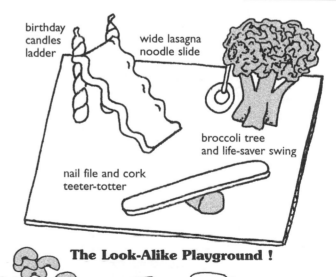

birthday candles ladder

wide lasagna noodle slide

broccoli tree and life-saver swing

nail file and cork teeter-totter

The Look-Alike Playground !

Tomi Ungerer November 28, 1931

Interpret Tomi Ungerer's snake illustrations. Create a long, segmented sock snake who will make reading, pretending, or acting out the story more fun than ever.

"I was raised with a respect and love of books. My sisters taught me to draw, my brother taught me to think, and my mother taught me to use my imagination."

- TOMI UNGERER
Tomi Ungerer's Reluctant Heroes, Lanes, Atlantic Monthly, 1/74, p. 87-90

by Monika Baranek, age 11

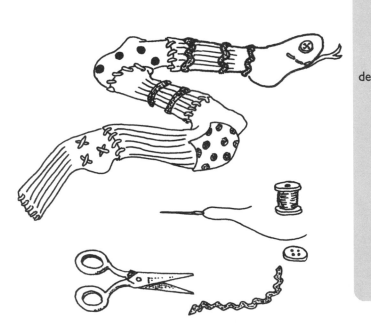

Crictor • *Jean-Thomas Ungerer, author*

Madam Louise Bodot receives an unusual gift from her son – a snake! Crictor the snake proves to be not only fun, but helpful through progressive happenings in the classic story.

A READING RAINBOW BOOK

Crazy-for-Crictor Socks

Materials
4 or more spare socks*
  (orphan, non-matching
  socks are a good
  choice) *long socks
  are best)
stuffing materials –
    old rags
    newspaper
    cotton batting
    scraps of fabric
    more old socks
    paper towels
decorating materials –
    buttons
    colored yarn
    embroidery floss
    felt scraps
    sewing trims
    fabric scraps
    ribbons
    beads
    sequins, faux jewels
    iron-on patches
    fabric glue
    fabric paints in
        squeeze bottles
    needle & thread

Process
1. Stuff one orphan sock with stuffing materials until completely packed and stretched to its full length and width. To make an extra-long segmented sock snake, continue stuffing three more socks (or 100 socks!). One sock makes a nice small snake.
2. To make a longer snake, sew the opening of the first sock to the toe of a second sock, and then repeat the joining steps with more socks. (Sew the opening of the second to the toe of the third, the opening of the third to the toe of the fourth, and so on. Stitch the opening of the last sock closed.)
3. Decorate the snake in any way imagined using materials on hand. There is no right way or wrong way to decorate a sock-snake! Try any or all of these ideas –
   - Sew eyes and other features onto the stuffed socks to make it look like a real or imaginary snake. (Felt is a good fabric for making details to sew on with needle and thread, and should also stick on with fabric glue.)
   - Fabric glue will work for sticking different types materials, but will take extra drying time during which the snake art should be left undisturbed.
   - Fabric paints in squeeze bottles can be used for adding outlines or designs, also needing sufficient drying time.
   - Buttons are good for eyes, spots, or colorful texture.
   - Yarn or embroidery floss can be sewn into a fluffy hair-do.
   - Ribbons can make designs or can be wrapped around and around the snake for colorful decoration.
4. A snake sock can be twisted or bent into letters or numerals as told in the story of Crictor. Snuggle with the soft snake while reading or listening to a book.

Variation
• Squishy snakes can be made from – clay, playdough, pretzel dough, bread dough or cookie dough.

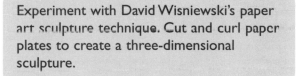

Golem • *David Wisniewski , author*

A saintly rabbi brings a clay giant to life in 16th Century Jewish Prague. Illustrations are paper cut-outs in extraordinary detail.

CALDECOTT MEDAL 1967

Experiment with David Wisniewski's paper art sculpture technique. Cut and curl paper plates to create a three-dimensional sculpture.

Paper Plate Sculpture

Materials
good sharp scissors
10-15 white paper plates for each
    sculpture (thin style with rippled edges
    in several sizes)
stapler, tape, brads, glue
glue-gun, with adult supervision only
pinking shears with fancy edges, optional
puncturing tools, such as –
    pencil
    nail
    screwdriver
    large darning needle
    hole punch
curling tools, such as –
    dowel
    pencil
    nail
    bamboo skewer
    jumbo marker

Process

1. Create a 3-D sculpture that will stand, using all ten or more paper plates. Some suggestions for sculptures with interesting details are –

animals	fantasy creatures
people	tropical fish
aliens	imaginary characters
insects	plants

2. Assemble the plates using such techniques as –

attach...... with staples, brads, paperclips
curl.......... around a dowel, skewer, pencil, or pen
cut............with scissors, pain or fancy
edge.........with pinking shears, tearing,
                or snipping fringe
fold.......... press-in the crease with a ruler or spoon
poke........ with any sharp tool or hole punch
score.......with scissors points
stick.........with tape, glue, paste
tear.......... with fingers

3. Add details with scraps from paper plates, such as – hair, eye-lashes, wings, scales, or fur.

Variations
- Decorate the sculptures with yarn, colorful scraps, and other collage materials.
- Pre-paint the paper plates with light watercolors first. Then use in sculpture.

by Mikal Olson, age 8

"Sometimes, people ask me why I bother with such a complicated and time-consuming art technique when I could simply draw or paint. One answer is that other artists draw much better than I do, and almost anybody (including your dog) paints better than I do. The other answer is that cut-paper gives me a recognizable style that no one else has duplicated, and that's important in the increasingly crowded and sophisticated world of children's picture books. As Anne Diebel, the art director for Clarion Books, once told me,'When it come to cutting paper, you da MAN!'"
    -DAVID WISNIEWSKI

The Children's Book Council ©1998-2002 www.cbcbooks.org

Don Wood May 4, 1945

Don Wood's illustrations can inspire young artists to follow King Bidgood's unusually clean example. Transform bath-time into a colorful painting session that washes away, just like mud off the pig in the story.

"As I contemplate illustrating a new picture book, I get the same feeling of exhilaration potential that used to come over me as a kid when I was given the huge sheet of tan paper the laundry came wrapped in."

-DON WOOD
letter to MaryAnn Kohl 2002,
www.audreywood.com,
interview with Marguerite Feitlowitz
Something About the Author®,
Vol.50 p.225 ©2003
The Gale Group, Inc.

by Lauren
Kaemingk,
age 11

King Bidgood's in the Bathtub • Audrey Wood, author

A fun-loving king refuses to get out of the bathtub, despite pleas from his court.

CALDECOTT HONOR 1986

Bath-Time Paints

Materials
unflavored gelatin, instant (in a box)
medium saucepan or pot
1/4 cup [60ml] hot water in a small bowl
medium heat on stove
spoon
1/4 cup [60ml] mild dishwashing detergent
1/2 cup [120ml] cornstarch
small plastic bowls
3 tablespoons [45ml] sugar
food coloring
1 1/3 cups [320ml] cold water
adult supervision

Process
1. With adult supervision, add the box of unflavored gelatin to 1/4 cup [60ml] hot water in a small bowl. Mix with a spoon and let sit for 10 minutes.
2. Meanwhile, combine 1/2 cup [120ml] cornstarch, 3 T. [45ml] sugar, and 1 1/3 cups [320ml] cold water in the saucepan and stir until cloudy in appearance. The adult should cook the cornstarch mixture over medium heat, stirring occasionally, and then reduce the heat until the mixture is thick.
3. With adult help, add the gelatin mixture and the dishwashing detergent to the saucepan, stirring until smooth. Let the mixture cool.
4. Divide the mixture equally into several small plastic bowls, one for each color of bath-time paint. Add drops of food coloring (or 1/4 teaspoons of food coloring paste) to each bowl. Mix. Colors can be bright or muted.
5. Hooray, it's bath-time! Paint on a porcelain or fiberglass tub with the homemade paints and any paintbrush – or for even more fun, with hands (or feet)! When done, rinse and rub away paints with water and a sponge.

Variation
• Make **Mud Paint** that is a surprisingly impressive paint! Collect a cup or two of clean, soft dirt. Clean any sticks, bark, pebbles or foreign particles from the dirt. Stir the dirt in a bowl with some water until it is the consistency of tempera paint. Dip a paintbrush into the thick mud paint, and paint on paper or fabric. It's amazing what a great paint mud can be.

BATH-TIME PAINTS ARE NOT RECOMMENDED FOR USE ON POROUS TILE OR GROUT

Dare Wright

December 3, 1914 –2001

The Lonely Doll • *Dare Wright author/photographer*

Edith is a lonely little doll who longs for company. She meets Mr. Bear, a fatherly bear, and Little Bear, a very young bear, in her garden. Photographer, Dare Wright, poses the doll and two toy bears in cozy dollhouse style black and white photos that tell a cozy story of friendship. (Edith was the author's own doll from her childhood.)

Portraiture

Materials

camera with film
  (or digital camera
  and printer)
choice of toys to act
  as characters in a
  story –
    doll
    stuffed animal
    plastic people
    action figure
props to add to the
  scenes and help
  tell the story –
    table
    chairs
    curtains
    kitchen things
    small toys
    books
    flowers in pot
    food
stapler, glue, tape
poster board for
  story display

Process

1. Look at the illustration photos and notice how Dare Wright has positioned toys and props in different poses, and with changing background scenery. The scenes and poses tell a stor, just like actors on a stage. Still poses that tell a story are called *portraiture*. Find a few favorite toys, and imagine how they might help tell a photo-story. Some story suggestions are –
   – a little dog is lost and then found in the most unusual place
   – a grandmother lives alone in a tall apartment house, and someone visits with a big surprise
   – it's the day of the big race, and someone very unusual wins in an unusual way
   – all the toys in Santa's workshop are helping get ready for Christmas, but something has gone terribly wrong!
   – the cookies are missing from the cookie jar, and the culprit is a most unexpected thief

2. Gather toys and props. Set-up the first scene. Pose the toys and props. Then, snap the first picture!

3. Move props and toys around for the second scene to tell the second thing that happens in the story. Add or remove props and characters. Take the second picture.

4. Continue for as many scenes as it takes to tell the story. Keep in mind that most rolls of film are 24 pictures long. A digital camera should hold more. *A story can be told in one picture or many pictures.* With adult help, print out the photos. While waiting, put away the toys and props!

5. Sort the pictures into story order. Tape or staple them to the poster board. Leaving space for writing the story or a big fancy story title is a good additional idea.

6. When the storyboard is complete, gather a friend or two, the family, the dog, the cat, the fish, and a few special toy-friends. Gather 'round - it's Photo Story Time!

Variation

• Tape each photo on a separate sheet of paper, and staple together in a book. Leave space for writing a story on the pages. Add a decorated cover, and include the special author's and photographer's name.

Imitate Dare Wright's illustration style. Pose toys in *portraiture* scenes that tell a story. Take pictures of each scene with a camera. Display the photos on a storyboard, and retell the story to family and friends (also to toys who like stories).

by Laura Sanchez, age 9

"Dare Wright began as a high fashion model, then became a freelance photographer. Her photographs appeared in many important fashion magazines. She created books about her actual childhood doll, Edith, and her friends, including *The Lonely Doll* and *Edith and Mr. Bear.*"

- Periodicals:
Los Angeles Times 2/4/01 p.B7
New York Times 2/3/01 p.B7
Washington Post 2/4/01 p.C8

1. Let's play All-Go-Round!

2. Oh, no. Mikey fell off.

3. Quick, call for help!

4. Mikey will be fine, thanks to quick thinking & good friends.

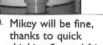

Resource Guide & Index
chapter 5

Mom's Portrait
by Victoria, age 3

Mom's Portrait
by Alexandra, age 3

Mom's Portrait
by Christopher, age 3

Fuzzy Girl Collage by unknown artist
based on
Zoo-Looking by Candace Whitman

Snowy Owl by Margaryta Lypova, age 7
based on
Owl Moon illus. by John Schoenherr

Resting Cat by Courtney Jackson, age 7
based on
The Empty Lot by Jim Arnosky

Little Man by Marty Finkbonner, age 7
based on
Where the Sidewalk Ends by Shel Silverstein

About Book Collecting:(about authors & illustrators)
collectbooks.about.com/cs/illustratorschild
ACHUKA: Author Interviews, United Kingdom
www.achuka.co.uk
America Writes for Kids
usawrites4kids.drury.edu
Author Chats
www.authorchats.com
Author Illustrator Source
www.author-illustr-source.com
Authors on the Web
www.authorsontheweb.com
Books Are Fun
www.booksarefun.com
Carol Hurst's Children's Literature Site
www.carolhurst.com
Castleton Public Library: Authors Illustrators
www.uhls.org/castleton/Author_Books.shtm
Children's Book Illustrators
www.ortakales.com/illustrators/index.html
Children's Literature Awards & Winners:
Directory of Prizes CLWG: Children's
Literature Web Guide – Authors &
Illustrators on the Web
www.ucalgary.ca/~dkbrown/authors.html
Cynthia Leitich Smith Children's Literature
Resources
www.cynthialeitichsmith.com/
authors-illustrators.htm
deGrummond Children's Literature Collection:
University of Southern Mississippi Libraries
www.lib.usm.edu/%7Edegrum
Educational Paperback Association
www.edupaperback.org
Fairrosa Cyber Library
www.fairrosa.info
Geebung SS: Authors' Birthdays
www.geebungss.qld.edu.au/birthdays.htm
Horn Book: Virtual History Exhibit
www.hbook.com
Index to Internet Sites: Children's & Young
Adults' Authors & Illustrators
falcon.jmu.edu/~ramseyil/biochildhome.htm
ISLMC: Index to Internet Sites: Children's &
Young Adults' Authors & Illustrators
falcon.jmu.edu/~ramseyil/biochildhome.htm
Kathy Schrock's Guide for Educators:
Author Illustrator Birthdays
school.discovery.com/schrockguide/authorname.html
KidSpace @ the Internet Public Library
www.ipl.org/div/kidspace/browse/rzn9000

Links to Children's Authors/Illustrators/Book
Publishers
www.thelibrarylady.net/Links%20to%20
Authors/links_to_authors_illustrators_
publishers.htm
Literary Birthdays by Month
www.waterboro.lib.me.us/birth.htm
Mona Kerby's Reading Corner
www.carr.org/read
More Children's Authors Biographies &
Autobiographies
falcon.jmu.edu/~ramseyil/mychauthor.htm
NLC: National Library of Canada
www.nlc-bnc.ca/
Pronouncing Dictionary of Authors' Names
mainst.monterey.k12.ca.us/library/libpg/
Dictionary/dict.html
Public Television
pbskids.org
Randolph Caldecott
www.randolphcaldecott.org.uk
Society of Children's Book Writers &
Illustrators   www.scbwi.org
Teacher's Corner
www.theteacherscorner.net
The White House
www.whitehouse.gov/kids
U.S. Department of Education
www.ericit.org/weblinks/weblinks.shtml
Vandergrift's Children's Literature Page
www.scils.rutgers.edu/~kvander/
ChildrenLit/index.html
Words Worth Books
www.wordsworth.com

deGrummond
Children's
Literature
Collection

What a Great Resource!
www.lib.usm.edu

AOL Time Warner Book Group/Little Brown
www.twbookmark.com
Barefoot Books
www.barefootbooks.com
Barron's Educational Series
www.barronseduc.com
Boyds Mills Press
www.boydsmillspress.com
Bright Ring Publishing
www.brightring.com
Candlewick Press
www.candlewick.com
Capstone Press, Inc.
www.capstone-press.com
Chicago Review Press
www.ipgbook.com
Children's Book Press
www.cbookpress.org
Chronicle Books
www.chronbooks.com
Farrar, Straus & Giroux
www.fsgbooks.com/fsg.htm
Firefly Books
www.fireflybooks.com
Fitzhenry & Whiteside
www.fitzhenry.ca
Gryphon House
www.ghbooks.com
Harcourt
www.harcourtbooks.com
HarperCollins
www.harperchildrens.com/hch
Hastings House
www.hastingshousebooks.com
Henry Holt
www.hholt.com
Holiday House
www.holidayhouse.com
Houghton Mifflin
www.eduplace.com &
www.houghtonmifflinbooks.com
Knopf
www.randomhouse.com/kids
Little Brown
www.twbookmark.com
Mondo Publishing
www.mondopub.com
North-South Books
www.northsouth.com
Penguin Putnam
www.penguinputnam.com
Random House & Golden Books
www.randomhouse.com/kids

Random House Children's Group
www.randomhouse.com/teachers
Random House (Knopf)
www.randomhouse.com/kids
Scholastic & Cartwheel Books
www.scholastic.com
Sierra Club Juveniles
www.sierraclub.org/books
Simon & Schuster / SimonSaysKids
www.simonsays.com
Ten Speed / Tricycle Press
www.tenspeed.com
Weekly Reader Corp.
www.weeklyreader.com

Whispering Coyote / Charlesbridge Publishing
www.charlesbridge.com/subwcp.htm
Winslow Press
www.winslowpress.com

Books Are By People
Hopkins, Lee Bennett. New York: Citation
Press, 1969
Illustrators of Children's Books 1744-1945
Mahoney, Bertha E. et al. Boston, Horn Book,
1947
Illustrators of Children's Books 1957-1966
Kingman, Lee et al. Boston: Horn Book, 1968
Meet the Authors & Illustrators, Vol. Two
Kovacs, Deborah & James Prelle. New York:
Scholastic, 1993
*Newbery & Caldecott Medal Books 1976-1985
& 1956-1965*, Kingman, Lee. Boston: Horn
Book
Something About the Author series, numerous
volumes, Gale Publishing Inc.
The Illustrator's Notebook
Kingman, Lee. Boston: Horn, Book, 1978

Visit favorite illustrators through the wonderful world of the **web**. The **internet** is a rich and varied source of information about illustrators, authors and picture books. Everyday on the web, something new emerges (or disappears)!

A
Arnosky, Jim
www.jimarnosky.com

B
Bang, Molly
www.mollybang.com
Bender, Robert
home.epix.net/~rbender/framesets/Meet.html
Benson, Patrick
www.bl.uk/whatson/exhibitions/magicpencil/learning_benson_interview_6.html
Brett, Jan
www.janbrett.com
Buehner, Mark
curry.edschool.virginia.edu/go/tempo/VCCB/Authorsets2/buehner/AuthorsetsBuehner.html
Burton, Virginia Lee
libweb.uoregon.edu/speccoll/mss/childrenslit/vlburton.html

C
Carle, Eric
www.eric-carle.com
Carter, David A.
www.popupbooks.com
Cooney, Barbara
www.ortakales.com (search-Cooney)
Crews, Donald
www.eduplace.com

D
Degen, Bruce
www.scholastic.com/magicschoolbus/books/
dePaola, Tomie
www.bookpage.com (search-DePaola)
Diaz, David
www.eduplace.com/kids/hmr/mtai/diaz.html
Donohue, Dorothy
www.author-illustr-source.com/DotDonohue.htm
Dorros, Arthur
www.arthurdorros.com
Dr. Seuss
www.seussville.com
Duvoisin, Roger
www.lib.usm.edu/ (search deGrummond, Duvoisin)

E
Ehlert, Lois
www.friend.ly.net/scoop/biographies/ehlertlois
Emberley, Ed
www.edemberley.com
Ets, Marie Hall
avatar.lib.usm.edu/~degrum/findaids/ets.htm

F
Falconer, Ian
www.simonsays.com/ (search-Falconer)
Fleming, Denise
www.denisefleming.com
Freeman, Don
www.edupaperback.org (search-Freeman)

G
Gág, Wanda
www.ortakales.com (search-Gág)
Gammell, Stephen
www.bookpage.com (search Gammell)
Garrison, Barbara
www.boydsmillspress.com
Geisel, Theodor
www.seussville.com
Geisert, Arthur
www.scbwi-illinois.org/Ageisert.html
Goble, Paul
www.turtletrack.org

H
Hurd, Clement
www.harperchildrens.com/features/ch.htm
Hutchins, Pat
www.titch.net/pat.htm

I J
Jenkins, Steve
www.jenkinspage.com
Jocelyn, Marthe
www.ala.org/booklist (search-Jocelyn)
Johnson, Crockett
www.ksu.edu/english/nelp/purple
Johnson, Stephen T.
www.stephentjohnson.com/bio.html
Jonas, Ann
www.harpercollins.com

K
Katz, Karen
www.simonsays.com (search-author, Katz)
Keats, Ezra Jack
www.ezra-jack-keats.org
Kirk, David
www.callaway.com/CK/CK-wodc.html
Kliros, Thea
www.wandanow.com/kliroskidshome.html
Knight, Christopher
www.newfilmco.com

Krommes, Beth
www.houghtonmifflinbooks.com

L
Lionni, Leo
www.edupaperback.org
Lobel, Anita
www.anitalobel.com

M
Macdonald, Suse
www.create4kids.com/about.html
McCloskey, Robert
www.friend.ly.net/scoop (search-McCloskey)
McKee, David
www.andersenpress.co.uk (search-McKee)
Meade, Holly
www.eduplace.com/kids/hmr/mtai/meade.html
Mills, Yaroslava
www.artukraine.com
Minor, Wendell
www.minorart.com
Montresor, Beni
special.lib.umn.edu/findaid/html/clrc/clrc0167.html

N
Newberry, Clare Turlay
www.rabbit.org/journal/3-2/marshmallow.html

O P
Parker, Nancy Winslow
www.nwparker.com
Pfister, Marcus
www.bravemonster.com/authors/marcuspfister.htm
Pinkwater, Daniel Manus
www.pinkwater.com/pzone
Polacco, Patricia
www.patriciapolacco.com
Pomeroy, Diana
www.potatoprint.com

Q R
Reid, Barbara
www.nlc-bnc.ca/read-up-on-it/t11-6054-e.html
Reisberg, Mira
www.mirareisberg.com
Ringgold, Faith
www.faithringgold.com
Roth, Susan L.
www.eduplace.com/kids/hmr/mtai/roth.html

S
Sabuda, Robert
www.robertsabuda.com
Saillard, Rémi
perso.wanadoo.fr/bijouxcailloux/tetes.htm (Fr.)

Saint James, Synthia
www.synthiasaintjames.com
Say, Allen
www.unomaha.edu/~unochlit/say.html
Schoenherr, John
www.spanierman.com/schoenherrbio.htm
Sendak, Maurice
www.pbs.org/ (search-Sendak)
Shaw, Charles G.
nmaa-ryder.si.edu/collections/exhibits/abstraction/shaw.html
Shulevitz, Uri
www.carolhurst.com
Silverstein, Shel
www.carolhurst.com
Simont, Marc
www.cbcbooks.org/html/marc_simont.html
Slobodkin, Louis
www.lib.usm.edu/libraryfocus/spring00/art.html
special.lib.umn.edu/findaid/html/clrc/clrc0171.html
Steig, William
www.williamsteig.com/williamsteig.htm
Steiner, Joan
www.twbookmark.com (search-Steiner)

T U V
Ungerer, Tomi
falcon.jmu.edu/~ramseyil/ungerer.html
Van Allsburg, Chris
www.eduplace.com

W X
Waldman, Neil
www.charlesbridge.com/waldman.htm
Walsh, Ellen Stoll
www.geocities.com/~teddarnold/ellen.html
Ward, Lynd
www.bpib.comlyndward.htm
Wexler, Jerome
www.lib.usm.edu/~degrum/html/ (search-Wexler)
Whitman, Candace
www.candacewhitman.com
Wiese, Kurt
www.lib.usm.edu/~degrum/html/ (search Wiese)
Wiesner, David
www.houghtonmifflin.com/ (search Wiesner)
Wisniewski, David
www.eduplace.com/ (search-Wisniewski)
Wood, Don
www.audreywood.com
Wright, Dare
www.logan.com/loganberry/most-wright.html

Y Z
Yashima, Taro
taroyashima.homestead.com
Young, Ed
www.nccil.org/artists/txt_ey.html

Contact Bright Ring with your discoveries of new links: books@brightring.com

Picture Book Publishers of some of the finest books for children

Publishers of picture books featured in *Storybook Art* are listed in **bold**. Their corresponding *TITLE* with **ISBN** follow. Use this publisher information for purchasing, special ordering, or online searches.

Barefoot Books
1841480770 *How Big is a Pig?*
Candlewick Press
1564021017 *Owl Babies*
Children's Book Press
0892391111 *Baby Rattlesnake*
Chronicle Books
081181842X *Mr. Fine, Porcupine*
Farrar, Straus & Giroux
0374370923 *Snow*
Firefly Books Ltd.
0920668372 *Love You Forever*
Harcourt
— **Gulliver**
0152000275 *Sea Shapes*
0152208704 *Light*
0152280502 *Fish Eyes*
0152427309 *King Bidgood's in the Bathtub*
0152518738 *Many Moons*
0152699546 *Smoky Night*
— **Silver Whistle**
0152014152 *Is that You, Winter?*
— **Voyager**
0152001182 *Mouse Paint*
0152003002 *One Potato*
HarperCollins
0060202130 *The Seashore Book*
0060207051 *Good Night Moon*
0060229365 *Harold & the Purple Crayon*
0060244615 *Marshmallow*
0060254920 *Where the Wild Things Are*
0060256672 *Where the Sidewalk Ends*
0060261552 *A Tree is Nice*
0060261803 *Crictor*
0064431592 *It Looked Like Spilt Milk*
— **Greenwillow**
0688009085 *Carousel*
0688038263 *The Quilt*
0688052525 *The Doorbell Rang*
0688088651 *Alison's Zinnia*
0688127029 *The Alphabet Tale*
0688161944 *Sand Castle*
— **Lothrop Lee & Shepard**
0688078885 *Balloon Farm*
0688086527 *Wake Up City!*
0688091717 *Elmer*
0688411614 *White Snow, Bright Snow*
— **Mulberry**
0688135749 *Ten Black Dots*
0688510531 *The Mitten*

— **Trophy**
0688132839 *Inch by Inch*
— **Ty Crowell**
0690006055 *Brown Bear, Brown Bear*
Henry Holt
080501957X *Barnyard Banter*
Holiday House
0823400913 *Rain Makes Applesauce*
Houghton Mifflin
0395148065 *The Biggest Bear*
039525938X *The Little House*
0395385091 *Pigs From A to Z*
0395389496 *The Polar Express*
0395570352 *Grandfather's Journey*
0395726654 *Looking Down*
0395883997 *Grandmother Winter*
— **Clarion**
0395551137 *Tuesday*
0395726182 *Golem*
Knopf
0394827996 *Fish is Fish*
Little Brown (Charlesbridge)
0316813079 *Look-Alikes Jr.*
Mondo
1572550112 *Zoo-Looking*
North-South
1558580093 *The Rainbow Fish*
0735817480 *The Rainbow Fish, 10th Anniversary Ed.*
Penguin Putnam
039922033X *Goldilocks & the Three Bears*
0670175919 *Blueberries for Sal*
0670241334 *Corduroy*
0670479586 *Miss Rumphius*
0698200918 *Millions of Cats*
— **Dial**
0803714572 *Snow on Snow on Snow*
0803717482 *How Thunder & Lightning Came to Be*
— **Dutton**
0525444289 *Alligator Shoes*
0525453636 *Everyday Mysteries*
0525459030 *The Snow Tree*
0525464425 *Hannah's Collection*
0525651160 *Only One*
— **Philomel**
0399214577 *Owl Moon*
0399222618 *Seven Blind Mice*
— **Puffin/Viking**
0140562133 *The A to Z Beastly Jamboree*
0670654000 *The Snowy Day*
— **Viking**
0670340251 *Gilberto & the Wind*
0670627100 *Seashore Story*
0670672238 *The Story About Ping*
0670856312 *Alphabet City*

Random House
039484484X *The Cat in the Hat*
— **Crown**
0517580314 *Tar Beach*
0517700476 *The Squiggle*
— **Zephyr**
0305150408 *The Lonely Doll*
Scholastic
0590405853 *Have You Seen Birds?*
0590445103 *The Big Orange Splot*
0590477242 *Miss Spider's Tea Party*
0590725998 *The Magic School Bus Lost in the Solar System*
— **Blue Sky**
0887765211 *When Sophie Gets Angry*
— **Cartwheel**
0590457837 *More Spaghetti I Say*
— **Orchard**
0531095002 *Hush! A Thai Lullaby*
Sierra Club
0871568594 *The Empty Lot*
Simon & Schuster
— **Books for Young Readers**
0671649639 *The Keeping Quilt*
067166154X *Sylvester & The Magic Pebble*
0671662481 *Drummer Hoff*
067166283X *Strega Nona*
067167949X *Chicka Chicka Boom Boom*
0878881212 *The Girl Who Loved Wild Horses*
— **Aladdin**
067166249X *Drummer Hoff*
0671662694 *Sylvester & the Magic Pebble*
0671666061 *Strega Nona*
068971081X *Sugaring Time*
0689713533 *May I Bring a Friend?*
068971503X *Oh, A Hunting We Will Go*
0689716966 *The Girl Who Loved Wild Horses*
0689718810 *Crocodile Beat (out of print)*
068983568X *Chicka Chicka Boom Boom*
0689844476 *The Keeping Quilt*
— **Atheneum**
0689206151 *May I Bring a Friend?*
0689829531 *Olivia / An Anne Schwartz Book*
0689845049 *The Girl Who Loved Wild Horses / A Richard Jackson Book*
— **Little Simon**
0671748947 *Chicka Chicka Boom Boom*
068980119X *Feely Bugs*
0689817649 *Strega Nona*
0689838999 *T'was the Night Before Christmas*
— **McElderry**
0689848730 *Twelve Hats for Lena*
Whispering Coyote (Charlesbridge)
1879085550 *There Was an Old Woman Who Lived in a Glove*
Winslow
189081721X *Veggie Soup*

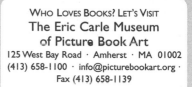

WHO LOVES BOOKS? LET'S VISIT
The Eric Carle Museum of Picture Book Art
125 West Bay Road · Amherst · MA 01002
(413) 658-1100 · info@picturebookart.org ·
Fax (413) 658-1139

FOR KIDS & ADULTS

www.picturebookart.org

ONLINE BOOK PURCHASE & SEARCH SITES

This is a beginning list ... add your favorites:
• www.addall.com (new, used, & out of print books - searches many other used book sites, such as Alibris, Powells, Bibliofind)
• www.amazon.com (book purchase)
• www.barnesandnoble.com (book purchase)
• www.borders.com (book purchase)
• www.ebay.com (new & used books)
• www.half.com (discount new & used books)

I like the prehistoric way to find a good book — I go to the library!

... and always remember your independent book store.

by Peter James, age 8

by Tatiana Huaracha, age 8

Arnosky: from interview by Lisa Horak, reprinted with permission from the 11/98 issue of *BookPage: America's Book Review*

Bang: Molly Bang's web page, www.mollybang.com

Batherman: from *Something About the Author®*, Vol.125 p.67 ©2003 The Gale Group, Inc.

Beaton: Barefoot Books letter to Kohl 2002, & Barefoot Books www.barefoot-books.com

Bender: Bender letter to Potter, phone Kohl 2003

Benson: Benson letter to Kohl 2003

Bileck: letter to Kohl 2003, *photo credit Emily Nelligan*

Brett: Brett letter to Kohl 2002 & from www.janbrett.com

Buehner: Virginia Center for Children's Books (VCCB) ©2001 Curry School of Education, curry.edschool.virginia.edu

Burton: www.libweb.uoregon.edu, Division of Special Collections & University Archives ©University of Oregon Library System

Carle: *Eighth Book of Junior Authors & Illustrators* 2000 ©HW Wilson Company

Carter: letter from Carter to Kohl 2003 & from www.popupbooks.com, *Patitucci photo credit, bug art okayed by David A. Carter*

Cooney: Denise Ortakales©1999-2002, www.ortakales.com & correspondence D.O.

Crews: interview with George Bodmer, Professor of English & Children's Literature Indiana University Northwest ©1998 *African American Review*, ©2000 Gale Group

Degen: from Scholastic Inc. Kids' Fun Online, *The Magic Schoolbus*™&© 2003-1996, www.scholastic.com/magicschoolbus/ books/authors/

dePaola: from BookPage: America's Book Review, www.bookpage.com & BookPage letter to Kohl 2003

Diaz: communication with Potter 2002 & Scholastic Inc.™ & © 2003–1996, *Celebrate Hispanic Heritage: Meet Famous Latinos*, interview by Scholastic students, www.teacher.scholastic.com

Donohue: from letter to Kohl 2002, cover ok D. Donohue

Dorros: from letter to Kohl 2002

Duvoisin: from deGrummond Collection, McCain Library & Archives, University Libraries, University of Southern Mississippi, Hattiesburg avatar.lib.usm.edu/~degrum/findaids/duvoisin.htm & letters Dee Jones

Ehlert: from *Something About the Author®*, Vol.128 ©2003 The Gale Group, Inc.

Emberley: from Emberley letter to Kohl 2002 & www.edemberley.com

Ets: from *Contemporary Authors Online*, The Gale Group, 2000 letters with Gale Group

Falconer: *Something About the Author®*, Vol.125 p.67 ©2003 The Gale Group, Inc.

Fleming: Fleming letter to Kohl 2002 & www.denisefleming.com

Freeman: www.edupaperback.org, originally from print volumes ©HW Wilson

Gág: Denise Ortakales ©1999–2002 www.ortakales.com & correspondence to D.O.

Gammell: *Something About the Author®*, Vol.128 p.78 ©2003 The Gale Group, Inc.

Garrison: letter from Garrison to Kohl 2002

Geisert: *Something About the Author®*, Vol.133 p.72 ©2003 The Gale Group, Inc., mail with Geisert office

Gerberg: Gerberg letter to Kohl 2003 (art/quote)

Goble: phone interview with Goble, & interview: Lynn Verschoor-director, Art Museum & South Dakota State University, *Honoring Paul Goble* 4/30/02, www.sdstate.edu

Hurd: Hurd letter to Kohl 1971

Hutchins: film company letter to Kohl 2002 & *Something About the Author®*, Vol.111 p.91 ©2003 The Gale Group, Inc.

Jenkins: Jenkins letter to Kohl 2002, & 20th Anniversary Children's Literature Conference, Ohio State University, Children's Literature www.childrenslit.com, & www.jenkinspage.com

Jocelyn: Trevor Day School's Intranet Site, www.trevornet.org, a description of Marthe Jocelyn's visit

Johnson, C.: Phil Nel ©1998-2003, Kansas State University, www.ksu.edu & letter P. Nel

Johnson, S.T.: K-State Media Relations & Marketing www.mediarelations.ksu.edu & www.stephentjohnson.com

Jonas: National Center for Children's Illustrated Literature, www.nccil.org, & letter NCCIL

Katz: letter & phone interview with Kohl 2003

Keats: deGrummond Children's Literature Collection, University of Southern Mississippi, www.lib.usm.edu & letter Dee Jones

Kirk: Kirk letter to Kohl 2002

Kliros: Hilary Kliros letter to Kohl 2002

Knight: Knight letter to Kohl 2002 & www.newfilmco.com

Krommes: Krommes letter to Kohl 2002 & phone

Lionni: Educational Paperback Association www.edupaperback.org, originally from *Junior Authors & Illustrators* ©HW Wilson Company

Lobel, A: www.anitalobel.com & Anita Lobel

Lodge: Lodge letter to Kohl 2003

Macdonald: MacDonald letter to Kohl 2002 & MacDonald website www.create4kids.com

Martin: comment from Kohl 2003

McCloskey: reprinted with permission from *The Horn Book, Inc.*, www.hbook.com, interview by Anita Silvey, Horn Book Radio Review, Virtual History Exhibit

McGraw: letter to Potter 2003, & from letter to Kohl 2002 & Firefly Books, www.fireflybooks.com

McKee: Andersen Press letter to Kohl, David McKee/Andersen Press. Andersen Press, London/original editions, www.andersenpress.co.uk, Harper Collins/USA editions

Meade: Educational Paperback Association, Houghton Mifflin ©2000 www.eduplace.com

Mills: *Something About the Author®*, Vol.35 p.171 ©2003 The Gale Group, Inc. & mailing to Kohl 2002

Minor: Minor letter to Kohl 2002 & www.minorart.com

Montresor: The University of Minnesota Libraries ©1999 by the Regents University of Minnesota, Twin Cities, & the University Libraries, special.lib.umn.edu/findaid/html/

Morgan: interview by Kohl 2002

Mullins: Scholastic/Australia letter to Kohl 2003 & Scholastic Australia Pty Ltd ©1997-2002 www.scholastic.com.au

Newberry: *The Unexpected Surrogate* (House Rabbit Society), Diana Murphy, www.rabbit.org

Parker: Parker letter to Kohl 2002 & www.nwparker.com

Pfister: *Something About the Author®*, Vol.83 p.168 ©2003 The Gale Group, Inc.

Pinkwater: *Daniel Pinkwater & the Afterlife Diet*, interview by Marilyn Wann, www.fatso.com & Wann letter 2003

Polacco: *Firetalking*, Richard C. Owen (Katonah, NY) 1994 & correspondence

Pomeroy: from www.potatoprint.com & interview with Kohl 2002

Reid: Reisberg letter to Kohl 2002 & National Library of Canada, biography 6/24/96 www.nlc-bnc.cal

Reisberg: Reisberg letter to Kohl 2002 & www.mirareisberg.com

Ringgold: Ringgold office contact with Kohl 2002, & www.faithringgold.com

Roth: Roth letter to Potter 2002

Sabuda: Sabuda letter to Kohl 2002 & www.robertsabuda.com

Saillard: Saillard letter to Kohl, 2003

Saint James: St. James letter, Synthia Saint James' website, www.synthiasaintjames.com

Say: University of Nebraska at Omaha, *Allen Say: Author/Illustrator*, prepared by Theresa A. Valish, www.unomaha.edu

Schoenherr: Schoenherr letter to Kohl 2003

Sendak: "Maurice Sendak" Factmonster ©2002 Family Education Network, 2/1/03, www.factmonster.com

Seuss: well-known, multiple sources, Seuss representation office email, fax, & telephone

Shaw: ArtArchives, recorded interview mailed to Kohl, 4/15/68, Paul Cummings interviewer, artarchives.si.edu/askus.cfm

Shulevitz: The University of Nebraska at Omaha, www.unomaha.edu

Silverstein: Jean F. Mercier, "Shel Silverstein", *Publishers Weekly*, 4/29/75

Simont: Lee Bennett Hopkins, *Books Are by People: Interviews with 104 Authors & Illustrators of Books for Young Children*, Citation Press, 1969

Slobodkin: letter interview with son, Lawrence Slobodkin 2003

Steig: Patrick Hearn, *Washington Post Book World* 5/11/80

Steiner: Steiner letter & fax to Potter 2002

Ungerer: Lanes, "Tomi Ungerer's Reluctant Heroes," *Atlantic Monthly*, January 1974, pp.87-90

Van Allsburg: Detroit Free Press, October 22, 1995, pp.7-9, Sunday Magazine, Lannon, Linnea, "The Van Allsburg Express"

Waldman: interview by Kohl 2003

Walsh: *Something About the Author®*, Vol.99 p.210 ©2003 The Gale Group, Inc.

Ward: from Jim Vadeboncoeur, Jr., Bud Plant Illustrated Books, www.bpib.com

Wexler: *Something About the Author®*, Vol.14 p.243 ©2003 The Gale Group, Inc.

Whitman: Whitman letter to Kohl 2002 & www.candacewhitman.com

Wiese: *Delaware Valley News*, 1/12/73, through Reference Department, Hunterdon County Library, Flemington, NJ, USA

Wiesner: *Something About the Author®*, Vol.117 p.197 ©2003 The Gale Group, Inc.

Wisniewski: www.cbcbooks.org, The Children's Book Council ©1998-2002

Wood: Wood letter to Kohl 2002 & www.audreywood.com, based on interview with Marguerite Feitlowitz, *Something About the Author®*, Vol.50 p.225 ©2003 The Gale Group

Wright: *Los Angeles Times* 2/4/01 p.B7, *New York Times* 2/3/01 p.B7, *Washington Post* 2/4/01 p.C8

Yashima: John O'Brien, former student of Taro Yashima, letter to Kohl 2003, writeman.homestead.com

Young: McIntosh & Otis correspondence & The National Center for Children's Illustrated Literature, interview, www.nccil.org

* CITATION/PERMISSION NOTE: *Significant effort was made to contact each illustrator, publisher, foundation, or other source for permission & proper use of all quotes, photos, or book covers. This includes direct correspondence, emails, letters, telephone contacts, faxes, and quotation/citation requests. Verification, proper citation, and solid permissions were of foremost importance. Please inform Bright Ring if you have corrections or comments, as we strive to represent everyone fairly and accurately.*

CALDECOTT MEDAL WINNERS & HONOR BOOKS 1938-2002

The highly respected and trusted *Caldecott Medal* is given annually for the best illustrated books. *Caldecott* titles, authors, or illustrators featured in **Storybook Art** will be shown in **bold**. View a complete list of *Caldecott* Medalists and honor books at:

www.ala.org/alsc/caldpast.html

2002 Medal Winner –
The Three Pigs by **David Wiesner** (Clarion/Houghton Mifflin)
Honor Books –
The Dinosaurs of Waterhouse Hawkins illustrator-Brian Selznick, author-Barbara Kerley (Scholastic)
Martin's Big Words: the Life of Dr. Martin Luther King, Jr. illustrator-Bryan Collier, author-Doreen Rappaport (Jump at the Sun/Hyperion)
The Stray Dog by **Marc Simont** (HarperCollins)

2001 Medal Winner –
So You Want to be President? illustrator-David Small & author-Judith St. George (Philomel Books)
Honor Books –
Casey at the Bat: A Ballad of the Republic Sung in the Year 1888 illustrator-Christopher Bing, author-Ernest Lawrence Thayer (Handprint Books)
Click, Clack, Moo: Cows that Type illustrator-Betsy Lewin, author-Doreen Cronin (Simon & Schuster)
Olivia by **Ian Falconer** (Simon & Schuster/Atheneum)

2000 Medal Winner –
Joseph Had a Little Overcoat by Simms Taback (Viking)
Honor Books: –
A Child's Calendar illustrator-Trina Schart Hyman Text: John Updike (Holiday House)
Sector 7 by **David Wiesner** (Clarion Books)
When Sophie Gets Angry-Really, Really Angry by **Molly Bang** (Scholastic)
The Ugly Duckling illustrator-Jerry Pinkney, Text-Hans Christian Andersen, adapted-Jerry Pinkney (Morrow)

1999 Medal Winner –
Snowflake Bentley illustrator-Mary Azarian, text-Jacqueline Briggs Martin (Houghton)

Honor Books –
Duke Ellington: The Piano Prince & the Orchestra illustrator-Brian Pinkney, Text-Andrea Davis Pinkney (Hyperion)
No, David! by David Shannon (Scholastic)
Snow by **Uri Shulevitz** (Farrar)
Tibet Through the Red Box by Peter Sis (Frances Foster)

1998 Medal Winner –
Rapunzel by Paul O. Zelinsky (Dutton)
Honor Books –
The Gardener illustrator-David Small, Text-Sarah Stewart (Farrar)
Harlem illustrator-Christopher Myers, Text-Walter Dean Myers (Scholastic)
There Was an Old Lady Who Swallowed a Fly by Simms Taback (Viking)

1997 Medal Winner –
Golem by **David Wisniewski** (Clarion)
Honor Books –
Hush! A Thai Lullaby illustrator-**Holly Meade**; text-**Minfong Ho** (Melanie Kroupa/Orchard Books)
The Graphic Alphabet by David Pelletier (Orchard Books)
The Paperboy by Dav Pilkey (Richard Jackson/Orchard Books)
Starry Messenger by Peter Sís (Frances Foster Books/Farrar Straus Giroux)

1996 Medal Winner –
Officer Buckle & Gloria by Peggy Rathmann (Putnam)
Honor Books –
Alphabet City by **Stephen T. Johnson** (Viking)
Zin! Zin! Zin! a Violin illustrator-Marjorie Priceman; text-Lloyd Moss (Simon & Schuster)
The Faithful Friend illustrator-Brian Pinkney; text-Robert D. San Souci (Simon & Schuster)
Tops & Bottoms adapted & illustrated-Janet Stevens (Harcourt)

1995 Medal Winner –
Smoky Night illustrator-**David Diaz**; text-**Eve Bunting** (Harcourt)
Honor Books –
John Henry illustrator-Jerry Pinkney; text-Julius Lester (Dial)
Swamp Angel illustrator-Paul O. Zelinsky; text-Anne Issacs (Dutton)
Time Flies by Eric Rohmann (Crown)

1994 Medal Winner –
Grandfather's Journey by **Allen Say**; text-edited by Walter Lorraine (Houghton)

Honor Books –
Peppe the Lamplighter illustrator-Ted Lewin; text-Elisa Bartone (Lothrop)
In the Small, Small Pond by **Denise Fleming** (Holt)
Raven: A Trickster Tale from the Pacific Northwest by Gerald McDermott (Harcourt)
Owen by Kevin Henkes (Greenwillow)
Yo! Yes? illustrator-Chris Raschka; text-edited by Richard Jackson (Orchard)

1993 Medal Winner –
Mirette on the High Wire by Emily Arnold McCully (Putnam)
Honor Books –
The Stinky Cheese Man & Other Fairly Stupid Tales illustrator-Lane Smith; text-Jon Scieszka (Viking)
Seven Blind Mice by **Ed Young** (Philomel Books)
Working Cotton illustrator-Carole Byard; text-Sherley Anne Williams (Harcourt)

1992 Medal Winner –
Tuesday by **David Wiesner** (Clarion Books)
Honor Book –
Tar Beach by **Faith Ringgold** (Crown/Random)

1991 Medal Winner –
Black & White by David Macaulay (Houghton)
Honor Books –
Puss in Boots illustrator-Fred Marcellino; text-Charles Perrault, trans-Malcolm Arthur (Di Capua/Farrar)
"More More More," Said the Baby: Three Love Stories by Vera B. Williams (Greenwillow)

1990 Medal Winner –
Lon Po Po: A Red-Riding Hood Story from China by **Ed Young** (Philomel)
Honor Books –
Bill Peet: An Autobiography by Bill Peet (Houghton)
Color Zoo by **Lois Ehlert** (Lippincott)
The Talking Eggs: A Folktale from the American South illustrator-Jerry Pinkney; text-Robert D. San Souci (Dial)
Hershel & the Hanukkah Goblins illustrator-Trina Schart Hyman; text-Eric Kimmel (Holiday House)

1989 Medal Winner –
Song & Dance Man illustrator-**Stephen Gammell**; text-Karen Ackerman (Knopf)
Honor Books –
The Boy of the Three-Year Nap illustrator-**Allen Say**; text-Diane Snyder (Houghton)
Free Fall by **David Wiesner** (Lothrop)

Goldilocks & the Three Bears by James Marshall (Dial)
Mirandy & Brother Wind illustrator-Jerry Pinkney; text-Patricia C. McKissack (Knopf)

1988 Medal Winner –
Owl Moon illustrator-**John Schoenherr**; text-Jane Yolen (Philomel)
Honor Book –
Mufaro's Beautiful Daughters: An African Tale by John Steptoe (Lothrop)

1987 Medal Winner –
Hey, Al illustrator-Richard Egielski; text-Arthur Yorinks (Farrar)
Honor Books –
The Village of Round & Square Houses by Ann Grifalconi (Little, Brown)
Alphabatics by **Suse MacDonald** (Bradbury)
Rumpelstiltskin by Paul O. Zelinsky (Dutton)

1986 Medal Winner –
The Polar Express by **Chris Van Allsburg** (Houghton)
Honor Books –
The Relatives Came illustrator-**Stephen Gammell**; text-Cynthia Rylant (Bradbury)
King Bidgood's in the Bathtub illustrator-**Don Wood**; text-**Audrey Wood** (Harcourt)

1985 Medal Winner –
Saint George & the Dragon illustrator-Trina Schart Hyman; text retold-Margaret Hodges (Little, Brown)
Honor Books –
Hansel & Gretel illustrator-Paul O. Zelinsky; text-retold by Rika Lesser (Dodd)
Have You Seen My Duckling? by Nancy Tafuri (Greenwillow)
The Story of Jumping Mouse: A Native American Legend retold & illustrated-John Steptoe (Lothrop)

1984 Medal Winner –
The Glorious Flight: Across the Channel with Louis Bleriot by Alice & Martin Provensen (Viking)

If I had to choose a book to win an award, I would choose all of them. I can make the awards all by myself so I can make 200. Or maybe 500.
Vivian

Honor Books –
Little Red Riding Hood retold & illustrated-Trina Schart Hyman (Holiday)
Ten, Nine, Eight by **Molly Bang** (Greenwillow)

1983 Medal Winner –
Shadow translated & illustrator-**Marcia Brown**, original French: Blaise Cendrars (Scribner)
Honor Books –
A Chair for My Mother by Vera B. Williams (Greenwillow)
When I Was Young in the Mountains illustrator-Diane Goode; text-Cynthia Rylant (Dutton)

1982 Medal Winner –
Jumanji by **Chris Van Allsburg** (Houghton)
Honor Books –
Where the Buffaloes Begin illustrator-**Stephen Gammell**; text-Olaf Baker (Warne)
On Market Street illustrator-**Anita Lobel**; text-Arnold Lobel (Greenwillow)
Outside Over There by **Maurice Sendak** (Harper)
A Visit to William Blake's Inn: Poems for Innocent & Experienced Travelers illustrator-Alice & Martin Provensen; text-Nancy Willard (Harcourt)

1981 Medal Winner –
Fables by Arnold Lobel (Harper)
Honor Books –
The Bremen-Town Musicians retold & illustrated-Ilse Plume (Doubleday)
The Grey Lady & the Strawberry Snatcher by **Molly Bang** (Four Winds)
Mice Twice by Joseph Low (McElderry/ Atheneum)
Truck by **Donald Crews** (Greenwillow)

1980 Medal Winner –
Ox-Cart Man illustrator-**Barbara Cooney**; text-Donald Hall (Viking)
Honor Books –
Ben's Trumpet by Rachel Isadora (Greenwillow)
The Garden Of Abdul Gasazi by **Chris Van Allsburg** (Houghton)
The Treasure by **Uri Shulevitz** (Farrar)

1979 Medal Winner –
The Girl Who Loved Wild Horses by **Paul Goble** (Bradbury)
Honor Books –
Freight Train by **Donald Crews** (Greenwillow)
The Way to Start a Day illustrator-Peter Parnall; text-Byrd Baylor (Scribner)

1978 Medal Winner –
Noah's Ark by Peter Spier (Doubleday)
Honor Books –
Castle by David Macaulay (Houghton)
It Could Always Be Worse retold & illustrated-Margot Zemach (Farrar)

1977 Medal Winner –
Ashanti to Zulu: African Traditions illustrator-Leo & Diane Dillon; text-Margaret Musgrove (Dial)
Honor Books –
The Amazing Bone by **William Steig** (Farrar)
The Contest retold & illustrator-Nonny Hogrogian (Greenwillow)
Fish for Supper by M. B. Goffstein (Dial)
The Golem: A Jewish Legend by Beverly Brodsky McDermott (Lippincott)
Hawk, I'm Your Brother illustrator-Peter Parnall; text-Byrd Baylor (Scribner)

1976 Medal Winner –
Why Mosquitoes Buzz in People's Ears illustrator-Leo & Diane Dillon; text & retold by-Verna Aardema (Dial)
Honor Books –
The Desert is Theirs illustrator-Peter Parnall; text-Byrd Baylor (Scribner)
Strega Nona by **Tomie dePaola** (Prentice-Hall)

1975 Medal Winner –
Arrow to the Sun by Gerald McDermott (Viking)
Honor Books –
Jambo Means Hello: A Swahili Alphabet Book illustrator-Tom Feelings; text-Muriel Feelings (Dial)

1974 Medal Winner –
Duffy & the Devil illustrator-Margot Zemach; retold-Harve Zemach (Farrar)
Honor Books –
Three Jovial Huntsmen by Susan Jeffers (Bradbury)
Cathedral by David Macaulay (Houghton)

1973 Medal Winner –
The Funny Little Woman illustrator-Blair Lent; text retold-Arlene Mosel (Dutton)
Honor Books –
Anansi the Spider: A Tale from the Ashanti adapted/illustrated-Gerald McDermott (Holt)
Hosie's Alphabet illustrator-Leonard Baskin; text-Hosea, Tobias & Lisa Baskin (Viking)
Snow-White & the Seven Dwarfs illustrator-Nancy Ekholm Burkert; text translated-Randall Jarrell retold from the Brothers Grimm (Farrar)

When Clay Sings illustrator-Tom Bahti; text-Byrd Baylor (Scribner)

1972 Medal Winner –
One Fine Day retold & illustrator-Nonny Hogrogian (Macmillan)
Honor Books –
Hildilid's Night illustrator-Arnold Lobel; text-Cheli Durán Ryan (Macmillan)
If All the Seas Were One Sea by Janina Domanska (Macmillan)
Moja Means One: Swahili Counting Book illustrator-Tom Feelings; text-Muriel Feelings (Dial)

1971 Medal Winner –
A Story A Story retold & illustrated-Gail E. Haley (Atheneum)
Honor Books –
The Angry Moon illustrator-Blair Lent; text retold-William Sleator (Atlantic)
Frog & Toad are Friends by Arnold Lobel (Harper)
In the Night Kitchen by **Maurice Sendak** (Harper)

1970 Medal Winner –
Sylvester & the Magic Pebble by **William Steig** (Windmill Books)
Honor Books –
Goggles! by **Ezra Jack Keats** (Macmillan)
Alexander & the Wind-Up Mouse by **Leo Lionni** (Pantheon)
Pop Corn & Ma Goodness illustrator-Robert Andrew Parker; text-Edna Mitchell Preston (Viking)
Thy Friend, Obadiah by Brinton Turkle (Viking)
The Judge: An Untrue Tale illustrator-Margot Zemach; text-Harve Zemach (Farrar)

1969 Medal Winner –
The Fool of the World & the Flying Ship illustrator-**Uri Shulevitz**; text & retold by-Arthur Ransome (Farrar)
Honor Books –
Why the Sun & the Moon Live in the Sky illustrator-Blair Lent; text-Elphinstone Dayrell (Houghton)

1968 Medal Winner –
Drummer Hoff illustrator-**Ed Emberley**; text adapted-**Barbara Emberley** (Prentice-Hall)
Honor Books –
Frederick by **Leo Lionni** (Pantheon)
Seashore Story by **Taro Yashima** (Viking)
The Emperor & the Kite illustrator-**Ed Young**; text-Jane Yolen (World)

1967 Medal Winner –
Sam, Bangs & Moonshine by Evaline Ness (Holt)
Honor Book –
One Wide River to Cross illustrator-**Ed Emberley**; text adapted-**Barbara Emberley** (Prentice-Hall)

1966 Medal Winner –
Always Room for One More illustrator-Nonny Hogrogian; text-Sorche Nic Leodhas, pseud. [Leclair Alger] (Holt)
Honor Books –
Hide & Seek Fog illustrator-Roger Duvoisin; text-Alvin Tresselt (Lothrop)
Just Me by **Marie Hall Ets** (Viking)
Tom Tit Tot retold & illustrator-Evaline Ness (Scribner)

1965 Medal Winner –
May I Bring a Friend? illustrator-**Beni Montresor**; text-**Beatrice Schenk de Regniers** (Atheneum)
Honor Books –
Rain Makes Applesauce illustrator-**Marvin Bileck**; text-**Julian Scheer** (Holiday)
The Wave illustrator-Blair Lent; text-Margaret Hodges (Houghton)
A Pocketful of Cricket illustrator-Evaline Ness; text-Rebecca Caudill (Holt)

1964 Medal Winner –
Where the Wild Things Are by **Maurice Sendak** (Harper)
Honor Books –
Swimmy by **Leo Lionni** (Pantheon)
All in the Morning Early illustrator-Evaline Ness; text-Sorche Nic Leodhas, Leclaire Alger (Holt)
Mother Goose & Nursery Rhymes illustrator-Philip Reed (Atheneum)

1963 Medal Winner –
The Snowy Day by **Ezra Jack Keats** (Viking)
Honor Books –
The Sun is a Golden Earring illustrator-Bernarda Bryson; text-Natalia M. Belting (Holt)
Mr. Rabbit & the Lovely Present illustrator-**Maurice Sendak**; text-**Charlotte Zolotow** (Harper)

1962 Medal Winner –
Once a Mouse retold & illustrated-**Marcia Brown** (Scribner)
Honor Books –
Fox Went out on a Chilly Night: An Old Song by Peter Spier (Doubleday)
Little Bear's Visit illustrator-**Maurice Sendak**; text-Else H. Minarik (Harper)

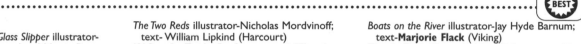

The Day We Saw the Sun Come Up illustrator-Adrienne Adams; text-Alice E. Goudey (Scribner)

1961 Medal Winner –
Baboushka & the Three Kings illustrator-Nicolas Sidjakov; text-Ruth Robbins (Parnassus)
Honor Book –
Inch by Inch, by **Leo Lionni** (Obolensky)

1960 Medal Winner –
Nine Days to Christmas illustrator-**Marie Hall Ets**; text-**Marie Hall Ets** & Aurora Labastida (Viking)
Honor Books –
Houses from the Sea illustrator-Adrienne Adams; text-Alice E. Goudey (Scribner)
The Moon Jumpers illustrator-**Maurice Sendak**; text-Janice May Udry (Harper)

1959 Medal Winner –
Chanticleer & the Fox illustrator-**Barbara Cooney**; text adapted-**Barbara Cooney** from Chaucer's Canterbury Tales (Crowell)
Honor Books –
The House that Jack Built: La Maison Que Jacques A Batie by Antonio Frasconi (Harcourt)
What Do You Say, Dear? illustrator-**Maurice Sendak**; text-Sesyle Joslin (W. R. Scott)
Umbrella by **Taro Yashima** (Viking)

1958 Medal Winner –
Time of Wonder by **Robert McCloskey** (Viking)
Honor Books –
Fly High, Fly Low by **Don Freeman** (Viking)
Anatole & the Cat illustrator-Paul Galdone; text-Eve Titus (McGraw-Hill)

1957 Medal Winner –
A Tree is Nice illustrator-**Marc Simont**; text-Janice Udry (Harper)
Honor Books –
Mr. Penny's Race Horse by **Marie Hall Ets** (Viking)
1 is One by Tasha Tudor (Walck)
Anatole illustrator-Paul Galdone; text-Eve Titus (McGraw-Hill)
Gillespie & the Guards illustrator-James Daugherty; text-Benjamin Elkin (Viking)
Lion by William Pène du Bois (Viking)

1956 Medal Winner –
Frog Went A-Courtin' illustrator-Feodor Rojankovsky; text retold-John Langstaff (Harcourt)
Honor Books –
Play With Me by **Marie Hall Ets** (Viking)
Crow Boy by **Taro Yashima** (Viking)

1955 Medal Winner –
Cinderella, or the Little Glass Slipper illustrator-Marcia Brown; text translated-Marcia Brown from Charles Perrault (Scribner)
Honor Books –
Book of Nursery & Mother Goose Rhymes illustrator-Marguerite de Angeli (Doubleday)
Wheel On The Chimney illustrator-Tibor Gergely; text-**Margaret Wise Brown** (Lippincott)
The Thanksgiving Story illustrator-Helen Sewell; text-Alice Dalgliesh (Scribner)

1954 Medal Winner –
Madeline's Rescue by Ludwig Bemelmans (Viking)
Honor Books –
Journey Cake, Ho! illustrator-**Robert McCloskey**; text-Ruth Sawyer (Viking)
When Will the World Be Mine? illustrator-Jean Charlot; text-Miriam Schlein (W. R. Scott)
The Steadfast Tin Soldier illustrator-Marcia Brown; text-Hans Christian Andersen, translated by M. R. James (Scribner)
A Very Special House illustrator-**Maurice Sendak**; text-Ruth Krauss (Harper)
Green Eyes by A. Birnbaum (Capitol)

1953 Medal Winner –
The Biggest Bear by **Lynd Ward** (Houghton)
Honor Books –
Puss in Boots illustrator-Marcia Brown; text translated-Marcia Brown from Charles Perrault (Scribner)
One Morning in Maine by **Robert McCloskey** (Viking)
Ape in a Cape: An Alphabet of Odd Animals by Fritz Eichenberg (Harcourt)
The Storm Book illustrator-Margaret Graham; text-**Charlotte Zolotow** (Harper)
Five Little Monkeys by Juliet Kepes (Houghton)

1952 Medal Winner –
Finders Keepers illustrator-Nicolas, Nicholas Mordvinoff; text- William Lipkind (Harcourt)
Honor Books –
Mr. T. W. Anthony Woo by **Marie Hall Ets** (Viking)
Skipper John's Cook by Marcia Brown (Scribner)
All Falling Down illustrator-Margaret Bloy Graham; text-Gene Zion (Harper)
Bear Party by William Pène du Bois (Viking)
Feather Mountain by Elizabeth Olds (Houghton)

1951 Medal Winner –
The Egg Tree by Katherine Milhous (Scribner)
Honor Books –
Dick Whittington & his Cat by Marcia Brown (Scribner)

The Two Reds illustrator-Nicholas Mordvinoff; text- William Lipkind (Harcourt)
If I Ran the Zoo by **Dr. Seuss**, pseud. **[Theodor Geisel]** (Random House)
The Most Wonderful Doll in the World illustrator-Helen Stone; text-Phyllis McGinley (Lippincott)
T-Bone, the Baby Sitter by **Clare Turlay Newberry** (Harper)

1950 Medal Winner –
Song of the Swallows by Leo Politi (Scribner)
Honor Books –
America's Ethan Allen illustrator-**Lynd Ward**; text-Stewart Holbrook (Houghton)
The Wild Birthday Cake illustrator-Hildegard Woodward; text-Lavinia R. Davis (Doubleday)
The Happy Day illustrator-**Marc Simont**; text-Ruth Krauss) (Harper)
Bartholomew & the Oobleck by **Dr. Seuss**, **[Theodor Geisel]** (Random House)
Henry Fisherman by Marcia Brown

1949 Medal Winner –
The Big Snow by Berta & Elmer Hader (Macmillan)
Honor Books –
Blueberries for Sal by **Robert McCloskey** (Viking)
All Around the Town illustrator-Helen Stone; text-Phyllis McGinley (Lippincott)
Juanita by Leo Politi (Scribner)
Fish in the Air by **Kurt Wiese** (Viking)

1948 Medal Winner –
White Snow, Bright Snow illustrator-**Roger Duvoisin**; text-**Alvin Tresselt** (Lothrop)
Honor Books –
Stone Soup by Marcia Brown (Scribner)
McElligot's Pool by **Dr. Seuss**, pseud. **[Theodor Geisel]** (Random House)
Bambino the Clown by Georges Schreiber (Viking)
Roger & the Fox illustrator-Hildegard Woodward; text-Lavinia R. Davis (Doubleday)
Song of Robin Hood illustrator-**Virginia Lee Burton**; text-edited Anne Malcolmson (Houghton)

1947 Medal Winner –
The Little Island illustrator-Leonard Weisgard; text-Golden MacDonald, **[Margaret Wise Brown]** (Doubleday)
Honor Books –
Rain Drop Splash illustrator-Leonard Weisgard; text-Alvin Tresselt (Lothrop)

Boats on the River illustrator-Jay Hyde Barnum; text-**Marjorie Flack** (Viking)
Timothy Turtle illustrator-Tony Palazzo; text-Al Graham (Welch)
Pedro, the Angel of Olvera Street by Leo Politi (Scribner)
Sing in Praise: A Collection of the Best Loved Hymns illustrator-Marjorie Torrey; text selected-Opal Wheeler (Dutton)

1946 Medal Winner –
The Rooster Crows by Maude & Miska Petersham (Macmillan)
Honor Books –
Little Lost Lamb illustrator-Leonard Weisgard; text-Golden MacDonald, **[Margaret Wise Brown]** (Doubleday)
Sing Mother Goose illustrator-Marjorie Torrey; music: Opal Wheeler (Dutton)
My Mother is the Most Beautiful Woman in the World illustrator-Ruth Gannett; text-Becky Reyher (Lothrop)
You Can Write Chinese by **Kurt Wiese** (Viking)

1945 Medal Winner –
Prayer for a Child illustrator-Elizabeth Orton Jones; text-Rachel Field (Macmillan)
Honor Books –
Mother Goose illustrator-Tasha Tudor (Oxford University Press)
In the Forest by **Marie Hall Ets** (Viking)
Yonie Wondernose by Marguerite de Angeli (Doubleday)
The Christmas Anna Angel illustrator-Kate Seredy; text-Ruth Sawyer (Viking)

1944 Medal Winner –
Many Moons illustrator-**Louis Slobodkin**; text-James Thurber (Harcourt)
Honor Books –
Small Rain: Verses From The Bible illustrator-Elizabeth Orton Jones; text selected-Jessie Orton Jones (Viking)
Pierre Pigeon illustrator-Arnold E. Bare; text-Lee Kingman (Houghton)
The Mighty Hunter by Berta & Elmer Hader (Macmillan)

You are the best!

A Child's Good Night Book illustrator-Jean Charlot; text-**Margaret Wise Brown** (W. R. Scott)
Good-Luck Horse illustrator-Plato Chan; text-Chih-Yi Chan (Whittlesey)

1943 Medal Winner –
The Little House by **Virginia Lee Burton** (Houghton)
Honor Books –
Dash & Dart by Mary & Conrad Buff (Viking)
Marshmallow by *Clare Turlay Newberry* (Harper)

1942 Medal Winner –
Make Way for Ducklings by **Robert McCloskey** (Viking)
Honor Books –
An American ABC by Maud & Miska Petersham (Macmillan)
In *My Mother's House* illustrator-Velino Herrera; text-Ann Nolan Clark (Viking)
Paddle-To-The-Sea by Holling C. Holling (Houghton)
Nothing At All by **Wanda Gág** (Coward)

1941 Medal Winner –
They Were Strong & Good by Robert Lawson (Viking)
Honor Book –
April's Kittens by **Clare Turlay Newberry** (Harper)

1940 Medal Winner –
Abraham Lincoln by Ingri & Edgar Parin d'Aulaire (Doubleday)
Honor Books –
Cock-a-Doodle Doo by Berta & Elmer Hader (Macmillan)
Madeline by Ludwig Bemelmans (Viking)
The Ageless Story by Lauren Ford (Dodd)

1939 Medal Winner –
Mei Li by Thomas Handforth (Doubleday)
Honor Books –
Andy & the Lion by James Daugherty (Viking)
Barkis by **Clare Turlay Newberry** (Harper)
The Forest Pool by Laura Adams Armer (Longmans)
Snow White & the Seven Dwarfs by **Wanda Gág** (Coward)
Wee Gillis illustrator-Robert Lawson; text-Munro Leaf (Viking)

1938 Medal Winner –
Animals of the Bible, A Picture Book illustrator-Dorothy P. Lathrop; text selected-Helen Dean Fish (Lippincott)
Honor Books –
Four & Twenty Blackbirds illustrator-Robert Lawson; text compiled-Helen Dean Fish (Stokes)
Seven Simeons: A Russian Tale retold & illustrator-Boris Artzybasheff (Viking)

 **THE PARENTS' CHOICE AWARDS**

Parents' Choice has been reviewing children's media since 1978. The title winners featured in *Storybook Art* will be listed in *italic*. View award listings at: www.parents-choice.org

Baby Rattlesnake, T. Ata and L. Moroney, Mira Reisberg (Children'sBook Press), A 1990 Parents' Choice Approved Award Winner
Baby Rattlesnake, T. Ata and L. Moroney. Mira Reisberg (Children'sBook Press), A 1989 Parents' Choice Approved Award Winner
Chicka Chicka Boom Boom, Bill Martin, Lois Ehlert (Simon & Schuster), A 1990 Parents' Choice Silver Award Winner
Fish Eyes, Lois Ehlert (Harcourt Brace Jovanovich), A 1990 Parents' Choice Silver Award Winner*Goldilocks & the Three Bears*, James Marshall
(Dial) A 1988 Parents' Choice Gold Award Winner
Goldilocks & the Three Bears, Jan Brett (Putnam) A 1990 Parents' Choice Gold Award Winner
Grandfather's Journey, Allen Say (Houghton Mifflin) A 1993 Parents' Choice Gold Award Winner
Looking Down, Steve Jenkins (Houghton Mifflin) A 1995 Parents' Choice Silver Award Winner *Olivia*, Ian Falconer (Simon & Schuster) A 2000 Parents' Choice Gold Award Winner
Pigs From A to Z, Arthur Geisert (Houghton Mifflin) A 1996 Parents' Choice Silver Award Winner
The Polar Express, Chris Van Allsberg (Houghton Mifflin) A 1985 Parents' Choice Gold Award Winner
The Quilt, Ann Jonas (Greenwillow) A 1984 Parents' Choice Silver Award Winner
Smoky Night, Eve Bunting, David Diaz (Harcourt Brace) A 1994 Parents' Choice Gold Award Winner
Snow, Uri Shulevitz (FSG) A 1998 Parents' Choice Recommended Award Winner

 BOOKSENSE BOOK OF THE YEAR AWARD (formerly The ABBY Award)

BookSense winners are chosen by independent booksellers for titles they have most enjoyed selling the previous year. Titles, authors, or illustrators featured in **Storybook Art** will be highlighted in **bold**. View award listings at: www.bookweb.org/news/awards/3433.html

2002
Children's Literature WINNER –
The Sisterhood of the Traveling Pants by Ann Brashares
FINALISTS –
Love That Dog by Sharon Creech
Witness by Karen Hesse
You Read to Me & I'll Read to You ed. by Janet Schulman
Angus, Thongs, & Full-Frontal Snogging by Louise Rennison

Illustrated Children's Book WINNER –
Olivia Saves the Circus by **Ian Falconer**
FINALISTS –
Stand Tall, Molly Lou Melon by Patty Lovell illustrator-David Catrow
Take Me Out of the Bathtub by Alan Katz illustrator-David Catrow
The Water Hole by Graeme Base
The Dinosaurs of Waterhouse Hawkins by Barbara Kerley illustrator-Brain Selznick

Rediscovery WINNER –
My Father's Dragon by Ruth Stiles Gannett
Freddy The Detective by Walter Brooks
Handling Sin by Michael Malone
Time Stops For No Mouse by Michael Hoeye
Enchantress From the Stars by Sylvia Louis Engdah

2001
Children's Literature WINNER –
Because of Winn-Dixie by Kate DiCamillo
FINALISTS –
Bad Beginning by Lemony Snicket
The Giggler Treatment by Roddy Doyle
Stargirl by Jerry Spinelli
The Wanderer by Sharon Creech, **David Diaz**-illustrator

Illustrated Children's Book WINNER –
Olivia by **Ian Falconer**-illustrator/author
FINALISTS –
Click Clack Moo: Cows That Type by Doreen Cronin, Betsy Lewin-illustrator

How Do Dinosaurs Say Goodnight? by Jane Yolen, Mark Teague-illustrator
I Love You Like Crazy Cakes by Rose A. Lewis, Jane Dyer-illustrator
Stranger in the Woods by Jean Stoick, Carl R. Sams, II-illustrator

Children's WINNER –
The Quiltmaker's Gift Jeff Brumbeau illustrator-Gail de Marcken (Pfeiffer-Hamilton)
FINALISTS –
Amelia & Eleanor Go for a Ride Pam Muñoz Ryan illustrator-Brian Selznick (Scholastic)
Bud, Not Buddy by Christopher Paul Curtis (Delacorte)
Sector 7 by **David Wiesner** (Houghton)
The 20th Century Children's Poetry Treasury edited by Jack Prelutsky illustrator-Meilo So (Knopf)

1999
Children's ABBY WINNER –
Harry Potter & the Sorcerer's Stone by J.K. Rowling illustrator-Mary Grandpré (Scholastic)
ABBY Children's Honor Books –
If You Give a Pig a Pancake by Laura Numeroff illustrator-Felicia Bond (HarperCollins)
Look Alikes by **Joan Steiner** (Little, Brown & Company)
Squids Will Be Squids: Fresh Morals, Beastly Fables by Jon Scieszka illustrator-Lane Smith (Viking)
Today I Feel Silly & Other Moods That Make My Day by Jamie Lee Curtis illustrator-Laura Cornell (Joanna Cotler Books)

1998
Children's ABBY WINNER –
The Hat by **Jan Brett** (Putnam Publishing Group)
ABBY Children's Honor Books –
The Gardener by Sarah Stewart illustrator-David Small (Farrar, Straus & Giroux)
To Market, To Market by Anne Miranda illustrator-Janet Stevens (Harcourt)
Toot & Puddle, Holly Hobbie (Little, Brown)
When Jessie Came Across the Sea by Amy Hest illustrator-P. J. Lynch (Candlewick)

1997
Children's ABBY WINNER –
Lilly's Purple Plastic Purse by Kevin Henkes (Greenwillow)
Children's ABBY Honor Books –
Falling Up by **Shel Silverstein** (HarperCollins)
The Golden Compass by Philip Pullman (Alfred A. Knopf)

(1997 cont.)
My Many Colored Days by **Dr. Seuss**, paintings by Steve Johnson & Lou Fancher (Knopf)
My Very First Mother Goose edited by Iona Opie illustrator-Rosemary Wells (Candlewick)

1996
Children's ABBY WINNER –
Guess How Much I Love You by Sam McBratney illustrator-Anita Jeram (Candlewick)
Children's ABBY Honor Books (in alphabetical order) –
Catherine, Called Birdy by Karen Cushman (Clarion;Harper Trophy)
The Library by Sarah Stewart illustrator-David Small (Farrar, Straus & Giroux)
Math Curse by Jon Scieszka illustrator-Lane Smith (Viking)
Miss Spider's Tea Party by **David Kirk** (Scholastic)

1995
Children's ABBY WINNER –
The Rainbow Fish by **Marcus Pfister** (North-South)
Children's ABBY Nominees –
All the Places to Love by Patricia MacLachlan illustrator-Mike Wimmer (Charlotte Zolotow/HarperCollins)
The Giver by Lois Lowry (Houghton Mifflin;Dell)
Miss Spider's Tea Party by **David Kirk** (Scholastic)
Penguin Small by Mick Inkpen (Harcourt)
Pink & Say by **Patricia Polacco** (Philomel/Putnam)
Red Ranger Came Calling by Berkeley Breathed (Little, Brown)
Ship of Dreams by Dean Morrissey (Harry N. Abrams)
Time for Bed by Mem Fox illustrator-Jane Dyer (Harcourt)
Town Mouse, Country Mouse **Jan Brett** (Putnam)

1994
Children's ABBY WINNER –
Stellaluna by Janell Cannon (Harcourt)
Children's ABBY Nominees –
Emily by Michael Bedard, illustrator-**Barbara Cooney** (Doubleday)
The Giver by Lois Lowry (Houghton Mifflin)
Mama, Do You Love Me? by Barbara M. Joosse illustrator-Barbara Lavallee (Chronicle)
The Rainbabies by Laura Melmed illustrator-Jim LaMarche (Lothrop, Lee & Shepard)
Rainbow Fish by **Marcus Pfister** (North-South)
Santa Calls by William Joyce (HarperCollins)

The Stinky Cheese Man by Jon Scieszka illustrator-Lane Smith (Viking)
The Three Little Wolves & the Big Bad Pig by Eugene Trivizas illustrator-Helen Oxenbury (Macmillan)
Time for Bed by Mem Fox illustrator-Jane Dyer (Harcourt)

1993
Children's ABBY WINNER –
Old Turtle by Douglas Wood illustrator-Cheng-Khee Chee (Pfeifer-Hamilton)
Children's ABBY Nominees –
Dinotopia: A Land Apart from Time by James Gurney (Turner)
Emily by Michael Bedard illustrator-**Barbara Cooney** (Doubleday)
Love You Forever by **Robert Munsch** illustrator-**Sheila McGraw** (Firefly)
Martha Speaks by Susan Meddaugh (Houghton Mifflin)
On the Day You Were Born by Debra Frasier (Harcourt)
The Rainbabies by Laura Melmed illustrator-Jim LaMarche (Lothrop, Lee & Shepard)
The Stinky Cheese Man: And Other Fairly Stupid Tales by Jon Scieszka illustrator-Lane Smith (Viking)
The Trouble with Trolls by **Jan Brett** (Putnam)
The True Story of the Three Little Pigs by Jon Scieszka illustrator-Lane Smith (Viking)

1992
ABBY WINNER –
Brother Eagle, Sister Sky: A Message from Chief Seattle by Susan Jeffers, illus. (Dial)

THE CHARLOTTE ZOLOTOW AWARD

The annual **Charlotte Zolotow Award** is given to the author of the best picture book text published in the USA. The award honors Charlotte Zolotow, a children's book editor and author of 65+ picture books, including *Mr. Rabbit & the Lovely Present* and *William's Doll*. Titles, authors, or illustrators featured in *Storybook Art* will be highlighted in **bold**.

2002 WINNER –
Willey, Margaret. *Clever Beatrice*. Illustrator-Heather Solomon. Atheneum, 2001.
Honor Book –
Jenkins, Emily. *Five Creatures*. Frances Foster / Farrar Straus Giroux, 2001.

Highly Commended –
Look, Lenore. *Henry's First Moon Birthday*. Illustrator-Yumi Heo. Anne Schwartz/ Atheneum, 2001.
MacDonald, Margaret Read. *Mabela the Clever*. Illustrator-Tim Coffey. Albert Whitman, 2001.
Russo, Marisabina. *Come Back, Hannah*. Greenwillow/HarperCollins, 2001.
Stock, Catherine. *Gugu's House*. Clarion, 2001.
Wong, Janet S. *Grump*. Illustrator-John Wallace. Margaret K. McElderry, 2001.

2001 WINNER –
Banks, Kate. *The Night Worker*. Illustrator-Georg Hallensleben. Frances Foster / Farrar Straus Giroux, 2000.
Honor Book –
Myers, Christopher. *Wings*. Scholastic Press, 2000.
Highly Commended –
Christian, Peggy. *If You Find a Rock*. Illustrator-Barbara Hirsch Lember. Harcourt, 2000.
Cronin, Doreen. *Click Clack Moo: Cows that Type*. Illustrator-Betsy Lewin. Simon & Schuster, 2000.
Harjo, Joy. *The Good Luck Cat*. Illustrator-Paul Lee. Harcourt, 2000.
Kajikawa, Kimiko. *Yoshi's Feast*. Illustrator-Yumi Heo. Melanie Kroupa/DK Ink, 2000.
Pinkney, Sandra L. *Shades of Black: A Celebration of Our Children*. Photographs-Myles C. Pinkney. Scholastic, 2000.
Van Laan, Nancy. *When Winter Comes*. Illustrator-Susan Gaber. Anne Schwartz/Atheneum, 2000.

2000 WINNER –
Bang, Molly. *When Sophie Gets Angry- Really, Really Angry*, Blue Sky/Scholastic, 1999
Honor Books –
Best, Cari. *Three Cheers for Catherine the Great!* Illustrator-Giselle Potter. Melanie Kroupa/DK Ink, 1999.
Feiffer, Jules. *Bark, George*. Michael di Capua/HarperCollins, 1999
Highly Commended –
Diakité, Baba Wagué. *The Hatseller & the Monkeys*. Scholastic, 1999
George, Kristine O'Connell. *Little Dog Poems*. Illustrator-June Otani. Clarion, 1999
Graham, Joan Bransfield. *Flicker Flash*. Illustrator-Nancy Davis. Houghton Mifflin, 1999
Howard, Elizabeth Fitzgerald. *When Will Sarah Come?* Illustrator-Nina Crews. Greenwillow, 1999
Schwartz, Amy. *How to Catch an Elephant*. DK Ink, 1999

Thomas, Joyce Carol. *You Are My Perfect Baby*. Illustrator-Nneka Bennett. Harper Growing Tree/HarperCollins, 1999
Zimmerman, Andrea & David Clemesha. *Trashy Town*. HarperCollins, 1999

1999 WINNER –
Shulevitz, Uri. *Snow*. Farrar Straus Giroux, 1998
Honor Books –
Meade, Holly. *John Willy & Freddy McGee*. Marshall Cavendish, 1998
Steig, William. *Pete's a Pizza*. Michael di Capua/HarperCollins, 1998
Highly Commended –
Fleming, Denise. *Mama Cat Has Three Kittens*. Henry Holt, 1998
Henkes, Kevin. *Circle Dogs*. illustrator-Dan Yaccarino. Greenwillow, 1998
Jones, Bill T. & Susan Kuklin. *Dance*. photographs by Susan Kuklin. Hyperion, 1998
Reiser, Lynn. *Little Clam*. Greenwillow, 1998
Stuve-Bodeen, Stephanie. *Elizabeth's Doll*. illustrator-Christy Hale. Lee & Low, 1998

1998 WINNER –
Williams, Vera B. *Lucky Song*. Greenwillow, 1997
Honor Book –
Kasza, Keiko. *Don't Laugh, Joe!* Putnam, 1997
Highly Commended –
Bauer, Marion Dane. *If You Were Born a Kitten*. Illustrator-JoEllen McAllister Stammen. Simon & Schuster, 1997
Cooper, Elisha. *Country Fair*. Greenwillow, 1997
Fleming, Denise. *Time to Sleep*. Henry Holt, 1997

McKissack, Patricia C. *Ma Dear's Aprons*. Illustrator-Floyd Cooper. Anne Schwartz/Atheneum, 1997
Waber, Bernard. *Bearsie Bear & the Surprise Sleepover Party*. Houghton Mifflin, 1997
Wells, Rosemary. *Bunny Cakes*. Dial, 1997

As a rule, I tend to read books about worms - now and then, a book about bugs.

BIG AWARDS PARTY FRIDAY!

• • •

Dress as your favorite illustrator, author or book character!

• • •

AWARDS PARTY
2 PM Friday
! WEAR COSTUMES !

Love You Forever
Robert Munsch, illustrator - Sheila McGraw

1993 CHILDREN'S ABBY WINNER

Tar Beach
Faith Ringgold

1992 CALDECOTT HONOR

BOSTON GLOBE – HORN BOOK AWARDS

The **Boston Globe & The Horn Book, Inc.** recognize excellence in literature for children and young adults. Not all categories receive awards each year. Picture Book & Illustration categories are listed (youth awards for older children are omitted). Authors, illustrators and titles featured *StorybookArt* are highlighted in **bold**. View categories and recipients at: multimedia.tamucommerce.edu/library/boston.htm

2001 Picture Book –
Cold Feet author-Cynthia DeFelice
   illustrator-Robert Andrew Parker. (DK Ink)
Honor Books –
Five Creatures
   author-Emily Jenkins
   illustrator-Tomek Bogacki.(Foster/Farrar).
Stray Dog, The
   retold & illustrator-**Marc Simont**.
   (HarperCollins).

2000 Picture Book –
Henry Hikes to Fitchburg
   author/illustrator-D. B. Johnson. (Houghton).
Honor Books –
Buttons
   author/illustrator-Brock Cole. (Farrar).
A Day, A Dog
   illustrator-Gabrielle Vincent. (Front Street).

1999 Picture Book –
Red-Eyed Tree Frog
   author-Joy Cowley, photographer/illustrator-
   Nic Bishop. (Scholastic Press).
Honor Books –
Dance
   author-Bill T. Jones & Susan Kuklin,
   photographer/illustrator-Susan Kuklin.
   (Hyperion).
Owl & the Pussycat, The
   author-Edward Lear illustrator-James
   Marshall. (di Capus/ HarperCollins).
Special Citation –
Tibet: Through the Red Box
   author/illustrator-Peter Sis. (Foster/Farrar).

1998 Picture Book –
And If the Moon Could Talk
   author-Kate Banks illustrator-Georg
   Hallensleben. (Foster/Farrar).

Honor Books –
Seven Brave Women
   author-Betsy Hearne illustrator-Bethanne
   Anderson. (Greenwillow)
Popcorn: Poems
   author/illustrator James Stevenson.
   (Greenwillow).

1997 Picture Book –
Adventures of Sparrowboy, The
   author/illustrator-Brian Pinkney. (Simon)
Honor Books –
Home on the Bayou: A Cowboy's Story
   author/illustrator G. Brian Karas. (Simon)
Potato: A Tale from the Great Depression
   author-Kate Lied illustrator-Lisa Campbell
   Ernst. (National Geographic)

1996 Picture Book –
In the Rain with Baby Duck
   author Amy Hest illustrator-Jill Barton.
   (Candlewick).
Honor Books –
Fanny's Dream
   author-Caralyn Buehner illustrator-**Mark
   Buehner**. (Dial).
Home Lovely
   author-Lynne Rae Perkins. (Greenwillow)

1995 Picture Book –
John Henry
   retold by Julius Lester illustrator-Jerry
   Pinkney. (Dial).
Honor Books –
Swamp Angel
   author-Anne Isaacs illustrator-Paul O.
   Zelinsky. (Dutton).

1994 Picture Book –
Grandfather's Journey by **Allen Say**
(Houghton). [Caldecott]
Honor Books –
Owen
   author-Kevin Henkes. (Greenwillow).
Small Tall Tale from the Far Far North, A
   author-Peter Sis. (Knopf).

1993 Picture Book –
Fortune Tellers, The
   author-Lloyd Alexander
   illustrator-Trina Schart Hyman. (Dutton).
Honor Books
Komodo! by Peter Sis. (Greenwillow)
Raven: A Trickster Tale from the Pacific Northwest
   author-Gerald McDermott. (Harcourt).

1992 Picture Book –
Seven Blind Mice
   author-**Ed Young**. (Philomel).
Honor Book –
In the Tall, Tall Grass
   author-**Denise Fleming**. (Holt).
1991 Picture Book –
Tale of the Mandarin Ducks, The
   author-Katharine Paterson illustrator-Leo &
   Diane Dillon. (Lodestar).
Honor Books –
Aardvarks, Disembark!
   author-**Ann Jonas**. (Greenwillow).
Sophie & Lou
   author-Petra Mathers. (Harper).

1990 Picture Book –
Lon Po Po: A Red-Riding Hood Story from China
   translator/illustrator-**Ed Young**. (Philomel).
   [Caldecott 398.2]
Honor Books –
Chicka Chicka Boom Boom
   authors **Bill Martin, Jr.** & **John Archambault**
   & illustrator-**Lois Ehlert**. (Simon).
We're Going on a Bear Hunt
   retold by Michael Rosen illustrator-Helen
   Oxenbury. (McElderry).

1989 Picture Book –
Shy Charles author-Rosemary Wells. (Dial).
Honor Books –
Nativity, The
   illustrator-Julie Vivas. (Gulliver/Harcourt).
Island Boy
   author-**Barbara Cooney**. (Viking Kestrel).

1988 Picture Book –
Boy of the Three-Year Nap, The
   author-Dianne Snyder illustrator-**Allen Say**.
   (Houghton).
Honor Books –
Where the Forest Meets the Sea author-Jeannie
   Baker. Greenwillow).
Stringbean's Trip to the Shining Sea
   author Vera B. Williams, illustrator-Jennifer &
   Vera G. Williams. (Greenwillow).

1987 Picture Book –
Mufaro's Beautiful Daughters: An African Tale
   author-John Steptoe. (Lothrop).
Honor Books –
In Coal Country
   author-Judith Hendershot illustrator-Thomas
   B. Allen. (Knopf).
Cherries & Cherry Pits
   author-Vera B. Williams. (Greenwillow).

Old Henry
author-Joan W. Blos illustrator-**Stephen Gammell**. (Morrow).
1986 illustration –
Paper Crane, The
author-**Molly Bang**. (Greenwillow).
Honor Books
Gorilla
author-Anthony Browne. (Knopf)
Trek, The
author-**Ann Jonas**. (Greenwillow)
Polar Express, The
author-**Chris Van Allsburg**. (Houghton).
[Caldecott]

1985 Illustration –
Mama Don't Allow
author-Thacher Hurd. (Harper)
Honor Books –
Like Jake & Me
author-Mavis Jukes illustrator-Lloyd Bloom.(Knopf).
How Much Is a Million?
author-David Schwartz illustrator-Steven Kellogg. (Lothrop). *Mysteries of Harris Burdick, The* author-**Chris Van Allsburg**. (Houghton).

1984 Illustration –
Jonah & the Great Fish
retold/illustrator-Warwick Hutton. (McElderry/Atheneum).
Honor Books –
Dawn author-**Molly Bang**. (Morrow)
Guinea Pig ABC, The
author-Kate Duke. (Dutton)
Rose in My Garden, The
author-Arnold Lobel illustrator-**Anita Lobel.** (Greenwillow)

1983 Illustration –
Chair For My Mother, A
author-Vera B. Williams. (Greenwillow).
Honor Books –
Friends
author-Helme Heine. (Atheneum/ McElderry).
Yeh Shen: A Cinderella Story from China author-Ai-Ling Louie
illustrator-**Ed Young**. (Philomel).
Doctor De Soto author-**William Steig**. (Farrar).

1982 Illustration –
Visit to William Blake's Inn, A: Poems for Innocent & Experienced Travelers
author-Nancy Willard illustrator-Alice & Martin Provensen. (HBJ). [Newbery]

Honor Books –
Friendly Beasts, The: An Old English Christmas Carol
author-**Tomie dePaola**. (Putnam).

1981 Illustration –
Outside Over There author-**Maurice Sendak.** (Harper).
Honor Books –
Jumanji
author-**Chris Van Allsburg** (Houghton). [Caldecott]
On Market Street
author-Arnold Lobel illustrator-**Anita Lobel.** (Greenwillow)
Where the Buffaloes Begin
author-Olaf Baker illustrator-**Stephen Gammell**. (Warne).

1980
Illustration –
Garden of Abdul Gasazi, The
author-**Chris Van Allsburg**. (Houghton).
Honor Books –
Grey Lady & the Strawberry Snatcher, The
author-**Molly Bang**. (Four Winds).
Why the Tides Ebb & Flow
author-Joan Chase Bowden illustrator-Marc Brown. (Houghton).

1979 Illustration –
Snowman, The
author-Raymond Briggs. (Random).
Honor Books –
Ben's Trumpet
author-Rachel Isadora. (Greenwillow).
Cross-Country Cat
author-Mary Calhoun illustrator-Erick Ingraham. (Morrow)

1978 Illustration –
Anno's Journey
author-Mitsumasa Anno. (Philomel).
Honor Books
Story of Edward, The
author-Philippe Dumas. (Parents)
On to Widecombe Fair author-Patricia Lee Gauch illustrator-Trina Schart Hyman. (Putnam)
What Do You Feed Your Donkey On? Rhymes from a Belfast Childhood author-Collette O'Hare illustrator-Jenny Rodwell. (Collins-World)

1977 Illustration –
Granpa Grig Had a Pig & Other Rhymes Without Reason from Mother Goose
author-Wallace Tripp. (Little).
Honor Books –
Anno's Counting Book
author-Mitsumasa Anno. (Crowell).

Ashanti to Zulu: African Traditions
author-Margaret Musgrove illustrator-Leo & Diane Dillon. (Dial). [Caldecott]
Amazing Bone, The
author-**William Steig**. (Farrar).

1976
Illustration –
Thirteen
author-Remy Charlip & Jerry Joyner. (Four Winds).
Honor Books –
Desert is Theirs, The
author-Byrd Baylor illustrator-Peter Parnall. (Scribner).
Six Little Ducks
author-Chris Conover. (Crowell)
Song of the Boat
author-Lorenz Graham illustrator-Leo & Diane Dillon. (Crowell)
1975
Text –
Transport 7-41-R
author-T. Degens. (Viking)
Honor Book –
Hundred Penny Box, The
author-Sharon Bell Mathis illustrator-Leo & Diane Dillon. (Viking)
Illustration –
Anno's Alphabet
author-Mitsumasa Anno. (Crowell).

Honor Books –
She Come Bringing Me That Little Baby Girl
author-Eloise Greenfield illustrator-John Steptoe. (Lippincott).
Scram, Kid!
author-Ann McGovern illustrator-Nola Langer. (Viking)
Bear's Bicycle, The
author-Emilie Warren McLeod illustrator-David McPhil. (Atlantic-Little).

Capture a picture of a favorite book cover on film - then frame it, & display it on the wall!

1974
Text –
M.C. Higgins, the Great author-Virginia Hamilton. (Macmillan). [Newbery]
Honor Books –
And Then What Happened, Paul Revere? author-Jean Fritz.
Summer After the Funeral, The
author-Jane Gardam
Tough Chauncey
author-Doris Buchanan Smith

Illustration –
Jambo Means Hello
author-Muriel Feelings illustrator-Tom Feelings. (Dial).
Honor Books –
All Butterflies: An ABC Book
author Marcia Brown.
Herman the Helper
author-Robert Kraus illustrator-Jose Aruego & Ariane Dewey.
Prairie Boy's Winter, A
author-William Kurelek.

1973
Text –
Dark is Rising, The
author-Susan Cooper. (McElderry/Atheneum).
Honor Books –
Cat Who Wished To Be A Man, The
author-Lloyd Alexander.
An Island in the Green Sea author-Mabel Esther Allan
No Way of Telling author-Emma Smith

Illustration –
King Stork
illustrator-Trina Schart Hyman.
Honor Books –
Magic Tree, The
author-Gerald McDermott.
Who, Said Sue, Said Whoo?
author-Ellen Raskin.
Silver Pony, The
author-**Lynd Ward.**

1972
Text –
Tristan & Iseult
author-Rosemary Sutcliff. (Dutton).
illustration –
Mr. Gumpy's Outing
author-John Burningham. (Holt).

The Randolph Caldecott Medal

Embark on a *READING ADVENTURE!* Begin with a 1944 Caldecott award-winning book, and read each and every book through present day medalists.

READING *EVERY* CALDECOTT IS FUN !

So many books, and all the time you need!

Sometimes a good book just makes you want to turn yourself upside down and shout HIP HIP HOORAY !

...Indeed !

Portraiture Story Art based on The Lonely Doll by Dare Wright

Picture Book Index : Art Activity Index

.... EASY INDEX KEY ....
 i *illustrator*
 a *author*
 i a *illustrator & author*
 Picture Book Title
 ART ACTIVITY
 art materials

 A

A Tree is Nice, 61
ABC STICKS, 97
ACCENTED PENCIL, 49
acetate, 15, 112
ACETATE LAYERS, 15
acorn caps, 103
adding machine tape, 51
Alison's Zinnia, 25
ALL IN A ROW, ONE-LINE DESIGN, 51
Allen Say i a, **110**
Alligator Shoes, 95
ALPHA-BAGGIE BOOK, 25
Alphabet City, 73
aluminum foil, 100, 103
Alvin R. Tresselt a, **80, 96**
animals, stuffed, 117
Anita Lobel i a , **25**
Ann Jonas i a, **74**
art tissue, 34, 81, 83, 88
Arthur Dorros i a, **95**
Arthur Geisert i a, **97**
ASSEMBLED NOODLES, 107
ASSEMBLED TREE RUBBINGS, 61
Audrey Wood a, **116**

 B

Baby Rattlesnake, 83
bag (paper sack), 61
  grocery, 29
  bakery white, 111
baking pan, 19, 110
ball, 16, 18
BALLOON SCULPTURE, 93
balloons, 93
ballpoint pen, 38, 54, 59
bamboo skewer, 54, 107, 115
band-aids, 101
bar of soap, 26, 52
Barbara Emberley a, **48**
Barbara Garrison i a, **22**
Barbara Reid i, **108**

bare feet, 36
Barnyard Banter, 98
basket, 61
BATH-TIME PAINTS, 116
bathtub, 97, 116
beach pebbles, 105
beads, 72, 92, 94, 95, 105, 114
beans, dry, 113
Beatrice Orcutt Harrell (retold) a, **85**
Beatrice Schenk De Regniers a, **106**
beets, 37
BEHIND-THE-SCENE, 44
Beni Montresor i, **106**
Bernard Lodge i a, **26**
berry basket, plastic or paper, 113
Beth Krommes i, **52**
Bill Martin, Jr. a, **16**
birthday candles, 113
black & white film, 76
black paper circles 1"-2" [3cm-5cm], 46
blacktop, 36
blanket, old, 74
block, 26, 30
  Styrofoam, 96
  of wood, 20, 26
BLUE FINGERDOTS, 27
blueberries, 27
Blueberries for Sal, 27
BOLD MARKING, 48
books, 98, 117
bottle, spray, 112
bottle caps, 103, 113
bottle of ketchup, 87
bow pasta, noodles, 107
bows, 101
box, 38, 47, 61, 102
  cardboard, 21
brads, 102, 115
braid, 92
branches, evergreen, 110
branches, fresh, 97
bread dough, edible, 114
bricks, 98
bristle block, 28
BROWN BAG PAINTING, 29
Brown Bear, Brown Bear What Do You See?, 16
brown leaves, 37
Bruce Degen i, **47**
bunion pads, 26
burlap, 16, 28, 84, 92, 94
butcher paper, 28, 83
buttons, 19, 72, 92, 94, 95, 103, 105, 106, 113, 114

C

cake circle, 23
CALENDAR HAT, 101
camera, 73, 76, 117
Candace Whitman i a, **88**
candy sprinkles, 23
cardboard, 18, 20, 22, 28, 33, 67, 72, 75, 78, 84, 87, 88, 92, 93, 100, 102, 110, 113
  box, 21, 38, 57
  corrugated, 22, 53
  painter's bucket, 27
Carole Lexa Schaefer a, **29**
Caroline Repchuk a, **54**
Carousel, 17
carpet, 93, 102
carpet scrap, 113
carrot, 30, 66
cartoon drawings, 60
CAT & MOUSE PRINTS, 20
CD (compact disc), 106
CD (compact disc) box, 44
cellophane, 34, 94
cereal, 113
chairs, toy furniture, 117
chalk, 17, 35, 42, 45, 49, 51, 53, 54, 55, 60
charcoal, 55
charcoal drawing sticks, 55
CHARCOAL SKETCH, 55
Charles G. Shaw i a, **33**
Charlotte Zolotow a, **105**
charred wood, 55
checkers, 113
Cheryl Chapman a, **86**
Chris Van Allsburg i a, **34**
Christopher Knight i, **76**
Clare Beaton i, **92**
Clare Turlay Newberry i a, **55**
CLASSIC ILLUSTRATING, 63
clay ball, 38
clay or play clay, 103, 108, 114
CLAY TEA SET, 103
clear hobby sealer, 55
Clement Hurd i, **102**
CLONE COLLAGE, 90
clothes, old, 74, 84
cocktail straws, 107
coffee grounds, 37
coffee stir sticks, 107
collage items, 22, 23, 61, 72, 101, 103, 105, 106, 113, 115
COLLAGRAPH, 22
collection, 72
COLOR OUTLINE, 14
comb, 28
computer mouse pad, 20
confetti, 22, 93, 98, 100

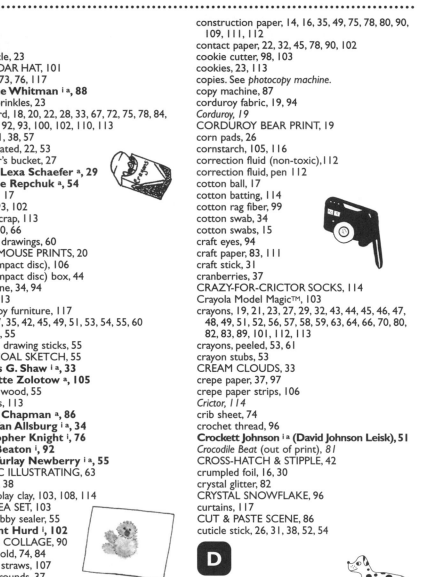

construction paper, 14, 16, 35, 49, 75, 78, 80, 90, 109, 111, 112
contact paper, 22, 32, 45, 78, 90, 102
cookie cutter, 98, 103
cookies, 23, 113
copies. See *photocopy machine.*
copy machine, 87
corduroy fabric, 19, 94
Corduroy, 19
CORDUROY BEAR PRINT, 19
corn pads, 26
cornstarch, 105, 116
correction fluid (non-toxic), 112
correction fluid, pen 112
cotton ball, 17
cotton batting, 114
cotton rag fiber, 99
cotton swab, 34
cotton swabs, 15
craft eyes, 94
craft paper, 83, 111
craft stick, 31
cranberries, 37
CRAZY-FOR-CRICTOR SOCKS, 114
Crayola Model Magic™, 103
crayons, 19, 21, 23, 27, 29, 32, 43, 44, 45, 46, 47, 48, 49, 51, 52, 56, 57, 58, 59, 63, 64, 66, 70, 80, 82, 83, 89, 101, 112, 113
crayons, peeled, 53, 61
crayon stubs, 53
CREAM CLOUDS, 33
crepe paper, 37, 97
crepe paper strips, 106
Crictor, 114
crib sheet, 74
crochet thread, 96
Crockett Johnson i a **(David Johnson Leisk), 51**
Crocodile Beat (out of print), *81*
CROSS-HATCH & STIPPLE, 42
crumpled foil, 16, 30
crystal glitter, 82
CRYSTAL SNOWFLAKE, 96
curtains, 117
CUT & PASTE SCENE, 86
cuticle stick, 26, 31, 38, 52, 54

D

Dale H. Fife a, **40**
Daniel Manus Pinkwater i a, **57**
Dare Wright i a, **117**
David A. Carter i a, **94**
David Johnson Leisk i a **(Crockett Johnson), 51**
David Kirk i a, **103**
David McKee i a, **28**
David Wiesner i a, **89**
David Wisniewski i a, **115**

Easy Index

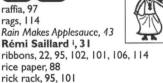

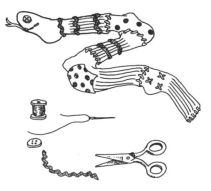

Art Activity • Page Order Index

A to Z Art Activities in the order in which they appear in Storybook Art.
(See the Chart of Contents for illustrator order of appearance.)

Mini-Gallery of Children's Fine Artworks in the Styles of Favorite Picture Book Illustrators

WHITE HOUSE STORY QUILT
artist unknown, age 8
in the style of
Tar Beach
by Faith Ringgold

DIVING DUCKS
by Jazmin Mendoza, age 8
in the style of
The Story About Ping
by Marjorie Flack
illustrator – Kurt Wiese

BLACK DOT MOUSE
artist unknown, age 6
in the style of
Ten Black Dots
by Donald Crews

SNOWY DAY SLED RIDE
by Morgan Van Slyke, age 7
in the style of
The Snowy Day
by Ezra Jack Keats

BOLD AIRPLANE
by Jalani Phelps, age 8
in the style of
Drummer Hoff
by Barbara & Ed Emberley

Because **Storybook Art** is a book about great illustrators and their art for children, it seems appropriate (and both fun and exciting) that **children illustrate their favorite illustrators.** The young Washington state artists range in age from 5-16, and individually chose an art method to create portrait sketches of 100 illustrators. Their choices of styles & techniques include: pencil, ink, crayon, marking pen, pen, and computer graphics. Most portraits were inspired by a photograph or photocopy of the book illustrator. These young artists are dedicated illustrators-to-be, putting forth amazing effort as well as cheerfully meeting deadlines. One day these kids may be among the highly respected Caldecott Medalists! Each young artist hopes the book illustrators will enjoy their portraits. All artwork is original (inspired by photographs in some cases), and is generously contributed to **Storybook Art**. ***Please join in thanking each and every one of these great kids.***

Student's Name	Town	Page #	Interests
Briley Ammons, 12	Lynden	45, 108	Singing, baseball, history, horses
Abby Asplund, 8	Bellingham	101	Reading, dance, piano, dolls
John Asplund, 13	Bellingham	21	Sports, piano, snowboarding, art
Monika Baranek, 11	Bellingham	72, 89, 114	Reading, singing, acting, art
Sonia Baranek, 8	Bellingham	64, 77	Writing, drawing, horse books
Abby Brandt, 5	Poulsbo	18, 55, 69, 70, 92	Dolls, Legos, singing
Molly Brandt, 7	Poulsbo	14, 17, 19, 46, 49, 80	Dolls, reading, art
Casey Collins, 11	Lynden	60	Basketball, swimming
Kayla Comstock, 8	Lynden	49, 65, 91, 108	Drawing, coloring, sleeping
Eleanor Davis, 12	Bainbridge Is	15, 16, 44, 56, 66, 83, 94, 98, 109	Music, clam-digging
Andrew DeMann, 10	Lynden	28	Sports, video games, pets, art
Derek DeMann, 12	Lynden	30	Sports, biking, skateboarding
Henry Dotson III, 8	Lynden	82	Hobbies
Jodi Drost, 15	Ferndale	48, 78, 82, 106	Read, swim, dance, violin
Jordan Drost, 16	Ferndale	13, 48, 75, 79, 86, 107	Swimming, piano, drawing
Christina Duim , 11	Bellingham	102	Drawing, playing piano, animals
Geneva Faulkner, 14	Ferndale	31, 110	Music, violin, piano, acting
Shon Gorsuch, 7	Lynden	24, 84	Playing soccer with friend
Lindsey Harkness, 12	Samish Is	12, 62	Writing, drawing, acting
Tatiana Huaracha, 8	Lynden	121	Hobbies
Peter James, 8	Lynden	121	Hobbies
Kayla Johnston, 8	Lynden	29	Art, playing with friends
Lauren Kaemingk, 11	Lynden	57, 73, 95, 97, 116	Draw, swim, basketball, writing
Elizabeth Kayser, 11	Lynden	52	Baseball, reading, watercolors
Meagan Kivlighn , 9	Lynden	37	Playing basketball, drawing
Molly Koker, 9	Lynden	13	Playing basketball
Torie Lee, 10	Lynden	105	Crafts, art, horses, dogs, cats
Jazmin Mendoza, 8	Lynden	46, 65, 139	Soccer, writing, drawing

Student's Name	Town	Page #	Interests
Adriana Mitchell, 8	Lynden	48	Hobbies
Taylor Niemi, 11	Lynden	27, 112	Football, sports, drawing
Kailey Olson, 9	Lynden	29, 58, 113	Dogs, cats, drawing, friends
Lauren Olson, 10	Lynden	67, 85, 109	Dogs, reading, drawing animals
Mikal Olson, 8	Lynden	115	Drawing, street hockey
Brittany Peterson, 9	Lynden	32	Studying planets, drawing
Jalani Phelps, 8	Lynden	139	Sports
Kate Propersi, 11	Lynden	50	Horses, movies, watercolors
Valeria Quiroz-Nava, 8	Lynden	13, 39, 46, 56	Reading, exercising, painting
Jennifer Reinstra, 9	Lynden	20, 25, 51, 60, 76, 87, 88, 93, 96, 143	Swim, draw, paint, read
Hannah Robinson, 9	Lynden	36, 64	Drawing
Kenzi Robinson, 9	Lynden	53, 63, 104	Horses, drawing animals, soccer
Carley Roddy, 8	Lynden	13, 57	Reading, drawing, T-Ball
Laura Sanchez, 9	Lynden	26, 33, 42, 61, 117	Drawing, vacations, cats/dogs
Courtney Shoemake, 9	Lynden	47, 111	Drawing, reading, horses, art
Tabitha Silva, 9	Lynden	83	Playing with friends, drawing
Nicholas Snydar, 9	Lynden	35	Farming, model farm display
Kelly Switzer, 7	-	91, 103	Hobbies
Meagan VanBerkum, 8	Lynden	68, 100	Read, draw, write, ice skating
Taylor Van Daylen, 8	Lynden	47	Hobbies
Morgan Van Slyke, 7	Bellingham	23, 41, 54, 55, 59, 78, 89, 90, 139	Reading, writing, playing with her dog
Abby Walters, 9	Lynden	38	Drawing cats
Chelsea Whitener, 11	Everson	74	Playing piano, basketball, reading
Weston Whitener, 8	Everson	43, 71	Playing baseball, history, science
Sarah Wiley-Jones, 14	Bellingham	22, 34, 40, 81	Drawing dragons, paintball
David Williams, 8	Lynden	16, 55	Playing with trains, Legos
Karla Witte, 10	Lynden	44, 59, 103	Swim, sports, draw, write
Christopher, Victoria, & Alexandra, 3	Charleston, WV	118	Picture books, playing, art

Meet the Authors & Illustrator

author illustrator portraits by Jennifer Reinstra, age 9

MaryAnn Faubion Kohl is the award-winning author of 20 books on creative art for children. She is an educational and publishing consultant who is a regular contributing author to *Scholastic Parent&Child* and *Parenting* magazine. MaryAnn is a recognized keynote speaker at educational conferences and was an elementary education teacher before starting Bright Ring Publishing, Inc. in 1985. Living in Bellingham, Washington with her husband, a dog, and two cats, she enjoys gardening, skiing, and playing at the beach (just like Jean). Both of MaryAnn's daughters are involved in the creative arts — acting, dance, music composition, and the visual arts.

Jean Potter, an experienced early childhood consultant, is the award-winning author of ten activity books which focus on art and science. Jean believes in making learning fun! Her career includes — classroom teacher, director of a state ECE program, and Deputy Assistant, and Acting Assistant Secretary of Education, for the US Department of Education, Washington, DC. Jean lives in Charleston, West Virginia with her husband & three children. She enjoys gardening, skiing, and playing at the beach (just like MaryAnn).

Rebecca Van Slyke lives on a small farm near Bellingham, Washington with her husband, daughter, and numerous creatures great and small. She has been an elementary teacher and art instructor since 1985. In addition to writing and illustrating, Rebecca enjoys cooking, gardening, reading, and speaking at Young Authors' Conferences. Becky has illustrated *Discovering Great Artists* (Bright Ring) and *Global Art* (Gryphon House), among other works. Rollo Van Slyke, MaryAnn's insurance agent, introduced Rebecca and MaryAnn.

TITLES BY MARYANN -

- *Discovering Great Artists: Hands-On Art for Kids in the Styles of the Great Masters* (illus. by Van Slyke)
- *Scribble Art: Independent Creative Art Experiences for Children*
- *Mudworks: Creative Clay, Dough & Modeling Experiences*
- *Mudworks Bilingual: same as Mudworks, in both Spanish & English, on facing pages*
- *ScienceArts: Discovering Science Through Art Experiences* (with Potter)
- *Good Earth Art: Environmental Art for Kids*
- *Preschool Art: It's the Process, Not the Product*
- *First Art: Art for Toddlers and Two's*
- *MathArts: Discovering Math Through Art Experiences*
- *Cooking Art: Edible Art for Kids* (with Potter)
- *Global Art: Activities, Projects, & Inventions from Around the Word* (with Potter / illus. by Van Slyke)
- *Making Make-Believe: Props, Costumes & Creative Play Ideas*

TITLES BY JEAN -

- *Science in Seconds for Kids: Over 100 Experiments You Can Do in Ten Minutes or Less*
- *Nature in a Nutshell for Kids: Over 100 Activities You Can Do in Ten Minutes or Less*
- *Science in Seconds with Toys: Over 100 Experiments You Can Do in Ten Minutes or Less*
- *Science in Seconds at the Beach: Exciting Experiments You Can Do in Ten Minutes or Less*
- *ScienceArts: Discovering Science Through Art Experiences* (with Kohl)
- *Global Art: Activities, Projects, & Inventions from Around the World* (with Kohl / illus. by Van Slyke)
- *Cooking Art: Easy Edible Art for Kids* (with Kohl)

Guess who?
hint: Think POP-UP!

Storybook Art ILLUSTRATOR HALL OF FAME

Can you name these 45 smiling picture book illustrators? Hints Everywhere ······ Answers Below ······

 1. alligators

2. mysteries

 3. that bugs me!

4. glove

 5. one is one

6. mitten

 7. cold time

8. bake it

9. so fine

 10. cold,cold,cold

11. seaside fun

12. soldiers

 13. dreamer

 14. white puff

15. geometric

 16. Z for zoo

17. squeaks

18. beastly !

 19. scrappy

20. papermaker

 21. blonde girl

22. green

 23. whoo! whoo!

 24. calendar

25. far out

26. funny birds

27. meow !

28. pop-up

29. galloping girl

30. squiggly

31. creation

32. recycle

 33. moon gift

34. sing a song

35. one potato

 36. smoky

 37. by the sea

 38. just a baby

39. sprinkle & fruit

40. trees

 41. shiny swimmer

42. ABC flowers

 43. just ducky

 44. dairy puddles

 45. garden party

Can you guess *who's who* in the ILLUSTRATOR HALL OF FAME?
100 picture book illustrators are found in **Storybook Art.**
Many shared their photographs, and 45 are part of this guessing page.

Hints are sometimes easy, sometimes puzzling, exactly as hints should be!
What books did each artist illustrate? Who is both author *and* illustrator?
One more hint: *Storybook Art* has a nice big *Index* with all the answers.

ANSWER KEY	
45	Mark Buehner
44	Charles G. Shaw
43	Kurt Wiese
42	Anita Lobel
41	Marcus Pfister
40	Marc Simont
39	Marvin Bileck
38	Mira Reisberg
37	Taro Yashima
36	David Diaz
35	Diana Pomeroy
34	Nancy Winslow Parker
33	Louis Slobodkin
32	Joan Steiner
31	Neil Waldman
30	Pierr Morgan
29	Paul Goble
28	Robert Sabuda
27	Wanda Gag
26	Susan Roth
25	Steve Jenkins
24	Karen Katz
23	John Schoenherr
22	James Arnosky
21	Jan Brett
20	Denise Fleming
19	David McKee
18	Robert Bender
17	Ed Young
16	Candace Whitman
15	Suse MacDonald
14	Clare Turlay Newberry
13	Faith Ringgold
12	Ed Emberley
11	Thea Kliros
10	Synthia Saint James
9	Rémi Saillard
8	Pat Hutchins
7	Beth Krommes
6	Yaroslava Mills
5	Barbara Garrison
4	Bernard Lodge
3	David Carter
2	Wendell Minor
1	Arthur Dorros

Bright Ideas Bookshelf ··· Art Resource Books by MaryAnn F. Kohl

NEW

STORYBOOK ART
Hands-On Art for Children in the Styles of 100 Great Picture Book Illustrators
MaryAnn Kohl & Jean Potter
ISBN 0-935607-03-X
   100 easy literature based art ideas in the styles of favorite picture book illustrators. Preschool through elementary. Extensive indexes.

$14.95 • 144 pages
Bright Ring • Ages 4–12

author's favorite

DISCOVERING GREAT ARTISTS
Hands-On Art in the Styles of the Great Masters
MaryAnn Kohl & Kim Solga
ISBN 0-935607-09-9
   100+ easy art ideas focusing on the style of a great master from the past or present. More than 80 artists featured including Picasso, Monet, & O'Keeffe. Most popular art book title of all.

$14.95 • 144 pages
Bright Ring • Ages 3–12

SCIENCE ARTS
Discovering Science Through Art Experiences
MaryAnn Kohl & Jean Potter
ISBN 0-935607-04-8
   200+ art experiences explore basic science concepts. Amazing ooo-ahh projects to entice even the most reluctant artist into exploration, discovery, and creativity.

$15.95 • 144 pages
Bright Ring • Ages 3–10

PRESCHOOL ART
It's the Process, Not the Product
MaryAnn Kohl
ISBN 0-87659-168-3
   Over 250 process-oriented art projects designed for children 3-6, but enjoyed by kids of all ages. Uses materials found commonly at home or school. Organized by months, seasons, and art technique.

$19.95 • 260 pages
Gryphon House • Ages 3–12

MAKING MAKE-BELIEVE
Fun Props, Costumes, & Creative Play Ideas
MaryAnn Kohl
ISBN 0-87659-198-5
   125+ ideas for pretend and make-believe through storybook play, games, cooking, mini-plays, dress-up and masks, imagination spaces, puppets, and more enrich children's playtime.

$14.95 • 190 pages
Gryphon House • Ages 1–8

NEW

MUDWORKS – Bilingüe / Bilingual
Experiencias creativas con arcilla, masa, y modelado
Creative Clay, Dough, & Modeling Experiences
ISBN 0-935607-17-X
   50+ of the best projects from the original edition of Mudworks, translated into both Spanish and English on facing pages, for children and adults - all ages.

$14.95 • 160 pages
Bright Ring • All Ages
Bilingual • Edición bilingüe

GOOD EARTH ART
Environmental Art for Kids
MaryAnn Kohl & Cindy Gainer
ISBN 0-935607-01-3
   200+ art explorations using common materials collected from nature or recycled from throw-aways. Filled with easy ideas for appreciating the earth through art.

$16.95 • 224 pages
Bright Ring • Ages 4–10

The BIG MESSY ART Book
***Easy to Clean Up**
MaryAnn Kohl
ISBN 0-87659-206-X
   100+ adventurous activities beyond the ordinary for exploration of art on a grander more expressive scale. Hundreds of bonus variations included.

$14.95 • 144 pages
Gryphon House • All Ages

GLOBAL ART
Activities, Projects, and Inventions from Around the World
MaryAnn Kohl & Jean Potter
ISBN 0-87659-190-X
   135+ easy-to-do art projects exploring collage, painting, drawing, construction, and sculpture while introducing kids to cultures and people worldwide. Uses art materials and kitchen supplies.

$14.95 • 190 pages
Gryphon House • All Ages

SNACKTIVITIES
50 Edible Activities for Parents & Young Children
ISBN 1-58904-010-4
   50+ fun, creative concoctions in minutes for snacktime or any time. Dinosaur eggs, tomato towers, star buscuits, alphabet sandwiches and more. 50 favorite recipes selected from *Cooking Art*.

$9.95 • 128 pages
Robins Lane Press • All Ages

MUDWORKS
Creative Clay, Dough & Modeling Experiences
MaryAnn Kohl
ISBN 0-935607-02-1
   100+ modeling and play-art ideas using play dough, mud, papier-mâché, plaster of Paris, and other mixtures from household supplies. Award Winning Best Seller. An arts and crafts classic!

$14.95 • 152 pages
Bright Ring • All Ages

SCRIBBLE ART *Newest Edition*
Independent Creative Art Experiences for Children
MaryAnn Kohl
ISBN 0-935607-05-6
   200+ process art ideas that applaud exploring in an indepen-dent, non-competitive, open-ended setting. Only basic art materials and kitchen supplies needed. (Originally published as *Scribble Cookies*.)

$14.95 • 144 pages
Bright Ring • Ages 2–12

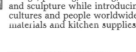

COOKING ART
MaryAnn Kohl & Jean Potter
ISBN 0-87659-184-5
   150+ artistic, edible recipes for learning the joys of food design. Food is designed, prepared and eaten as part of meals, snacks, parties (some for pets and outdoor friends too). 3/4 of the recipes require no cooking or baking.

$14.95 • 160 pages
Gryphon House • Ages 3–10

MATH ARTS
Exploring Math through Art for 3-6 Year Olds
MaryAnn Kohl & Cindy Gainer
ISBN 0-87659-177-2
   200+ innovative activities to introduce preschoolers through second graders to early math concepts through art projects. Essential math skills without pain!

$19.95 • 260 pages
Gryphon House • Ages 3–6+

NEW

FIRST ART
Art Experienes for Toddlers & Twos
MaryAnn Kohl
ISBN 0-87659-222-1
   75+ art experiences are specifically designed for the little guys, including tips for success. Filled with art exploration especially for toddlers and two year olds.

$14.95 • 160 pages
Gryphon House • Ages 1–5

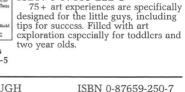

PRESCHOOL ART SERIES
5 books of art fun for preschool kids & older, excerpted from the award winning single volume, *Preschool Art*.
64 pages each • $7.95 each

• CLAY & DOUGH	ISBN 0-87659-250-7
• CONSTRUCTION	ISBN 0-87659-251-5
• PAINTING	ISBN 0-87659-224-8
• DRAWING	ISBN 0-87659-223-X
• COLLAGE & PAPER	ISBN 0-87659-252-3

Bright Ring Publishing, Inc.

P.O. Box 31338 • Bellingham, WA 98228-3338
800.480.4278 • FAX 360.383.0001 • 360.398.9801
www.brightring.com • books@brightring.com

Bill to:

Name_____

Address_____

City_____ State_____ Zip_____

Phone (_____)_____ Email _____

Ship to: *(if different from billing address)*

Name_____

Address_____

City_____ State_____ Zip_____

Phone (_____)_____ Email _____

Qty.	Title of Book	Book Cost Each	Price
	DISCOVERING GREAT ARTISTS *Hands-On Art for Children in the Styles of the Great Masters*	$14.95	
	MUDWORKS *Creative Clay, Dough, and Modeling Experiences*	$14.95	
	MUDWORKS EDICIÓN BILINGÜE ~ BILINGUAL EDITION *(Spanish & English in one book) Experiencias creativas con arcilla, masa, y modelado*	$14.95	
	SCRIBBLE ART *Independent Creative Art Experiences for Children*	$14.95	
	SCIENCEARTS *Discovering Science Through Art Experiences*	$15.95	
	GOOD EARTH ART *Environmental Art for Kids*	$16.95	
	COOKING ART *Easy Edible Art for Young Children*	$14.95	
	PRESCHOOL ART *It's the Process Not the Product*	$19.95	
	MAKING MAKE-BELIEVE *Fun Props, Costumes, and Creative Play Ideas*	$14.95	
	GLOBAL ART *Easy Edible Art for Young Children*	$14.95	
	MATHARTS *Exploring Math through Art for 3-6 Year Olds*	$19.95	
	THE BIG MESSY ART BOOK *But Easy to Clean-Up*	$14.95	
	PRESCHOOL ART: CLAY & DOUGH	$ 7.95	
	PRESCHOOL ART: CRAFT & CONSTRUCTION	$ 7.95	
	PRESCHOOL ART: PAINTING	$ 7.95	
	PRESCHOOL ART: DRAWING	$ 7.95	
	PRESCHOOL ART: COLLAGE & PAPER	$ 7.95	
	SNACKTIVITIES *50 Edible Activities for Parents and Young Children*	$ 9.95	
	FIRST ART *Art Experiences for Toddlers and Twos*	$14.95	
	STORYBOOK ART *Hands-On Art for Children in the Styles of 100 Great Picture Book Illustrators*	$14.95	
	PRIMARY ART *Art Experiences for Kids 5-10* (COMING SOON)	soon	
	DISCOVERING AMERICAN ARTISTS *Hands-On Art in the Styles of Great American Masters* (COMING SOON)	soon	
	MUSIC ARTS *Instruments, Composition, and Musical Arts* (COMING SOON)	soon	

Book Amount	
Shipping Amount *(See Chart)*	
Subtotal *(Book Amount plus Shipping Amount)*	
Washington State Residents Only **Sales Tax** 8.2% *on Subtotal*	
TOTAL ENCLOSED *(add WA Tax plus Subtotal)*	

Please pay by check to Bright Ring Publishing, Inc.